"Everything is permissible
as long as it is fantastic." — Carlo Mollino

COLLECTING DESIGN

Adam Lindemann

TASCHEN

Contents

Preface

What is design? This book is about the 20th century furniture that is valued by deal-ers and auction houses and coveted by collectors. "Design" is the catchword for the fur-niture that best represents our recent history and cultural legacy. Indeed, there are sep-arate and, at times, intersecting fields of design that can lead to confusion. There is car design, watch design, interior design and architecture; the focus of this book is on under-standing the collector's market for 20th century furniture.

Thirty-two international experts and market movers fill you in on how and why the most valuable furniture in the world is not what you think it is. Antiques, 18th century French furniture, André-Charles Boulle commodes and the like have become less valuable than the top icons of the 20th century. Art Deco prices started ramping up in the 1980s with celebrity collectors like Yves Saint Laurent and Andy Warhol; fast-forward to the art boom of the last several years, and we have seen prices that set a whole new threshold for the decorative arts.

How and why this happened is the focus of hours of conversation, research and thorough analysis. Not only did Art Deco by Eileen Gray fly high (the Dragons leather armchair made $27.8 million at Christie's in February 2009) but mid-century Italian design by Carlo Mollino reached extraordinary levels (a dining table made $3.8 million at Christie's in June 2005) and several galleries began to produce limited-edition pieces of furniture that were sold as instant collectibles. Designers like Ron Arad and Marc Newson created work selling in galleries for hundreds of thousands of dollars, making some art dealers jump into the design arena and causing many more traditional decorative arts collectors to wrinkle their noses in disapproval.

Trying to cover in one book everything from Gustav Stickley and Art Nouveau through modernism and contemporary is an impossible task. Collectors tend to focus on a specific style or period, and if they favour French metal pieces by Jean Prouvé, they most probably dislike the surrealist touch of the Lalannes or the playfulness of Mattia Bonetti. Even within the field there are tremendous differences of taste and opinion, and the rivalries are fierce and sometimes even bitter. More traditional collectors, those who have been committed for years, scoff at much of the work produced more recently, and openly express their beliefs that a good part of what was done in the past decade was strictly market-driven, and therefore lacks authenticity and integrity. Only the future knows which designers and which pieces will truly stand the test of time, and until then the race is on. This book will not provide conclusions, but it will present a range of options and enough market information to jump-start your own exploration of this fascinating field.

Now that we've witnessed a major economic reversal, how will this phenomenon change? Can these limited-edition design objects hold their value or are they the product of an over-stimulated, hyped-up art market the likes of which we may never see again? Will historic 20th century design continue to rise in value, or have we seen the top of the cycle, and soon the design world will look like the ragged tail of an art market that has lost its mojo?

In *Collecting Design,* we'll try to tackle all this and more, and the experts will teach you, try to convince you and point to where we go from here.

Adam Lindemann
Spring 2010

Opposite title
Jean Royère
Bar d'appartement dit "Mon cœur balance",
1954, bar with four garden seats in the form
of swings, wood, fabric Royère, tubular metal,
patinated iron, dimesions variable

p. 4
Gaetano Pesce
Moloch floor lamp, 1971, partially painted
metal, plastic, wood and glass,
92 in. (233.7 cm) high as shown

Introduction

by Adam Lindemann

The design world never held much interest for me. From a purely investment per-spective, art always looked more promising. Exceptional prices for extremely desirable works of art have been a recurring phenomenon for centuries, but ten years ago, the contemporary art world began to feel energised and sexy in a whole new way. I became obsessed with discovering and collecting the most explosive artists I could find. The art market was beginning to take off into uncharted territory. By 2005, works by Takashi Murakami, Damien Hirst, Richard Prince and many more were hard to get and selling for huge premiums at auction and on the secondary market.

My first book, *Collecting Contemporary,* was released in June 2006, just before we witnessed the highest prices ever achieved for the work of living artists. When a Damien Hirst pill cabinet could fetch over $19 million, a Peter Doig painting rocketed to $11 million and Jeff Koons' *Hanging Heart* hammered at almost $24 million, any sane collector had to wonder how long the run would last.

Design dealers latched on to this bullish exuberance by offering limited-edition works by contemporary stars and "rare" mid-century furniture that the auction houses promoted and glorified. Suddenly the design market looked like a microcosm of the art market, one that was built to lure in art collectors like me, and that's just what it did. The design bug bit me in a big way, it offered a window into an all-new universe, a growing market with the promise of real investment potential. I learned to enjoy design as much as art, if not more. After all, you can't sit in a painting, you can't cuddle up with a bronze, but you can sink into a chair and fall in love with the vintage patina of a desk or the original paint on a lamp. I've always been drawn to objects that show their history, and in design, patina is a good thing, with original condition selling for a premium; what a difference from the art world where a single scratch or chip is a flaw that can radically impair the value of a work.

I reasoned by analogy that just as Caravaggio had once been the most famous painter in Rome, and André-Charles Boulle was once the most coveted cabinetmaker in Paris,

"I learned to enjoy design as much as art, if not more. After all, you can't sit in a painting, you can't cuddle up with a bronze."

today Jeff Koons was our Caravaggio, so why couldn't Marc Newson be our Boulle? Luxurious appointments have appealed to society's moneyed classes in every age, the history of what was valued and collected becomes a part of our cultural heritage. For example, the advent of modernism in the mid-20th century redefined traditional concepts of luxury; architectural designs and machine-made furniture formed of metal and glass replaced the ideals of master craftsmanship and ornamentation. Today, with hindsight, we see that rare and beautiful things will always be studied and collected; what matters is their place in history. The value is in their design, not in the quality of their materials.

Pierre Paulin
Elysee table with interior light, 1971, white opaque Plexiglas and smoked glass, 12 ½ x ø 47 ½ in. (31.7 x ø 120.6 cm)

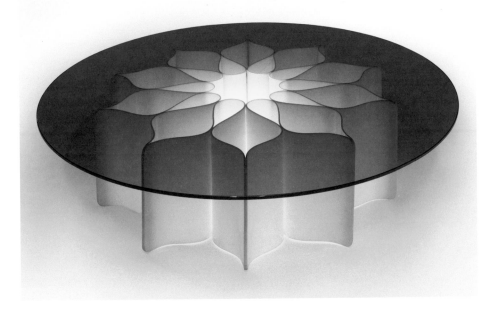

Value in the market rests on critical consensus and the laws of supply and demand. Since the 1980s, the value of important design, whether originally conceived for mass production or as a luxurious appointment, continues to grow. Though some may shake their heads in disbelief that classroom chairs designed by Jean Prouvé in the 1950s are more valuable than some fine antiques, or that the desire to own a new limited-edition piece by a fashionable designer can be stronger than the desire to own Louis XIV furniture, this has been a trend with strong momentum. Let's keep in mind that the generation of collectors buying 20th century design is still in its 40s and 50s, the peak income-generating years, therefore it is reasonable to assume that this market has real legs for the foreseeable future.

Several design dealers sensed that art collectors like me would begin to cross over from the art world, and they commissioned designers to produce works in limited editions in order to satisfy the demand. Design stars like Ron Arad and starchitects like Zaha Hadid jumped into the game; soon industrial designers like Jasper Morrison and Tom Dixon were on the bandwagon with editioned pieces; all of a sudden, a whole new market was taking off. A number of older designers like Maria Pergay and Wendell Castle were happily brought out of retirement and they began to produce new works for the first time in years.

From 2003 to 2008, the world of contemporary design was exploding and things were exceptionally bullish right up until the world markets took a nose dive. Suddenly, after the crash of 2008, the design market applied the brakes. Although prices for mega-blue-chip names like Carlo Mollino, Eileen Gray, Emile-Jacques Ruhlmann and Armand-Albert Rateau still held their ground, the prospects of record prices for mid-century favourites like Prouvé, Jean Royère, George Nakashima and Paul Evans looked dim. Somehow, the markets have remained relatively strong. The most contemporary pieces are the most vulnerable to weakening prices, especially works that had rapidly soared ten to twenty times their former value, but there are always exceptions, and the Lockheed Lounge, for example, recently traded at over $2 million, more than 50 times its original cost. Irrespective of the marketplace, the fact remains that amazing and expensive new work has been created and this has enriched the history of contemporary design and will continue to do so.

Today I have become design-obsessed, the discovery and study of new worlds of design is a consuming fascination, and thus the timing is just right for this second book, *Collecting Design*. Now, at the beginning of the 21st century, is a perfect time to collect the best design of the 20th century and beyond, and the experts and connoisseurs collected for this project over the past three years will explain why and show you how.

Tom Dixon
Pylon Chair, 1992, soldered wire, made by hand,
50 x 25 ¼ x 21 in. (127 x 64.1 x 53.3 cm)

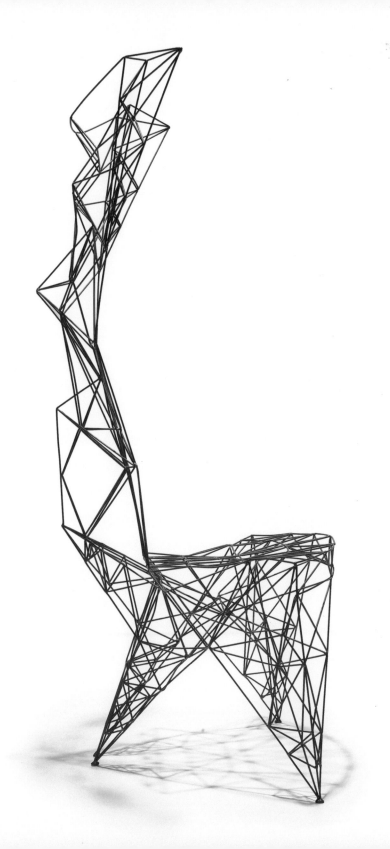

THE FIVE DESIGN PLAYERS

The design world is far more fragmented than the art world, and far less structured. Initially I feared that making a book about the design market would be of little consequence because the field is in its infancy. The truth is quite the opposite; the design market is actually much bigger than the art world if one considers the quantity of vintage furniture shops, small regional auction houses and especially the huge number of decorators and interior designers all over the world. Whereas only a small number of the elite are interested and passionate enough about art to spend their time and money collecting it, and few can at today's prices, everyone in the world interacts with furniture design whether they know it or not.

For this book, I omitted the design museums only because they are so varied and have many different views. MoMA, for example, only collects and exhibits pieces that have been mass-produced, and that pretty much excludes half the works in this entire book! There are a few critics who do some good writing but, unlike in the art world, these journalists are few, far between and have little impact on pricing and values. In the end I decided to keep it simple with only five categories. The designers head the group, and some words about them will explain why they are not given a separate chapter of their own.

TYPES OF MARKET

They are followed by the collectors who are the sine qua non category we all need to study; next, the dealers who are the de facto experts in their areas of specialisation (I have excluded generalists); and last, the auction house experts who really create the only public market for the field – they set price estimates and set the stage for growth.

As I moved amongst the players, I was left with a number of extremely influential people who shape our tastes, our preferences and the unconscious and unspoken feel of what's hot, what's trendy, what's a masterpiece and what is not. I felt that the reader needed to have a feel for the way a fashion designer, an interior designer or a hotelier can change and influence the way we see our world, and the objects we choose to buy and include in our lives – they are the tastemakers.

These five categories complete the overall picture of the buyers, sellers, auction experts and influencers who make up the design market. This book studies them, contextualizes them, and will bring you closer to understanding great design and its market.

THE
DESI

In *Collecting Contemporary*, I decided not to interview any artists, for which I was criticised extensively. What has always seemed strange to me is that these critiques seemed to completely overlook the fact that this was a deliberate decision; it was not that I simply forgot them.

The idea of doing an art book without artists is provocative and subversive. There are several reasons to exclude them; for example, if we were to add them, which ones would we add? Is it appropriate to put in those who sell for the most money, or the least, or somewhere in between?

Artists are rarely straightforward and they are sparing in sharing information. Often they can put you on to the wrong course, or speak in circles. Andy Warhol was quite adept at speaking in circles and platitudes, and expressly preventing his interlocutor from gaining access to his inner thinking. The same is true of Damien Hirst or Jeff Koons, amongst others. I believe that even if the artist tried to give a genuine explanation, this could be enlightening, but not conclusive. Works of art need to

GNER

speak on their own, an artist's words are much less meaningful than actions, paintings and sculptures.

Most of the designers of the past century are now old or gone. Still, it would have been possible to speak to a number of living designers, old and young, and indeed I encourage the reader to seek them out and pick their brains. Most are obsessed and immersed in their own work. Their views on other designers is an "artist's look", a personal feeling or sympathy. I have almost never spoken to an artist or designer who truly has a collector's mind. For these reasons, I have excluded the designers from the book, although again I urge the reader to go out and meet them, see what they are about, test their knowledge of design history and learn from them. If you are serious about collecting, stick to other collectors and trusted dealers who have expertise and commitment in their respective specialties. The design market is made of buyers and sellers, and therefore so is this book.

THE
COLLE

Collectors come in varying sizes and shapes. In design you'll find the Art Deco crowd – they bought Emile-Jacques Ruhlmann and Armand-Albert Rateau when it was affordable and they still do because they know it's a buy at almost any price. Then there are the French-mid-century fanatics who devour Jean Prouvé, Charlotte Perriand and Pierre Jeanneret. They just can't get enough of the folded metal and stylised wooden pieces with the exotic provenance of Africa and India. They may also add a healthy dose of the 1950s French decorator Jean Royère, some Georges Jouve ceramics and lighting by Serge Mouille to create that perfect mid-century look.

Then there are the contemporary design collectors, they have been buying Ron Arad and Marc Newson from the early days, and now they are including Martin Szekely or Konstantin Grcic. At

CTOR

some point, they may add the Campana brothers and a piece by Joris Laarman and perhaps another by Maarten Baas.

Most of them remain consistent to a certain period or aesthetic and they like to be coherent. For example, the modernist addicts buy a Marcel Breuer piece and mix it with their Gerrit Rietveld, but they will never add a French 1970s piece of Pierre Paulin or Maria Pergay, nor will they consider a contemporary commission of Mattia Bonetti for that matter. In the design world, collectors are quite fractured and come from radically different viewpoints. They can be broadly characterised in terms of two main schools of thought: the architectural/conceptual viewpoint, or the preference for aesthetic/stylistic creation.

Bruno Bischofberger

Collector, Zurich

Bruno Bischofberger's art gallery in Zurich is one of the best known and most respected in Europe. He has represented Andy Warhol and Jean-Michel Basquiat as well as Julian Schnabel, Sandro Chia and Francesco Clemente. He is a thorough and acknowledged connoisseur of 20th century design, with deep collections of Alvar Aalto, Carlo Mollino, Ettore Sottsass, Gerrit Thomas Rietveld and more.

The difference between art and decorative art or design

A piece of decorative art is usually something that is utilitarian. It can be a piece of furniture that you sit on, or work on, or store things in…if it is glass or ceramic, perhaps it is a vase that can hold flowers, even if you do not actually use it for that. But artistically, for me, there is absolutely no difference between a piece of decorative arts or design, and a piece of art like a painting or sculpture.

The difference lies in the quality of the work, but that is only half the story. The other very important half is how the work is embedded in the history of art or design and how much it drives history when it appears. The knowledge of the past decades, centuries and even millennia helps you to realise how a designer or artist transforms his time, invents a new style and mood, or reveals a new way of seeing and thinking. The work's effect on other designers or artists establishes its future importance.

Is a table by Carlo Mollino as valid and valuable as a painting by Warhol or Basquiat?

If you mean monetary value, maybe not, but its beauty and its place in history can be of similar importance. Therefore, a great Carlo Mollino table is very valuable today, but a great Andy Warhol or Jean-Michel Basquiat is more valuable because of its much greater recognition in the history of art. The painters have written a page of art history that has strongly influenced generations up to the present day.

Artworks are almost always unique pieces, while works of design are often produced in series. Serial or mass-produced works are of lesser individual value than a unique creation, just as a lithograph or multiple would cost less than a painting or sculpture. This fact has led a number of contemporary designers to produce their design pieces in small editions, mostly between three and twelve, as an artist would do when producing

sculptures. The designs are then sold through galleries with prices that are in line with the work of artists. Their ability to do this is based on their own convictions, and on the acceptance of designers as artists by the art world.

Design vs. decorative arts

"Decorative" has become almost a swear word in the art world. This is ridiculous because an art work that is decorative means it offers another dimension, which is fantastic.

If you think of Henri Matisse, most of his works are extremely decorative. True, if you say a piece of art is just decorative, meaning its value lies only in decoration and nothing more, the criticism is valid. But decorativeness in itself is a wonderful quality. Because "decorative" has now become interpreted in a negative way, the art world no longer speaks of decorative arts, instead it uses the word "design". This refers to simple, possibly mass-produced types of work that today make more sense as "design" rather than "decorative art". But basically, the two are more or less the same.

Finn Juhl
Pelikan Chair, 1940, leather upholstered chair, maple legs, 27 ½ x 31 ½ x 23 ⅝ in. (70 x 88 x 60 cm)

A better investment – art or decorative arts?

I would never call it investment. When I buy something for my "study" collection, I do not think in terms of investment. As

Marcel Breuer
Wassily easy chair B3, 1925, tubular steel frame and
cloth, 30 ¾ x 30 ⅛ x 27 ¼ in. (78 x 76.5 x 69 cm)

an art dealer, I buy many works, especially from earlier periods, because the prices often are very low in comparison to some works of contemporary art or design sold by art galleries in small editions. So you could call this an investment factor.

But when it comes to my collection, everything I spend is on the object itself – without much thought of investment. I do buy some things that are *way* overpriced because I feel I need them for the collection. I also try to buy what is out of favour, or against the current mainstream.

Today, many young collectors who have made a lot of money in their investments, or in banking, and have been successful in entrepreneurial ventures, are after contemporary art. They all want to buy young art, meaning work that can be bought at low cost, thinking it will be worth much more in the future. Of course, these collectors are interested in the art itself and the art of their own time, but they also love to make a lot of money on what they buy, at least hypothetically, because even if they don't sell the artwork, they want to know that that it is worth a lot. It proves to them and to their egos that they were able to find something very early. Today, there is such a big audience for this that if an artist is even halfway interesting, the buyers at auction sometimes overpay to such an absurd extent that it is crazy...despite the fact that I personally don't see too many really great artists around.

What he collects

Basically, I collect things that I love. Every collector buys only what he likes, but if limited to this attitude, one can put together a terrible collection. Personal taste is not enough. The collector also needs knowledge.

I collect Swiss design from the 20th century, Scandinavian design from Sweden, Denmark and from Finland, of which I have a wonderful and important collection of glass, ceramics, furniture etc. By Alvar Aalto I own perhaps the best collection of furniture, glass and other objects. I also collect, in depth, works by Carlo Mollino, Adolf Loos, Le Corbusier, Mies van der Rohe, Marcel Breuer, Frank Lloyd Wright, Max Bill, Ettore Sottsass and many others.

I have a great collection of ceramics and glass in which the work of the great masters working from circa 1925 to 1968 is represented in depth, as well as ceramics and glass pieces by artists like Lucio Fontana, Pablo Picasso and Joan Miró.

Alvar Aalto
Easy chair, 1930s, frame: bent laminated birch,
seating: black stained molded plywood,
30 ½ x 98 ⅜ x 30 ¾ in. (95.5 x 64.5 x 91 cm)

How does an art dealer have money to buy all those great things?

I became an art dealer because I always needed money to buy pieces. The profit from any sales went mostly into the collection. Most of my life, I was in debt. I sometimes had sleepless nights. I also studied art history at university and have had an art gallery for 45 years. I tried to concentrate on showing artists that I felt would emerge as the most important figures of our time, historically. Over the past few years, this approach has put me in a more comfortable position to collect, and to show works in the gallery. About half of my exhibitions are not commercial, meaning that nothing in the show is for sale.

About George Nakashima

I have a few pieces by Nakashima, but I was slightly disenchanted when I went to visit him many, many years ago. Francesco Clemente and I were in Philadelphia to see a show and on the way home I said to him: "Let's go to visit Nakashima." Francesco didn't know well who Nakashima was at the time. I did not know the level of Francesco's interest in decorative arts, but he has a beautiful collection of all kinds of things, especially early Frank Lloyd Wright furniture that he lives with and uses in his studio. So we went to see Nakashima and this was the first time I had met him. I don't know why, but in a way I was expecting some kind of saint, or Japanese or Buddhist monk, or something like that.

Ettore Sottsass
Mobile a tre ante wardrobe, 1979,
plastic laminated wood, aluminium borders,
70 ⅞ x 84 ¼ x 28 ¼ in. (180 x 214 x 72 cm)

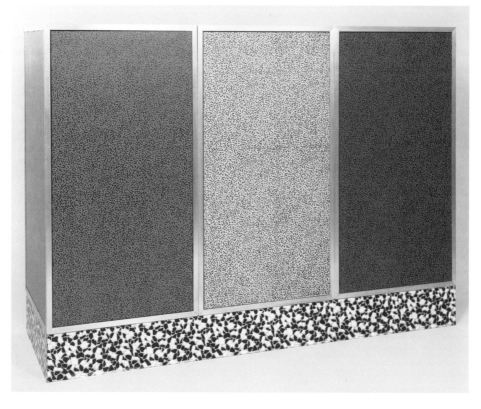

Instead, I found an interesting person, a strong businessman trying to sell us great pieces of wood to make a table for $60,000 or $100,000. I just did not like the encounter much, although I still think his work is interesting. I have some excellent pieces by Nakashima but I would not want to have a large collection of his work, even though it shows an interesting mixture of beautiful craft, influenced by Japanese or Eastern art and 1950s modernism, which work together wonderfully. I just would not want it in real depth.

Ettore Sottsass

I more or less stopped collecting design works that were produced after around 1968 except for Ettore Sottsass, who became a dear and close friend. He built my house outside Zurich and I have a wonderful collection of his creations. Sottsass is, for me, the most important and influential designer Italy has ever had. He was great in many fields: architecture, the design of furniture, glass, ceramics and many other objects, photography, writing, teaching. He was one of my mentors.

> "Personal taste is not enough. The collector also needs knowledge."

Ettore Sottsass was originally part of Alchimia. He and Alessandro Mendini and a few others were members of that studio. Sottsass also was the spiritual director of the so-called Memphis group. Memphis became the general title for post-modern furniture and design about 15 or 20 years ago in Europe. But names can be misleading. Just think of how *Art Nouveau* is a funny name in French, meaning "new art"; in Germany it is called *Jugendstil*, "youth style", because there was a review called *Jugend*. But in Italy, *Art Nouveau* is called "Liberty", after the name of a London department store, which was promoting the new style in England around 1900.

So post-modern furniture was widely identified as Memphis, and at the time you would often hear people ask: "Are you collecting Memphis?" The name became a collective, so that any and all furnishings that were a little colourful and new and different were called Memphis. For a long time, Sottsass was stamped as "Mr. Memphis". The reality is that after Memphis, he created unbelievable things, perhaps his best work came later in his career.

overleaf: **Carlo Mollino**
Tavolo a vertebre (Vertebrae table), 1950, bent laminated wood with glass top and brass fittings, 30 ½ x 98 ⅜ x 30 ¾ in. (77.5 x 250 x 78 cm)

Michael Boyd

Collector, Los Angeles

Michael Boyd, a recognised Los Angeles collector, was originally a commercial music writer. He is now focused on design and also works as a consultant on the restoration of architecturally important houses. He is also an advisor and private dealer, and has offered several successful single-owner sales through auction.

How he started

The market for design in 1980 was nowhere when I started, and I certainly was not able to compete in the cutting-edge transactions of the day. But Philippe Garner, who is now the International Head of 20th Century Decorative Art and Design at Christie's, was doing some pioneering auctions in Monaco; in the late 1970s and early 1980s he included designers like Eileen Gray, Emile-Jacques Ruhlmann and Pierre Chareau. French Art Deco was popular with the fashion designers like Karl Lagerfeld, Yves Saint Laurent and others – they collected it quite seriously. So for me that is where it started.

What is 20th century design or decorative arts?

In 20th century modernism there are two tracks. One is when the designer is trying to achieve mass production, hoping to bring well-designed objects to the general public. That started in Vienna with Josef Hoffmann, Otto Wagner and Adolf Loos and continued in the 1920s in Germany with the Bauhaus, in Amsterdam in the 1920s and 1930s with Gerrit Rietveld and Theo van Doesburg, Paris in the 1930s and early 1940s with Le Corbusier, Pierre Jeanneret and Charlotte Perriand, in Scandinavia just after World War II with Arne Jacobsen and through the 1950s and early 1960s, perhaps culminating here in Los Angeles with Charles and Ray Eames.

At the same time, there was another track: private commissions for the well-to-do. The interior and exterior metal fittings in Pierre Chareau's Maison de Verre in Paris took a team of locksmiths seven years to execute at an astronomical cost.

That's a long way from modernist architects who generally sought universal solutions to the problems of public housing and design. Chareau's project really went against this tenet.

Eileen Gray
Satellite hanging lamp, ca. 1925,
painted aluminium,
53 ⅛ x ø 18 ⅞ in. (135 x ø 48 cm)

Serge Mouille
Three-arm ceiling light, ca. 1950,
painted aluminium, painted steel and brass,
39 x 65 x 39 in. (99.1 x 165.1 x 99.1 cm)

Even someone like Josef Hoffmann, the quintessentially Viennese architect, had a foot in both worlds. He created many mass-produced designs that he sold through Wiener Werkstätte, which had galleries as far away as New York City, but he also designed a masterwork, a palais in Brussels, Villa Stoclet, which was the most lavish, no-holds-barred, high-budget commission that any modernist architect had ever undertaken. It is undeniably powerful and a hugely important work – but it's completely over the top.

There has always been this division between private commissions – creating exclusive, beautiful, precious objects for rich people on the one hand – and the inclusive, socialist program in architecture and design which sought to produce great and affordable designs for everybody.

Ironically, these days, there is a kind of subversion of functionalism in design. Anti-design was a late 1960s and early 1970s European avant-garde movement that subverted the classical modernist ideal in a more interesting and provocative way. As recently as a few years ago, in the heyday of so-called design art, Maarten Baas' *Where There's Smoke* includes a Gerrit Rietveld Zig-Zag chair that's been burned to a crisp. I guess it's witty, but it's a somewhat gimmicky one-liner. Tejo Remy's *You Can't Lay Down Your Memory,* a chest formed from recycled drawers held together with a shipping strap at all angles, is a totally useless object. If you put something in a drawer, it will fall to the side, leaving much of the volume of the space unusable. Ron Arad's bookshelf that swirls its way up the wall is equally absurd. Not only is it damaging to the bindings of any books shelved there, but it tries to defy gravity. I'm all for questioning accepted practices, but I'm afraid gravity is not debatable.

> "Pursuing the new for its own sake is neither meaningful nor valid."

Caveat emptor...fakes

The biggest issue plaguing us today is the prevalence of fakes and forgeries. It's only natural that, as the prices for the best material get stratospheric, industrious criminal types make a few more. If something is too good to be true, it is generally not true. Demand for historical pieces has far outstripped supply and it can make people overly eager. There's a great line about the French painter Camille Corot: it's said he painted 200 pictures and there are 500 in American collections.

All the dealers, auctioneers and experts need to band together to stop this sort of thing. People are very excited about some of the material, but we all need to take a sober look at how much the forgeries, fakes and frauds damage the market and public confidence about the works in general. If you're going to spend $50,000 on a Jean Prouvé chair, you need an experienced expert to advise you. So, caveat emptor! Do your homework or hire someone who has done theirs.

Collecting with a point of view

When I work with a client who is building a collection, it is all about his or her point of view. If someone says, "Look, I really want a George Nakashima piece," I will say: "If you want to get Nakashima, don't get a piece by his daughter, Mira, get an original piece by him. Look at the piece, make sure it's got the original patina." And I would direct them towards his three-legged, or tripod, items that are a little more avant-garde. It is important to get Nakashima pieces that are modernist in inclination and not too entrenched in the traditional Japanese woodworking world.

I would say the same about Maria Pergay. She has done some interesting things, she has also done some silly things. I recommend to clients who collect design that they stick with things that are *conceptually* advanced and perhaps *technically* challenged, over things that are *technically* advanced and *conceptually* challenged – Gerrit Rietveld and Rudolph Schindler over Maria Pergay and John Dickinson any day. There are always exceptions. Jean Royère is interesting because he has a foot in both worlds. There is a structural vision there as well as a strong French style, which is very important. Royère's work is not just total whimsy and a "birthday cake" kind of decorating and surface application. I think Royère is definitely someone to take seriously.

French and Dutch designs are the most interesting to me. My favorite design is the work of the harder French modernists – creators like Le Corbusier, Jean Prouvé,

René Herbst
Sandows no. 5 chair, 1929, chromium-plated tubular steel and rubber, 33 ⅞ in. (86 cm) high. From the apartment of René Herbst, Paris

Charlotte Perriand, René Herbst and Serge Mouille. And Dutch functionalism will always have a place in my heart. Bart van der Leck, Theo van Doesburg, Gerrit Rietveld, Piet Zwart and others seemed to zero in on the essential.

The end date for pieces in my collection is 1965 – the year Le Corbusier died. The following year, Robert Venturi published *Complexity and Contradiction in Architecture,* announcing the beginning of Post-modernism. When he shows up, I bow out. His Queen Anne chairs for Memphis are appalling. This is the guy who coined the phrase "less is a bore". It may sound like a clever response to Mies, but in my opinion it's definitely not true. To Venturi, I respond with another Mies line: "You can't invent a new architecture every Monday morning." The implication is that pursuing the new for its own sake is neither meaningful nor valid. It may be better to develop a philosophy that is already sound and grounded. Building a collection is all about creating an engaging narrative.

Ups and downs in the design market

A perfect example today is the work of Charles and Ray Eames, who were very, very hot in the 1990s. Then replica companies started re-releasing everything and suddenly people could buy a reissued piece for a few hundred dollars, and that made the entire market collapse.

Other examples of that kind of vacillation in the marketplace would be the performance of the Pierre Jeanneret furniture from Chandigarh. People may think, "This is incredible, the pieces embody the spirit of Le Corbusier, the prices would have to be huge," but then they realise: "Well, this just keeps coming out at every auction…I guess there's a lot of it…it's not as rare as I thought." In the future, after this plentiful wave has been snatched up, it could very well become rare and expensive again. However, I have my suspicions about how much of this was made after the fact, without supervision or input

from Jeanneret or Le Corbusier. After all, we've all seen a 1957 Thunderbird and a Thunderbird today; although they have the same name, they are entirely different animals.

Gerrit Rietveld, Mies van der Rohe and Pierre Chareau

Gerrit Thomas Rietveld is a personal favourite because he introduced designs in 1918 that look radical to this day. With the simplest of means, a humble cabinet maker-cum-architect went all the way down the line without necessarily intending to. It amazes me that something that is virtually turn-of-the-century is still so up-to-the-minute.

He was a Dutch visionary who eliminated the superfluous in his work. His pieces look like a three-dimensional Mondrian. His most famous work, where he's just reducing the loftiest ideas to these simple planes, is his Red-Blue chair of 1918. An early Red-Blue chair sold recently at auction for $375,000. It came from the Brugman family and had been commissioned in 1923 for the Dutch poet Til Brugman.

Charlotte Perriand
Shadow chair, ca. 1956, stained bent plywood, 26 ½ in. (67.3 cm) high

Rietveld's Zig-Zag chair of 1934 is another masterpiece of abbreviation. With respect to its value, you'd have to rely on curators at the Stedelijk Museum in Amsterdam or the Centraal Museum in Utrecht. There were so many variations of his Zig-Zag chair, you would really have to wade through the editions of Metz & Co. [Amsterdam department store] or van de Groenekan [manufacturer] or other contractors executing his designs to find what the real Rietveld is.

Unfortunately, it's a different situation with Mies van der Rohe's classic Barcelona chair or ottoman. A pair of early chairs just sold at auction for a give-away price, in the range of many reproductions. It is so ubiquitous, we have seen it so many times, there are so many copies, versions and perversions of the seminal design. It is over-exposed. Only a limited number of people get really excited about the original issue any more, so the market is down considerably. But this is a market issue and has no place in a discussion on the historical importance of the piece.

Pierre Chareau had a foot in both the decorative and functionalist worlds, like Eileen Gray. He did some things that would make you think: "That one looks really French Deco...it's very ornate." On the other hand, some of the pieces, along with his Maison de Verre, are a self-contained manifesto of modernism – a total program that inspired subsequent generations of architects and designers. His importance cannot be overemphasised.

Ludwig Mies van der Rohe
Barcelona chair and ottoman nos. MR 90 and MR 80, ca. 1931, chromium-plated metal with second generation leather strapping, chair: 29 ¾ in. (75.5 cm) high

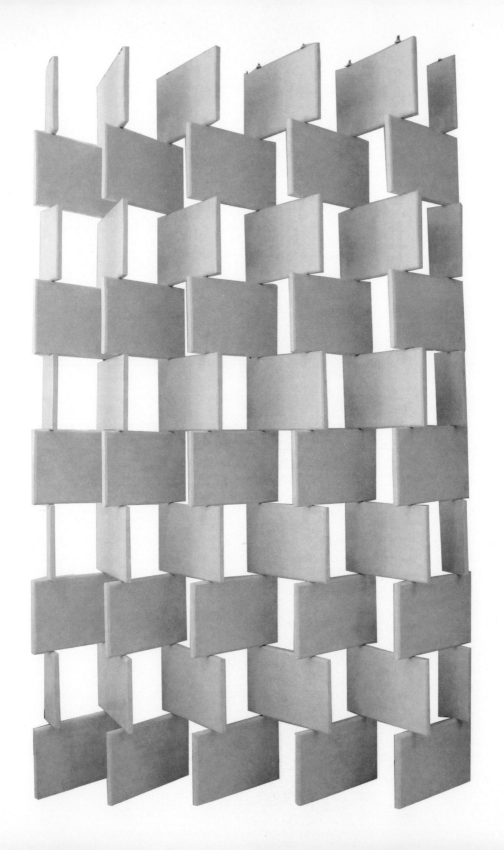

Eileen Gray

Another influential designer from the Art Deco period is Eileen Gray. Gray was Irish but she worked in Paris and had a gallery to sell some of her work. Although never trained as an architect, she designed a couple of houses that Le Corbusier and other major modernist architects, especially members of the Dutch de Stijl movement, thought were first-rate examples of *the new architecture*. She spent most of her time and energy on the production of decorative arts. Some of her pieces can be described as Deco, but she completely transcended that category and can be regarded as an important functionalist as well.

Today the value of her work can run into millions of dollars. She was a pioneer; she studied Japanese and other Asian lacquer techniques and developed many prototype matte and eggshell finishes. We would all see those works in the Philippe Garner catalogues in the late 1970s and early 1980s, and say: "Wow, look at that!" or "What is that? I've never seen *that* before."

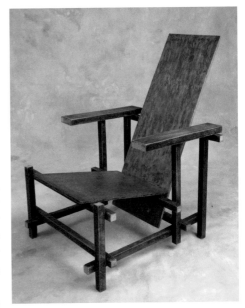

Gerrit Thomas Rietveld
Red-Blue chair, ca. 1919 (designed 1918), deal wood with coloured stains, 34 x 25 ⅝ x 33 in. (86.4 x 64.9 x 83.8 cm)

His taste in contemporary design

What I love are all the pioneering architects and designers who are visionaries. They are not cynical – they are really trying to build a better world, which takes a lot more courage and perseverance than snarky footnotes from the sidelines.

Shiro Kuramata's work is quite poetic and very consistent. Terence Woodgate designed a beautiful, thin-profile carbon table just recently that I like very much. I love Marc Newson's work; his designs are spot-on. I tend to like the more silent types, if you will: Jasper Morrison, Maya Lin, Robert Wilson, and Kuramata – where there is some restraint even in the presence of poetics.

Thank goodness we've come to the end of the era of bling. I'm afraid that we are going to look at the first decade of the 21st century and we'll feel like a dejected Flavor Flav with a big golden cheap fake clock around his neck. It can't go on. Where can it go? The motivation needs to be the benefit of Humanity with a capital H, or even just art culture, but not personal egos and blockbuster sales getting all the boosting. It all seems slightly immoral.

Eileen Gray
White painted wood block screen, ca. 1922–1925, painted wood and steel rods, 84 ¼ in. (214 cm) high

Peter M. Brant

Collector, Greenwich, Connecticut

Peter Brant, publisher and businessman, is one of the most savvy and dedicated collectors of his generation. He owns great works by Andy Warhol, Jean-Michel Basquiat, Jeff Koons, Julian Schnabel, Richard Prince, and has long had a passion for 20th century design. He is a connoisseur of design from American Empire all the way to Zaha Hadid and Marc Newson. He is also the owner of *The Magazine Antiques, Art in America* and *Interview.*

Getting started

I started out collecting in the late 1960s. I became interested in Art Deco furniture when I was just out of college. When I came to New York, I bought an apartment and I wanted to buy some furniture and express my tastes, so I hired a decorator, Michael Greer, who was famous at that time – he had helped Jackie Kennedy redecorate the White House. He was a very good decorator, but he was primarily interested in Directoire furniture. My interest was in more modern furniture, and in looking around I got to know the work of Ward Bennett. He is a very famous furniture designer of the 1960s and early 1970s. So I did my apartment in mostly Ward Bennett furniture – sofas, chairs – and that got me interested in design.

I liked some of the Art Deco pieces and Tiffany lamps I found at Lillian Nassau on 57th Street. At the time, I was very close with Fred Hughes, Andy Warhol's business manager, who was also interested in Art Deco. We kind of influenced Andy to focus on French Art Deco, because Andy really preferred American painted furniture, folk art type furniture – American, Maryland, Baltimore decorated painted furniture. That was his first choice, and his other favourite was Gustav Stickley who is so well known for his Arts and Crafts furniture.

Then he got interested in Art Deco, really through Fred, and that's how Jed Johnson, Warhol's companion and friend, became interested in being a great decorator. Jed passed away in the airplane tragedy, TWA flight 800 en route from New York to Paris in 1996. We miss him.

Fred Hughes had one of the really great eyes for the decorative arts, he understood it, was interested in it and studied it. Besides working for Andy as a business

Carlo Mollino
Chair, 1953, curved maple, plywood and ash, joints: brass, seat: red leatherette, 35 x 15 ⅜ x 18 ¾ in. (89 x 39 x 47.5 cm). From the Casa Editrice publishing house, Turin

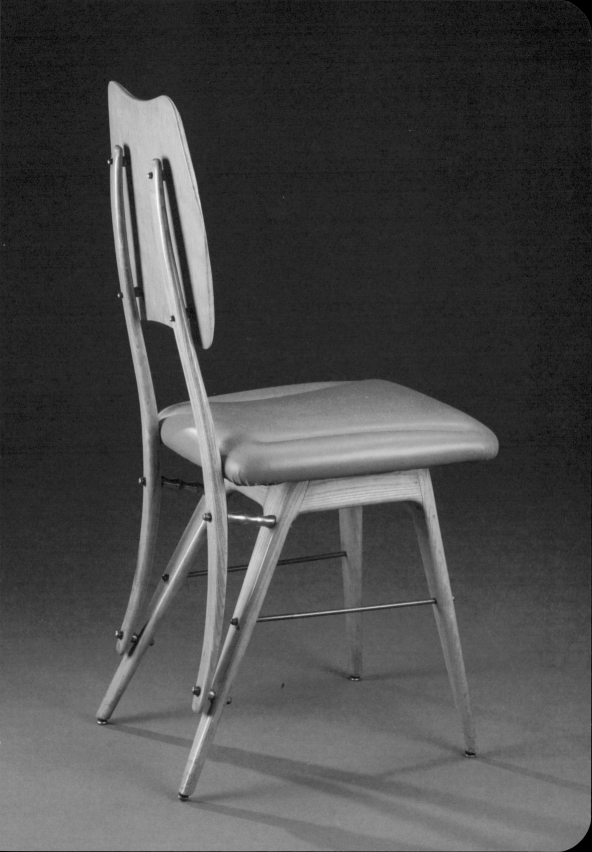

Charles Rennie Mackintosh
Side chair, 1909–1911, stained oak and rush,
28 ¾ in. (73 cm) high. From the Ingram Street
tea rooms, Glasgow

manager and art dealer, he had a broad interest in many things and probably could have been one of the great decorators of our time. I have enormously high regard for him. I would say that in decorative arts he had among the best eyes of anybody I have ever met and he certainly had a stronger influence on me than Andy.

During the period of the late 1960s, I was also buying art from people like Ileana Sonnabend and Antonio Homem – they were collecting Art Deco furiously. Then I became interested in early American furniture like Duncan Phyfe, around 1970 or 1971. I was also collecting Art Deco silver very seriously, like Jean Puiforcat, and was spending a lot of time in Paris, from 1969 to 1972. I did a movie with Andy in Paris in 1973 and lived in Paris for about two months during the filming and spent most of that time antiquing.

Actually, I was always collecting. In the 1980s, when I was playing polo in England and everybody would be out there watching the games and fishing in the afternoons, I would be in London going antiquing because I really liked Edward William Godwin, Charles Mackintosh, William Morris, Philip Webb and the Aesthetic and the Arts and Crafts movements. So I was buying that furniture which cost very little then, just as Art Deco furniture was inexpensive in the early 1970s. What generally happens to great furniture when it gets out of vogue, like post-modern furniture today, is that it suddenly appears bulky and cumbersome and is ejected by the market for a ten to 20-year period of time.

The Crocker collection

In 1972, I bought the Templeton Crocker collection which was one of the great Art Deco collections of the 1920s. That came about because, being interested in Art Deco furniture, I would go through the old *Vogues* and 1920s magazines, and I frequently came across the name Crocker. He was an American from a banking family. The articles did not really say what he did other than he was living in Paris, he wrote an opera and was friendly with all the big designers.

He had an apartment in Russian Hill in San Francisco, and so he got all these designers from Paris to design for him. He gave them the exact dimensions of the apartment rooms and as a result, these great decorators – like Jean Dunand and Jean-Michel Frank – did some of their best work for that apartment. So here was Crocker, a guy who lived

Jean Dunand
Poisson screen, ca. 1924, lacquered
wood, six panels, each 51 ½ x 9 ¾ in.
(130.8 x 24.8 cm)

in Paris, who came from a very wealthy family – his grandfather was founder of Crocker National Bank in San Francisco – and he shipped all the stuff home. Then as soon as he passed away, everything was dismantled and put in a warehouse like it was out-of-style modern furniture.

It was stored for about eleven years when I sent two trucks out to San Francisco to get the whole collection and bring it back. I gave part of it to the Metropolitan Museum where it is today…20th century Orrefors glass and the Dunand furniture. They took all the pieces and they still have it – parts of it are shown in special exhibits from time to time.

I was also interested in architectural furniture. Bruno Bischofberger influenced me a great deal in collecting art when I met him in Switzerland. I used to go there with my parents, skiing, and got very friendly with Bruno – it was he who probably introduced me to Carlo Mollino's furniture. My collection spans from part of the 18th century up to now – it covers a very broad range of the decorative arts representing work from France, England, Italy and the United States.

Jean-Michel Frank
Club armchair, ca. 1930, sycamore
with original leather upholstery,
33 ⅜ in. (84.8 cm) high

Would he pay $2 million for a chair?
It depends on how much money you have. If I have the sufficient resources, I would not think twice before

George Nakashima
Burl walnut table, 1978, burl walnut, four rose-wood butterfly joints, 15 ⅞ x 50 ½ x 67 ¾ in. (40.2 x 128.3 x 172 cm)

buying an Armand Rateau chair, no matter what the cost, because Rateau was one of the great furniture makers of all time, especially his commissioned bath-rooms, which are really incredible works. I would pay anything for Carlo Mollino, who I think is one of the greatest designers of all time and I have paid very high prices for some of his things. I bought an Alexandre Noll chair that was very, very expensive but I have also bought Noll for very little. So to me, because it was an absolute masterpiece, and since I have a large collection of Noll, it makes sense.

The thing with prices – sometimes we paid very little for a piece and other times the higher prices...I mean, you can't always get everything for very little. For example, when

> "When I was a kid, do you know what influenced me in design? The television program *Playboy after Dark.*"

I started collecting 1950s fur-niture, it was during the 1980s. Normally, work that is 25 or 30 years old is kind of going out of style. Today, people are look-ing at design differently. Many designers are doing editions. In earlier times, they did not have editions, they just produced the piece and it wound up being as rare as an edition because no one wanted it.

Today, people are more aware of design and realise that it is a good investment, but I think you have to be careful. Be aware of what you are paying and know the costs of really nice furniture. Then you need to evaluate how important a piece is to the history of design, how fragile it is, where you are going to use it, what happens if something goes wrong – these are all factors. I bought a Marc Newson chair, the Lockheed Lounge, and paid a very, very high price for it at the time. It does not seem like a high price now, but at the time it seemed an unbelievably high price for a guy who was his age. I loved

it and bought it because I thought it was great design, but $150,000 was a lot of money for a chaise.

Influence of architects

I also collect Frank Gehry whose work I admire, and I like Zaha Hadid, as well as Amanda Levete who designs for Future Systems, in fact she is one of the partners there. She is an architect and designs furniture, and I have bought some of her pieces. I think it's important to look at the architects because if you go to history, so many of the great furniture makers were architects.

From the 18th century there is William Adam who was Scotland's foremost architect of his time, known for great fireplaces, and he did fabulous furniture...he had four sons and they were all famous architects and interior decorators. Later there is Charles Mackintosh, also from Scotland, and Samuel McIntire, the American architect, and then you have people like Edward William Godwin, Philip Webb and Augustus Welby

"The thing with prices – sometimes we paid very little for a piece and other times the higher prices... you can't always get everything for very little."

Pugin from England, all architects and great furniture makers. Mies van der Rohe designed buildings and was also a great furniture designer. Frank Gehry is another great furniture designer. Also Frank Lloyd Wright. So many of the great designers of furniture were architects. Today, you have to look at Zaha Hadid, a perfect example; I have one of her prototype desks, she is a fabulous designer.

Value of design and art

I do not consider a piece of furniture of mine in the same light as a work of art. Yes, it is an artistic creation and, in the decorative arts, it can be a masterpiece, but that is quite different from a work that changes the way you think about things. An artist should make you *think* differently when you look at a work that is really great. Design, however, is viewed more for its place in history. A great Philadelphia chair makes you think about great design from that period in Philadelphia, it's the history that comes to mind.

I have been involved with *The Magazine Antiques* over the years, since 1983. I see that the connoisseurship of collecting, in one respect, has diminished; it is simply too difficult to be an expert on everything from Arts and Crafts, to Philadelphia furniture, to Mollino, to everything else, because it really requires a lot of study. I think what is happening now is that a designer does something, produces an edition of it and we know exactly how many there are because it is well documented. For that reason, people feel more comfortable with contemporary design than they do with work from the prior periods. It is documented and that is important for the prospective buyer.

Think of Jean Prouvé...the market comes up with an African Prouvé table every other month. When I bought mine there were supposed to be only twelve in the world. How many are around now? I think about 25, and more might appear. On the other hand, if somebody shows you a Lockheed Lounge, most

Shiro Kuramata
Miss Blanche chair, 1988, thick acrylic resin, anodised aluminium and artificial roses, 36 ¾ x 24 ¾ x 22 ¾ in. (93.5 x 63 x 58 cm)

of the dealers know the name of everybody who owns one. So that brands it, in a dealer way, by knowing how rare it is.

These new editions are virtually packaged like works of art and they are selling for high prices. In the case of Marc Newson, he is certainly very high up there. I think he is one of the great designers of the 20th century because everything he has done from watches [Ikepod] to planes to furniture has just been genius. I think the idea of showing his work in an art gallery is fine. You know, Ileana Sonnabend was showing French 1950s design with Patrick Seguin because it's wonderful to do that. But as far as value goes, or packaging it as art, to me that's difficult. It is great furniture.

Early influences

When I was a kid, do you know what influenced me in design? One of the first influences was the television program *Playboy after Dark*. I guess its premise was to show pretty girls, at least that's what I felt when I was a teenager. Of course there were some beautiful girls there, starlets and some others, but then, in the background of that after-dark New York apartment was a Franz Kline painting, and then there was a Willem de Kooning that caught my eye.

Also the furniture looked kind of special. I do not remember what it was at the time but it looked special. It had a look, and modernism was in play, coming out of the 1950s, and

I think it embedded itself in my youthful mind. So everybody gets someplace for different reasons…I guess some people notice and others do not.

Advice for the new collector

I think the new collector should try to find something that he or she can afford on a reasonable budget, that perhaps has been overlooked temporarily, that perhaps was produced in the 1970s or 1980s, that has great quality and does not demand the higher prices. There are terrific auctions in Chicago, like Wright, great auctions that you can pick from. If you had collected George Nakashima ten years ago, you would be in the chips, right? I started collecting him 15 years ago, 20 years ago, because I thought it was great stuff. Now it is very expensive. So you have to look for things that are high quality, that people believed in and collected, and you have to become knowledgeable.

Alexandre Noll
Armchair, ca. 1947, mahogany,
34 ¾ in. (88.3 cm) high

My son Chris is a big collector of Ettore Sottsass. He started collecting it a few years back when the interest in Sottsass was low, but now people are starting to get interested again. A couple of big shows are coming up. His prices are not that high now, but it is very high-quality work so this could easily change.

I think that you have to look for design furniture done by architects, and great, well-known furniture makers, not guys who are totally unknown. Try to get the pieces when they are a little bit out of fashion, and live with the furniture. If you really believe in it, keep on buying it, I think that's the way to go. If you can afford it, you should just buy it, the best of what you think is the best, and the best of what you can afford.

Marc Newson
Orgone Stretch Lounge, 1993, aluminium
and enamel, 24 ⅜ x 70 ½ x 32 ⅝ in.
(62 x 179 x 83 cm)

Dennis Freedman

Collector, New York

Dennis Freedman is the former creative director of the fashion and style magazine *W*, and he has been instrumental in bringing the trendier side of the art world into the fashion world. He is a long-time, dedicated design connoisseur; his extensive collection focuses mainly on Italian Pop of the 1970s as well as up-and-coming new designers.

What makes a serious collector

I don't think it is possible to build a serious collection without some knowledge of the history of design. Of course, instinct plays a role, but it is the understanding of what has come before that allows you to connect the dots and see the relationship between pieces. Design moves along a continuum, and in order to appreciate the importance of a particular work, you have to be able to place it in historical context.

In my own collection, for example, I can draw a line between Achille Castiglioni's 1960 Taraxacum hanging shade, and Jurgen Bey's Chair-Table-Chair of 1999. Both are based on a similar action: stretching a pliable synthetic material over a fixed form. Only the materials and production methods differ. It is hard to imagine that Bey was not aware of Castiglioni's work and influenced by it in one way or another.

Difference between collecting art and collecting design

There is a fundamental difference between art and design. Art by its very definition is unconditional; there are no constraints. Design, on the other hand, begins with function. Even when a designer chooses to ignore function, the very act of rejecting it is an acknowledgement of its existence. The fact that design is an applied art does not limit creative expression; it just means that it is a different form of expression.

I have always been interested in the man-made. If I had to choose between visiting the Grand Canyon or the Salk Institute designed by Louis Kahn, I would choose the latter. I am fascinated by how man shapes his environment and by how different designers and architects respond to the same task.

What he collects

My first interest was Italian Radical design from the late 1960s through the early 1970s, a time of intense political and cultural debate. The work from that period inspires

André Dubreuil
Pendule Ostensoir, 2001, enamel,
copper, steel and glass, 32 x 20 ½ x 6 in.
(81.3 x 54.6 x 15.2 cm)

my collection to this day. In contrast to the early years of the 20th century, when architects were influenced by the aesthetics of industrial production, Italian designers of the late 1960s focused on the shift from mass production to mass consumption. The impact of the American Pop art movement was profound. What was once considered irrelevant and banal was now celebrated. The rules were rewritten.

Alessandro Mendini
Doriflora armchair, 1984, hand-painted carved wood and canvas,
42 ½ x 37 x 38 ½ (108 x 94 x 97.8 cm)

Against this background, a generation of architect-based collectives emerged. Two of the most prominent groups were Superstudio and Archizoom Associati; both wrote provocative manifestos describing utopian super cities of the future. Fortunately, for me, they were also interested in designing furniture and interiors – which gave them another way to express their visionary ideas.

As an art student at university in the 1970s, I remember seeing photographs in the magazines *Abitare* and *Domus,* of super-sized polyurethane foam pieces like the Capitello chair and the Pratone seating system. They did not look like any other furniture I had ever seen. The Capitello was designed by Studio 65 in 1971. It is a seminal work of the anti-design movement in which artistic expression took precedence over functionalism. By appropriating the form of an Ionic column turned on its side, this chair/object recalls both classical Roman architecture and Claes Oldenburg's soft sculptures of the 1960s.

My bible was the catalogue from the landmark 1972 exhibition *Italy: The New Domestic Landscape.* Curated by Emilio Ambasz for the Museum of Modern Art, it introduced contemporary Italian design to American audiences for the first time.

When I finally got a job and could scrape together enough money, I made my first purchase – a first edition Capitello from one of the Italian design sales at Christie's South Kensington. The piece had a beautifully aged golden patina, though I could barely fit it through the doorway of my small New York apartment.

Impact of Italian Radical design

People like Simon Andrews (Christie's), James Zemaitis (Sotheby's) and Alexander Payne (Phillips de Pury) were among those who fought hard to bring Italian Radical design to the attention of the public through their auction house sales, and I think it's important to credit their vanguard efforts.

In fact, it was at a sale at Phillips in 2002 that I acquired one of the key pieces of my collection: a prototype cube for the Misura series designed by Superstudio. This elemental cube,

Riccardo Dalisi
Pasternacchio chair, 1979,
hand-painted wood, 55 x 25 ¼ x 19 ¼ in.
(139.7 x 64.1 x 48.9 cm)

resembling a Sol LeWitt sculpture, was the primary form they used to test the "universal" application of their grid system, which began with the Misura series and evolved into the famous Quaderna line of furniture. Through this collection of formica-clad tables and benches, Superstudio expressed, on a domestic scale, their utopian concept of the "neutral grid" which could be imposed on entire environments.

It was only a matter of time before my curiosity led me to start looking at work made after 1975. Many of the same designers and architects involved in the Radical movement, like Ettore Sottsass and Andrea Branzi, along with Alessandro Guerriero and others, formed Studio Alchimia in 1976. Through a series of exhibitions and catalogues, the members of Alchimia designed furniture, clothing and small objects that achieved much of their impact through the bold use of decorative pattern, colour and form. It was, above all, a movement characterised by its opposition to conventional elegance and good taste. Ornamentation, so long anathema to Italian designers, arrived with a vengeance.

> "Art by its very definition is unconditional; there are no constraints. Design, on the other hand, begins with function."

I started to buy iconic pieces like Alessandro Mendini's Doriflora and Proust armchairs, Ettore Sottsass' Capodanno light fixture and Cioccolato centerpiece and Riccardo Dalisi's extraordinary Pasternacchio painted armchair.

Dixon and Dubreuil

I was also eager to learn more about furniture that was being made outside of Italy. Two designers in particular caught my attention: Tom Dixon and André Dubreuil, both of whom lived and worked in London. One of my favourite pieces is Dixon's prototype Watermine table base which I bought from David Gill Galleries. In my opinion, it is one of the great, little-known designs of the late 20th century. Dixon's works from the early 1990s – among them the Pylon chair and Pylon desk – made in his studio by hand, are underappreciated and undervalued. I think it is only a matter of time before collectors and curators realize the importance of these early pieces.

Dubreuil, on the other hand, utilised his knowledge of the master furniture makers of the 18th century, like André-Charles Boulle and Adam Weisweiler, to produce a body of work that recalls rather than imitates his predecessors. One of my most prized possessions is his Pendule Ostensoir of 2001. In this piece, one in a series of extraordinary clocks, Dubrueil combined enamel, copper, steel and glass to make an object that is as unsettling as it is beautiful. Dubrueil is more interested in experimentation than in telling time. As he once said: "Today everyone knows the time...the clock is a pretext for making small symbolic compositions."

Because he and his assistants make everything by hand, their output is very small. Some of the more elaborate cabinets can take a year or longer to produce. In a market flooded with editioned work, Dubrueil's commitment to the unique is admirable, as is his desire to work outside the mainstream, impervious to the twists and turns of the marketplace.

Joris Laarman
Bone Chair, 2006, aluminium,
30 ⅓ x 17 ¾ x 30 in. (77 x 45 x 76 cm)

overleaf: **Jurgen Bey**
Chair-Table-Chair, 1999, synthetic elastic skin over wooden chair and table,
31 x 63 x 30 ¼ in. (78.7 x 160 x 76.8 cm)

Campana brothers

About ten years ago, while on a photo shoot in São Paulo, I arranged to visit the Campana brothers, Fernando and Humberto. I was familiar with their work, having seen images from Project 66, the exhibition that Paola Antonelli curated on the Campanas and Ingo Maurer at the Museum of Modern Art in 1998. I was impressed by the way they transformed ordinary cast-off materials from the street into highly original design objects. Where Dubreuil favoured enamel, crystal and bronze, the Campanas used bubble wrap, rope and aluminium tubing.

When I walked into their studio, located in a working class section of São Paulo, I couldn't believe my eyes. Sitting in front of me was their very first Rope Chair as well as a large-scale prototype of the Favela Chair. Off to the side was a Bubble Wrap Chair. They also showed me a photograph of the first Sushi Sofa that had just been shipped to a museum show in London.

Martine Boileau
Resin chair, 1960, bronze-tinted resin, 41 ¼ x 24 ¼ x 21 ½ in.
(104.8 x 61.6 x 54.6 cm)

I spent a good part of the afternoon at the studio. I described the history of my collection and how it had evolved over the years. At that time there were no design art sales, so the Campanas were not besieged by auction houses or museum curators. I guess they realised how devoted I was to building a serious collection because they very graciously allowed me to purchase many of their prototype pieces.

With the addition of these prototypes, my collection stretched from the 1960s to the present. Over the past decade, I have seen and read and learned a lot. However, I still get excited every time a new auction catalogue arrives. There is always the chance of finding a missing piece to the puzzle.

Young designers he is collecting

These are tricky times. With the advent of CNC (computer-numerically controlled) technology and rapid prototyping, young designers have the technological capability to create work that was unimaginable a decade ago. However, technological advances do not translate into artistic achievement. As a result, most of what I see today has more to do with pyrotechnics than artistic vision. There are, however, a few exceptions.

Chief among these is the Dutch designer Joris Laarman, a graduate of the influential Design Academy Eindhoven in the Netherlands. Laarman's impressive works include his Bone Furniture series. Among them are a cast aluminium side chair, a translucent resin lounge chair and a molded marble, resin armchair. I acquired all three for my collection.

To design the Bone Chair, Joris utilised software first developed by the auto manufacturer Opel. This particular software is based on the principle of bone growth – adding mass where it is needed for support and removing it where it is not. The use of bionics (the application of biological principles to the practice of engineering) would not be of much interest were it not for Joris' sensitivity to form and materials. In an interview not long ago, he said: "Combining reason with emotion, that is the most difficult thing to do…"

I am also very interested in the work of Jeroen Verhoeven, another graduate of Design Academy Eindhoven. To my mind, his Cinderella table of 2005 is one of the first great pieces of 21st century design.

I had studied all the photographs of his work I could find, but it was not until I saw the table in person at Sotheby's that I could appreciate its beauty. Through experimentation with the computer, Jeroen digitally merged the shapes of various 17th and 18th century European furniture designs into a single three-dimensional form. With the aid of CNC machinery, he constructed a table consisting of 741 layers of plywood, arranged into 57 slices and finished entirely by hand.

Each angle along a 360-degree turn results in a new shape, sometimes hollow, other times oblique. Jeroen took plywood – the most humble building material – and layered and cut it in a way that revealed its inherent beauty. He later executed the same design in marble, which was disappointing. It makes me question whether the decision was predicated on the misguided notion that precious materials make an object more "important" and therefore more valuable.

Fernando and Humberto Campana
Sushi sofa, 2003 prototype, felt, fabric, carpet, rubber, PVC and stainless steel,
29 ¼ x 64 ¼ x 27 ¼ in. (74.3 x 163.2 x 69.2 cm)

Dakis Joannou

Collector, Athens

Dakis Joannou is one of the most visible contemporary art patrons in the world. In recent years, he has turned his attention to Italian designs of the 1960s and amassed a major collection which mirrors his taste for bright colours and bold statements. Joannou's DESTE Foundation for contemporary art has supported many exhibitions internationally and promoted emerging artists as well as established artists. He had Jeff Koons design his yacht and also curate an exhibit of his collection, *Skin Fruit,* at the New Museum in New York City. Joannou is an engineer and architect by training, born on the island of Cyprus, and lives in Athens with his wife, Lietta.

How he started

In the early 1990s, we started to extend our home to accommodate the art collection, and we needed to redecorate. I then had to figure out what to do, so I decided to acquire furniture pieces that spanned from Art Deco to the 1950s. At that point, I did not consider it a collection, it was simply furnishing the house with pieces from that period. Most of the pieces were at the edge of Art Deco going into the 1940s, and then on to the 1950s. I was trying to deal with the in-between periods, the grey areas.

Some pieces obviously intrigued me more than others, like the Carlo Mollino table, the Jean Royère suite, the Charlotte Perriand table, the Emile-Jacques Ruhlmann *bergere.* At the time, few people were looking at that period, and I was not trying to connect the art collection with what I was doing with the furniture.

Why he changed everything

By 2004 and 2005, when we had the *Monument to Now* show, this furniture had become almost classic, and very popular. I then decided that I had to do something different, something that would conceptually connect better with the art collection. After speaking with some friends and thinking about it, I had a discussion with Dennis Freedman, who recommended that I consider the period of radical design of the late 1960s. I found this intriguing and started to see the similarities in the spirit of that period with the way I was collecting.

Alessandro Mendini
Scivolando chair, 1983, mirrored glass and wood, 55 x 43 ¼ x 39 ⅜ in. (140 x 110 x 100 cm)

It was a time of fresh ideas, fresh looks and tremendous liberty for the designer. Utopian ideas, social liberation, technological innovations, new materials, newly found freedom and liberation…"Space Odyssey" had arrived. I think it was a moment that radically changed design…from then on a chair was not just the four legs and a seat with a back…it was more than that.

So the house was literally emptied…everything was gone, and my "1968" collection had started. I did then and I do still enjoy and feel excited about the new thinking and the daring approach of that period. It was more about ideas than style. Of course, one's sitting comfort was sacrificed, so I had to compromise by adding a contemporary Jasper Morrison sofa!

> "Utopian ideas, social liberation, technological innovations, new materials, newly found freedom and liberation… 'Space Odyssey' had arrived."

The loss of traditional craftsmanship

Traditional craftsmanship gave way to testing and experimentation. Quality is achieved using new methods and new ideas. This time, my aim is not just about furnishing the house, but about creating a collection of that period, making it as comprehensive as possible and trying to connect ideas. New names are now added to our vocabulary, like Superstudio, Archizoom, Cini Boeri and Ettore Sottsass.

Buying more than one can use

In the context of building a collection, certainly, I buy more than I can use. In fact I even venture beyond "1968". I am testing the waters with some contemporary pieces, but I am not sure how this connects and where it will take me.

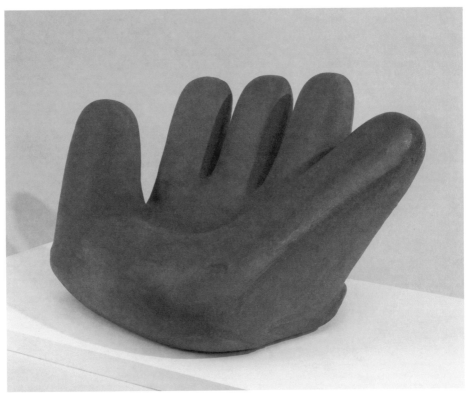

Jonathan De Pas, Donato D'Urbino and Paolo Lomazzi
Joe Chair, 1969 prototype, coated and
molded polyurethane foam, 34 x 31 ½ x 47 ¼ in.
(86.7 x 80 x 120 cm)

Design as investment

When I started buying the Art Deco, 1940s and 1950s furniture, prices were not very high; they were, in fact, comparable to buying new pieces. As it turned out, that was a good investment, but that was simply luck, it was not planned

Today's prices are higher and so, obviously, one must be more careful. One does not want to throw money away, but I think the buyer must focus on what is really meaningful. It is the job of the dealer to buy for investment, not that of the collector. To be honest, I really do not know to what extent the "1968" collection will perform as an investment, and I am not focusing on that.

His favourite pieces

A really extraordinary piece is the Cini Boeri Serpentine Couch – her rubber couch. I have a few pieces and I would love to buy some more and be able to recreate that famous photo of the serpent curving around the trees in a forest.

I also like the Superstudio's Bazaar. It's an incredible concept, creating this kind of cocoon where people sitting next to each other are almost forced to adjust their relationship and behaviour to one another. You really have to experience it – it plays with the emotions and I find it extraordinary that a piece of furniture can have this incredible power.

Cini Boeri
Serpentine couch, 1971, black polyurethane
foam and metal, 21 ¾ x 66 ¾ x 35 ½ in.
(55 x 169.5 x 90.2 cm)

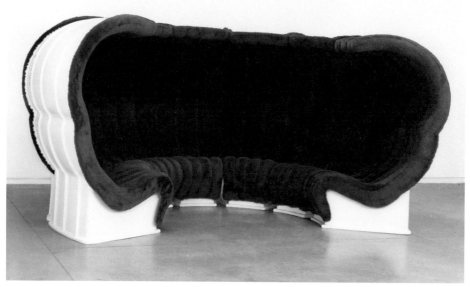

Superstudio

Bazaar sofa, 1968, white fibreglass
and brown beaver fabric, each unit:
58 ¼ x 33 x 35 ⅜ in. (148 x 84 x 90 cm),
assembled overall: 126 in. (320 cm)

How design changes your life

Design does change your life, for sure. Especially
if you keep changing things around, you find
yourself in a different environment and you are
always energised by it (I am not sure if this is good or bad!). You experience new feelings
even in your own house, sometimes even in the same place, you look around and see
something that changes your perception.

And sometimes you change your mind about something, one way or another. And that
is the greatest pleasure, the greatest freedom and the greatest luxury – to be able to
change your mind!

Alessandro Guerriero
Chair, 1978, painted metal,
43 ⅜ x 17 ¾ x 47 ¼ in.
(110.2 x 45 x 120 cm)

Reed Krakoff

Collector, New York

Reed Krakoff is the president and executive creative director of *Coach,* and is a well-known collector and connoisseur of design. He has published several monographs on designers, one on the Lalannes, another on Ron Arad and a volume on Mattia Bonetti.

His collecting strategy

Collecting, for me, is not necessarily about buying something for a good value, it's more about getting the best work of the people I like. To put it differently, the price is sort of unrelated. I never want to buy a mediocre work by someone, even a major artist. If I can't afford it or I do not want to spend X dollars to buy the artist's best work, I won't buy something mediocre – it's nonsensical.

Art collecting

One of the reasons I've enjoyed buying mid-century art, like the Colour Field painters or Louise Nevelson, is that it is more interesting to mix it with contemporary design – as opposed to everything being contemporary: art, furniture and decoration. I think it's more personal to mix things in a way that feels right to you. Good or bad, it's your footprint, as opposed to the same old expected array: a minimalist interior with a Barcelona table, a Jean-Michel Frank reproduction sofa and a couple of Basquiats.

What I find interesting is to mix elements like vintage Tiffany with Marc Newson and Jean-Michel Frank with Louise Nevelson – then you're creating something. As a designer, what is exciting to me is to do something different, as opposed to being too tasteful, which I see all the time. Too much good taste is boring. Having things that work together too obviously or literally – there's no challenge, there's no discovery, no journey, it doesn't feel worth doing.

Design collectors vs. art collectors

Traditionally, people collecting design are more understated than the art collectors. Design collectors will spend $1 million on a table that might not even be recognized for what it is, because it sort of disappears into a room.

When you spend the same amount on art, everybody knows what it is and how much you paid. To me, that is

François-Xavier Lalanne
Babouin, 1984, cast iron, 54 ¾ x 31 ½ x 27 ½ in. (139 x 80 x 70 cm)

Frank Lloyd Wright
Table lamp, ca. 1903, leaded glass
and bronze, 22 ¼ x 32 ¼ x 19 ⅛ in.
(56.5 x 81.9 x 48.6 cm)

the fundamental difference between design and art collectors.

It takes a different kind of person to collect design as opposed to art. I want to be careful not to insult art collectors but the fact is that – to paraphrase – you'd do better just writing a check for $1 million and nailing it to the wall. I do believe that for many people who collect contemporary art in particular, it's about that. Otherwise why would they spend $3,000 on a sofa and $3 million on a painting? It's because of the outward appearance of "Look at my wall, see what I can afford," and that is the reality…I know many others in the design world who would agree.

Trendiness in the market

The design market has become more of a popularity-driven market than it once was. If you were to look at Sotheby's catalogues say, from 20 years ago, you would see Tiffany, Emile Gallé, Daum glass, Arts and Crafts, and Art Nouveau. Take the Sotheby's or Christie's catalogues today, and there is a little bit of Tiffany, almost no Gallé at all, no Daum and a little Art Nouveau. The market moved into Jean Prouvé, Charlotte Perriand and Jean Royère, and now there is also a lot of Contemporary.

Three or four years ago, the 1940s were really popular, one could not open a home magazine without seeing André Arbus, Gilbert Poillerat, Jacques Adnet, Paul Dupré-Lafon to some extent – all that group. Their prices went way up and then came down again. Serge Roche is another one whose work went up and then

Maria Pergay
Drape Cabinets, 2005, stainless steel,
ebony macassar and palm wood,
35 ½ x 54 ¼ x 25 in. (90 x 138 x 63.5 cm)

down again. Now, prices are lower than they were several years ago. That happened because of the trendiness of the market.

On the other hand, the Deco market is somewhat different. Remember that Deco was the expensive furniture of its time. When you think of high Deco, there is Emile-Jacques Ruhlmann, Jean-Michel Frank, Armand-Albert Rateau and others. There is not that much Ruhlmann available now, it's a tiny market and the prices are in the multiple millions, $3 million or $4 million for a desk or an important cabinet...Ruhlmann is a mature market.

"There is always a wall to hang a painting...In a way, it can be much more personal to buy furniture...if you buy a pair of Ruhlmann chairs, you've got to have a place to put them."

Buying design is different from buying art

I believe that buying a pair of chairs is harder to rationalise than buying a piece of art. There is always a wall to hang a painting, and if you do not hang it, you put it in a rack. In a way, it can be much more personal to buy furniture. It is harder to fit – if you buy a pair of Ruhlmann chairs, you've got to have a place to put them, you can't just trot them out and have them in your house for a while, then take them out, and bring them back in again.

On the Lalannes

Claude and François-Xavier Lalanne are a special case because, in Europe, they are thought of only as fine artists. If you go to the auctions, they are part of the painting and sculpture sales, exclusively. In Europe you will not find their pieces sold as decorative art. In the States you do, which says a lot about the difference in how Europeans approach them versus the Americans who, I think, are more regimented about how they

perceive the work. Europeans have traditionally had a much better understanding of the Lalannes' work.

They are not that well-known here, except for few designers who work with them, and a few collectors. Recently they've had a lot of press and that has reignited their market. But here, I think, people seem to go by what they see, so if they are at a Sotheby's auction and there are three sheep sitting next to a Prouvé table, they'll say: "Okay, it's decorative arts."

I believe that the Lalannes' market is highly undervalued and I'll tell you why. First, they have an amazing history. The Lalannes have been working for 40 years, and they are sculptors. They have done show after show at European museums, as well as gallery exhibits and amazing installations. They represent an extended body of work. As François Lalanne once said, and he summed it up very well: "Just because it is furniture and functional does not mean it's not art."

A good way to compare their work is to look at a market like Diego Giacometti's furniture. Well, Diego Giacometti, to me – and what I'm going to say won't be very popular – is hugely overvalued. He made the same pieces, some of them for many years. Today, you can find a dining table on the market for $1 million and more, but who knows how many of this same table have been made? I have some of his pieces, I happen to like them, but the relative value of his pieces is astronomical.

Tony Duquette
Console, glass plate and mirror, 1990, gilt cast-resin, glass and mirror, console: 33 x 59 x 33 in. (83.8 x 150 x 84 cm), mirror: 50 x 36 x 3 ½ in. (127 x 91.5 x 9 cm)

American designers of the 1960s and 1970s

Vladimir Kagan, to me, is overrated, along with Paul Evans. Paul Evans' output is kitsch and I find the prices being paid totally appalling. Actually I do understand, because it is a fashion thing and it's "three decorators and two dealers" showing up at an auction house who drive the market up. This market will fall off the cliff, it absolutely will. Look

Jacques Adnet
Desk, ca. 1950, leather, iron, brass and St. Gobain Nile glass, 29 ⅛ x 80 ⅛ x 38 in. (74 x 204.5 x 96.5 cm)

at what happened with Charles and Ray Eames, and all that Herman Miller stuff. All the Eames cabinets and armoires were so expensive, briefly, and then dropped down because there were tons of it around and it was just fashion-driven. Anything that is too trendy is never sustainable

How to collect

What I always do is to study the interior design books from a specific period, like the 1960s and 1970s. When you look at the homes of stylish people who were respected, who had money and great collections, you see all the pieces that are desirable now. You can look through a 1970s book and there are photos of Maria Pergay's pieces, and Lalanne, and you'll probably see some Ruhlmann. If you want to study Tiffany, the same thing applies. You explore certain periods, certain types of people, certain areas of the world and you start to understand how cyclical the market is.

Ronald Lauder

Collector, New York

Ronald Lauder, businessman and philanthropist, created his own museum, the Neue Galerie, in 2001. The museum focuses on his great passion, German and Austrian art and design from the early 20th century. In 2006, the Neue Galerie paid $135 million for the portrait of Adele Bloch-Bauer by Gustav Klimt. He is a consummate art and design collector and is known to collect everything from Josef Hoffmann and Isamu Noguchi furniture all the way up to Vladimir Kagan.

Decorative arts versus the fine arts

I am not so much a patron of the arts as I am a collector. I look at paintings, sculpture, furniture and decorative objects as one category, one creative process. I have as much passion about buying a great drawing or painting as I do about acquiring a great decorative object.

I buy specific objects with the idea of possessing a complete collection. Whenever possible, I like to collect in depth. I will buy Carlo Mollino furniture, Alvar Aalto, Jean Prouvé, Jean Royère, Shiro Kuramata, Le Corbusier, Isamu Noguchi. I have been collecting Noguchi furniture for years, and it is a great passion of mine. I now have 25 of his pieces – in one case, all six versions of a coffee table he designed.

Contemporary design is also an area I follow with interest...I have started to look at Ron Arad with the idea of buying some of his unique pieces. I love all the decorative objects from the Bauhaus, and I very much admire the creations of the Wiener Werkstätte. I am also interested in many different types of silver. I have a set of 27 chafing dishes – I think from a hotel in Rome – done by Gio Ponti. These are some of my areas of interest.

Where the design collection is housed

Something like the chafing dishes are usually put into storage, to be used a few times a year for large dinners. At the Neue Galerie, there are two complete Josef Hoffmann rooms that I have purchased. All together, I have perhaps 4,000 objects of decorative arts. I may not look at the pieces in storage all the time, but I know that they are there; sometimes, I go to visit them and they give me great pleasure.

Isamu Noguchi
Table no. IN-62, ca. 1948, marble, ebonised wood and aluminium, 18 ¾ x 38 ¼ x 26 ½ in. (47.6 x 97.2 x 67.3 cm)

Koloman Moser
Centrepiece, 1904, silver, ivory and inlaid lapis lazuli,
14 ⅝ x 14 ⅛ x 13 in. (37 x 36 x 33 cm). Executed by Josef Holi
for the Wiener Werkstätte ca. 1905

Value of design

A chair is never as valuable as a painting, but the idea of the chair is no less difficult to create than a painting. For example, I have the greatest wood piece made by El Lissitzky, a chair made in 1915–1916 for a special theatre that was open for only six months. All the chairs in the theatre were destroyed except the one I have. For me, it has as much value as a painting – in the chair, you can see what the artist has expressed in three dimensions.

Design and functionality

Function does not have primary meaning for me. Of course, a chair has to function as a chair, a table has to function as a table, and a chest of drawers is made to hold clothes. But these pieces can still be objects of art, and that is the way I look at them.

Importance of Wiener Werkstätte and Bauhaus movements

Only twice that I know of did an artistic style influence all of society: once in Vienna with the Wiener Werkstätte, when furniture, clothes, writing, art and architecture came together as a whole way of life, and another in Germany when the Bauhaus had a direct influence on architecture, on the way people set their tables, the fabrics they used, the dresses they wore, the book covers they made. We saw a little of it in the United States in Art Deco, which took over many areas of our lives for a period of time.

The Wiener Werkstätte was probably the most important of these movements; it was concentrated in a relatively small area in Vienna. It came to an end because of World War I when all the great craftsmen were either sent to the front with the army, or they left the city. Also, tastes changed.

On changing tastes

When I was growing up, I loved Art Nouveau; I could not get enough of it. All of a sudden, I got tired of it and I liked Art Deco...then Wiener Werkstätte, then Bauhaus. With each

Josef Hoffmann
Sitzmaschine (Sitting machine) no. 670,
ca. 1905, stained beechwood,
42 x 25 x 32 in. (106.7 x 63.5 x 81.3 cm)

overleaf: **Josef Hoffmann**
Pair of Buenos Aires armchairs no. 675,
ca. 1909, ebonised bentwood and leather
upholstery, 30 in. (76.2 cm) high

of these, I changed my whole personality – my apartment, my way of living, every-thing.

The Wiener Werkstätte taught the world that it could change, and the Bauhaus comes out of that world. Without the one, there might not have been the other.

Then modernism came out of the Bauhaus movement. The term modernism was coined by The Museum of Modern Art, and people like Philip Johnson.

Every ten or 15 years, tastes change, and we do not dress or act or decorate our homes the same way as before. People evolve, and things we once enjoyed are no longer pleasing to us. The world comes and goes in cycles, and there is not one single move-ment – in architecture, for instance – that has a truly permanent effect.

Architecture today vs. Bauhaus and modernism

Today, we are in the digital age where instead of having five TV channels, which is what I grew up with, we have a choice of 500; everything is fragmented. As a result, there is a greater sense of individualism now than there has ever been. In the time of the Wiener Werkstätte, for instance, people had special things made for them, but the designs were still within the vernacular of that movement. Today, there are so many possibilities – in a design store, for instance, there are many different styles of couches to look at.

Design as investment

I am not an investor as much as an emotional junkie about the things I collect. At the same time, there is always at the back of my mind the thought that whatever I think is great will go up in value. So far, I have been right. Great art, great furniture, great architec-ture, always goes up in value.

> "A chair is never as valuable as a painting, but the idea of the chair is no less difficult to create than a painting."

Collecting design vs. collecting art

If you collect design, you must realise that you will never be able to show your entire collection, whereas if you collect drawings and paintings, you can.

I buy design because it is a piece of history. I hang great paintings, but a wonderful piece of Alvar Aalto might have to be put in storage. Five or ten paintings in a room can hold together, but if you put five or ten different pieces of furniture in a room, it looks like a furniture showroom; it does not work the same way. That is why you can have thou-sands of paintings – an unending number of paintings – but with three-dimensional objects, at some point you are done.

Koloman Moser
Coat rack no. W675, ca. 1904,
lacquered beech and copper, 42 x 24 x 24 in.
(106.7 x 61 x 61 cm)

THE DEAL

Most dealers in 20th-century design are specialists in a specific market and era. You have the Danish-1960s experts, the experts of Brazilians Joaquim Tenreiro and Oscar Niemeyer, and the powerful French Prouvé consortium. Then there are the Art Deco heavies, those who specialise in the American 1970s Arts and Crafts movement of George Nakashima and Paul Evans and those who focus on French 1960s and 1970s like Pierre Paulin, Maria Pergay, Pierre Guariche and Joseph-André Motte.

The dealers chosen for this book each represent a specific focus; they are also developing and supporting the market of certain designers. There can be no underestimating the importance of having a network of strong dealers to support a type of work and to hold up prices at auction, or develop a clientele who will. I have also included some galleries that specialise in the development of contemporary designers' work, issued mainly in limited editions. These dedicated galleries develop the

markets for a Ron Arad or a Marc Newson and then continue to produce new designers like Konstantin Grcic or Joris Laarman, amongst others. There are also the hybrids, dealers who sell mainly historic works but have invited legendary figures to jump back in and start to create again, and thus designers like Maria Pergay and Wendell Castle have been brought out of retirement and are designing again.

For the most part, dealers of 20th century design are poorly capitalised but extremely committed. They differ greatly from what one finds in the art world: their margins are slimmer, their collector-base is smaller, and since most people will buy many more paintings than chairs, their market is smaller. Despite these handicaps, the field has grown in the past few years and is expected to continue doing so. There is a lot to learn from the great dealers, they've done all the heavy lifting, let's make sure to benefit from it.

Anthony DeLorenzo

Dealer, New York

Anthony DeLorenzo is undoubtedly one of the best Art Deco dealers in the world. His inventory always includes unparalleled masterpieces of Deco by designers like Emile-Jacques Ruhlmann, Armand-Albert Rateau, Eugene Printz, André Groult and Eileen Gray in his uptown New York gallery on Madison Avenue. Downtown he shows mid-century designers like George Nakashima, Maria Pergay and Guy de Rougemont, and he is well known to be generous with his candid advice and opinions.

How he started

I have been a dealer since 1979…before that, I was a collector. I had a small shop out on Long Island specialising in Tiffany lamps. I had a great, really great collection of Tiffany lamps. One day, some European dealers were in and I said: "Look, I have some other pieces at home, come over."

They came to the house and, by luck, I had two pieces of Emile-Jacques Ruhlmann and one tall Edgar Brandt lamp. They paid no attention to the Tiffany lamps, they only wanted prices on the Brandt and the two pieces of Ruhlmann. I said to myself, "These lamps are only a domestic – not a global – market and I have my life savings invested here," so I immediately moved along into the French Art Deco market.

On October the 4th, 1980, the same day I opened up on Madison Avenue to sell French Art Deco, I sold my entire American Deco collection in a single-owner sale at Christie's.

Beginnings of the Deco market

I think the recognition of the Deco market started in the 1970s. The auction houses realised that major collectors and trendsetters were moving into the market, so they started to seek consignments. Also, magazines started running stories on who was buying Deco, and so went the market.

One of the trendsetters was Andy Warhol, another was Peter Brant. It is my understanding that they used to go on buying trips to Paris together in the very late 1960s and early 1970s. We bought a lot of the Deco pieces from Andy Warhol's

Jean Dunand / Jean Lambert-Rucki
Smoking room cabinet, ca. 1925, wood, black lacquer with engraved puppies motif, interior: red lacquer, 68 x 45 x 14 in. (172.7 x 114.3 x 35.5 cm)

collection at auction in 1988, the year after he died. Other notable early collectors were Karl Lagerfeld, Yves Saint Laurent and Ileana Sonnabend, the legendary art dealer who was also a Deco collector.

There is also Michael Chow of Mr. Chow's restaurants. In 1973, in Paris, there was a really important exhibit of Deco – Ruhlmann and Jean Dunand – at the Galerie Luxembourg and Michael bought all of the most important pieces. We were friendly with him because ours was one of the only galleries in the States dealing in Deco. In 1988, the same year we bought the Warhol pieces, we bought Michael's entire collection for

> "The only people who really get hurt are the ones who are looking for bargains."

what was a lot of money in those days. *The New York Times* covered the sale and said that it was one of the finest Deco collections ever put together. There were tables, chairs, desks, cabinets and vases by Ruhlmann, Dunand, Eileen Gray, Jean-Michel Frank – almost 100 items.

Then, in 1989, there was the Robin Symes sale at Sotheby's. He was an antiquities dealer in London who bought a townhouse in Manhattan that Philip Johnson had originally designed for Blanchette Rockefeller. He decorated the townhouse with Art Deco – including major pieces you'll never see again by Eileen Gray, and Pierre Legrain's African-inspired forms. He sold everything, including the townhouse, and we bought most of the important pieces at that sale.

Armand-Albert Rateau
Vanity, ca. 1925, wood, natural coral lacquer, gilt-bronze base, 33 x ø 17 ½ in.
(83.8 x ø 44.5 cm)

Views on the future of the Deco market

The Deco market is now truly global, with a very strong foundation. I am very happy to say I am part of that foundation. The future of the Deco market is pretty much assured because it's supported by collectors and dealers worldwide, including myself. Asians, South Americans, Central Americans, Europeans, Mid-Easterners, Australians and Americans are all buying. We now have a couple of Eastern European clients who have become strong collectors.

As we speak, museums worldwide, like The National Museum of Modern Art in Tokyo and the National Gallery of Victoria in Melbourne are doing Deco exhibits. In 2004, the Metropolitan Museum here in New York did a major exhibit of Ruhlmann, to which we contributed pieces, and it was well attended.

Armand-Albert Rateau
Armchair no. 1793, ca. 1919, bronze, 35 ½ x 24 ½ x 19 ½ in. (91.5 x 61 x 52 cm)

Going forward as a dealer, my intention now is to buy single-owner and limited production pieces. This attracts a collector who is willing to pay the price for a piece that has indisputable provenance. I want to be able to say to that client: "See this? It came from so-and-so's house, and that's it."

I am trying desperately to deal in known quantities, like these Armand Rateau chairs. I know these chairs very well, they were mine. I know they come from the Blumenthal's Manhattan townhouse and nowhere else. Back in 1985 or 1986, I bought a pair of these chairs for $125,000. Twenty years later, I paid over 20 times that amount at one of the recent auctions. Why? Because on the scale of one to ten, these chairs are a twelve.

Re-creations and fakes

There are some fakes in the Deco market and you've got to be careful. The only people who really get hurt are the ones who are looking for bargains. The only bargain in any market is a fair price.

There's also the problem of over-restoration. For example, take Jean Dunand lacquer. The value of his pieces is not just in the design but in the lacquer. He worked with natural lacquer, a painstaking process that involved 30, 40, even 50 coats with the last ten processed under a full moon. You buy a Dunand table but it is damaged so you go out and get it restored. But the artistic lacquer work is lost if it is at all refinished, so the table has now lost most of its value.

Design as investment

I ultimately always think financially...that is the way for me. Someone else might buy a piece to furnish with, but for me it's financial. I consider myself the best Deco dealer in the world. What other dealer spent millions of dollars on collections in the 1980s? If I spend $2 million for a chair, in my mind I am thinking that next year or five years from now the same chair will be $3.5 million.

That same vision extends to my clients' purchases. I am banking on the pieces they bought from me being worth more in one year, five years, ten years from the date of purchase. We've helped put together many collections

> "I do not know contemporary design and so I am afraid of it. Besides, I am an antiques dealer – I like old, not new."

that we have bought back, with the seller making a profit. Therefore, a piece or a collection has become a kind of currency. After all, we are only the custodians of any art.

Take, for example, this sharkskin cabinet by André Groult. He was a French decorator and designer of Art Deco furniture. I paid a lot for this piece, but I believe in it so strongly I would have paid 40 percent more to buy it. And I priced this piece according to the amount I was willing to spend, not what I actually paid.

Ruhlmann vs. Prouvé and the market

Emile-Jacques Ruhlmann is an important figure in the French lineage of ébénistes, cabinetmakers, master craftsmen who used the best materials and designed for the most prominent people of the day. Ruhlmann did not make a lot of money on furniture, which is why he was financially troubled when he died in 1933.

His pieces were not only made from the finest materials but were often important commissions from people like Lord Rothermere, the British press baron, and the Maharajah of Indore, a very wealthy Indian Prince. Ruhlmann is one of the best, if not *the* best, of his period. He was a *genius.*

Prouvé's pieces, by contrast, were all machine-made. And nobody knows how many pieces he made or where they all ended up. I did the first Prouvé show in the United States in 1985, a joint exhibit with lamps by Serge Mouille, so I am largely credited with bringing the 1950s market to this country. I like the 1950s period but I do not agree with the prices in this market right now; they are too high. It is one of the reasons I moved to buying George

Armand-Albert Rateau
Pair of torchères, ca. 1922, shade: alabaster, 66 ¼ in. (168.3 cm) high

Nakashima. I am still a Mouille buyer, though, and I probably have the best Mouille around. I knew him, knew what kind of man he was, and I love his creations. I once asked Serge whom he was inspired by and he said, "No one," but he was friendly with Alexander Calder. You figure that one out for yourself…I did.

Pergay and De Muzac

I am a strong supporter of Maria Pergay and Claude de Muzac who did work in the 1970s. I like their collaborative pieces the best.

George Nakashima

Nakashima is a designer whose work I admire…I am a huge believer in his creations. I recognised the emergence of his secondary market and pushed the market, putting away a lot of his pieces. His work is timeless and his archives are impeccable, so you

André Groult

Raised cabinet, ca. 1927–1928, green shagreen, amazonite top, 35 ¼ x 49 ½ x 17 in. (89.5 x 125.7 x 43.2 cm)

know what's what. My focus now is to buy up his more important pieces whenever they become available. I recently bought a Nakashima desk that the Rockefellers de-accessioned from Pocantico, and a monumental coffee table from the International Paper Company in New York.

Contemporary design

I do not know contemporary design and so I am afraid of it. Besides, I am an antiques dealer – I like old, not new. Everybody is in that market and I do not really want to be in the most popular market of the day. If everyone were to come into the market that I am in now, I would be gone. I prefer to be somewhere a little bit above where everybody else is. Even if I don't understand a piece, if I like it, I'll buy it for myself. Marc Newson – I don't understand that market. It might be good. I do not know, so I am not there. I would rather put my money in Claude de Muzac, a confirmed genius of the 1970s. There isn't enough of her work, unfortunately.

His advice for the new collector

Buy from a reputable dealer or a reputable auction house. I go back to my previous statement: the only bargain is a fair price.

Emile-Jacques Ruhlmann

Corner cabinet, ca. 1920, burr amboina with inlaid ivory, interior drawers with gilt-bronze handles, 49 ⅞ x 23 ⅞ x 20 ⅛ in. (126.5 x 60.5 x 51 cm)

Suzanne Demisch

Dealer, New York

Suzanne Demisch started out as a "picker", meaning one who scours flea markets and vintage shops, looking to discover pieces to sell to the bigger dealers. Today, Demisch Danant, her Chelsea gallery in New York's art district, specialises in European designs of the 1970s. Her book on Maria Pergay helped to stimulate the Pergay market and the 1970s design market. She is also involved with several other French designers like Pierre Paulin and has curated shows on German design of the 1980s among other, as yet, undervalued genres.

How she started

I started as a picker, more or less, selling to other dealers. I was much more versed in Americana then and not anywhere near this world at all. A few years later, I started bringing back containers filled with things from France, again selling to dealers and shops here in the United States.

I met Stephane Danant, my business partner, at the Paris flea market. I had already been buying pieces from the 1970s by this time, and because he was also into that period, we decided to collaborate – this was at the very beginning of the Maria Pergay resurgence in 1998.

Most of the information I had came from reading magazine articles, and so the whole time both Stephane and I were approaching it from an academic point of view; that is, we were really into the research and all the documentation. We would buy years and years of old magazines like *Maison Francaise,* and that was the only way one could identify things because there were no books about Pergay at the time, there was nothing.

When we started buying and identifying work from the 1970s, it was the very beginning of interest in the period; people were just discovering new names, but even so there weren't that many doing it. You could find things in the Paris flea market, including works of Pierre Paulin and Jean Prouvé. It's more difficult to find great pieces in the flea market now, but it used to be the starting point for many discoveries.

Jean-Pierre Vitrac
Flower lamp, 1970, stainless steel,
30 ¾ x 11 ¾ in. (78 x 30 cm)

Her book on Maria Pergay

Maria Pergay
Ring Chair, 1968, stainless steel,
28 ½ x 23 x 32 in.
(72.4 x 58.4 x 81.3 cm)

I started writing the book on Pergay before I met her, and I spent a couple of years on it. I felt that she deserved some recognition, it was really an academic pursuit on my part. Most of the book is about her vintage historical career and less about the newer pieces, because she started to produce those when I was almost at the end of the book.

I went to Morocco to sit with her and talk about her career. It was during those meetings that she told me about some of her ideas for new pieces. I think it has been amazing to watch someone who has continued to have ideas, she has never actually stopped working – but never in the way she's working now.

Her gallery

Our primary scope starts from the late 1950s and goes to the early 1980s. From the late 1950s you have the French modernists: Pierre Guariche, Antoine Philippon and Jacqueline LeCoq, René-Jean Caillette and Joseph-André Motte. It is an area that has been under-recognised in general; French collectors know the artists better because the work never came to this country; it was never distributed here.

The thing is to be able to know what to buy and what not to buy. When you enter into a period like the 1970s, this is still a relatively new area. When Pergay and Michel Boyer and all these names came on the scene, no one really knew who was going to stay or what was going to rise.

Maria Pergay
Broken Cabinet, 2007, stainless steel,
41 ⅞ x 61 x 22 ⅝ in. (106.5 x 155 x 57.5 cm)

Today, the Flying Carpet by Pergay is about $200,000, or almost double what it

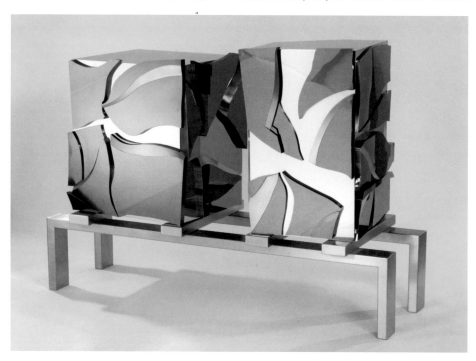

sold for in 2007. But on the other hand, two Ring Chairs suddenly don't sell at auction. How do you explain that?

As you know, the auction market reflects different factors. First, there have to be enough collectors, at that particular moment, to drive the price. Then, in the background, there is great effort from dealers to support pricing at auction, although this is not transparent in the results. But at the same time dealers are not always in the position to support every piece, even when there's a good deal to be made. Think of the Ring Chair – it should have sold – it was a fluke!

Contemporary design

Anyone who goes to the fairs is bombarded by lots of new stuff. I am not going to say whether it is good or bad, there's just a lot more of it. I think the design market has really evolved in the past three years with the advent of the design fairs, the attention and spotlight on design and also the new generation of young designers. Add to that a new group of collectors who are coming from the art market.

We have all enjoyed the conversations, "Is design art?" and "Is a chair a sculpture?"... We've beaten that subject to death. It has been press driven, too, which spurred a lot of activity in contemporary design. Prices got high and there was a lot more speculation as the market developed and became commercial. Historical design, which is what we do, was never about the commercial market, it was about design and technology and materials.

What confuses the situation is that everyone is trying to sell something new at a

> "With design collecting, you never know when and where you are going to find it – it's the hunt that's exciting."

Pierre Paulin
Cathedral table, 1981, aluminium base, glass, 29 ½ x 55 x 55 in. (74 x 140 x 140 cm)

Stefan Zwicky
Concrete chair, 1980, reinforced
concrete and iron, 26 ⅜ x 29 ⅞ x 27 ½ in.
(67 x 76 x 70 cm)

time when the market has really driven up
the prices. Recently there has definitely been
a step back and I think it's a good thing.
There isn't anything wrong at all with collecting contemporary design, but one must also
have a historical balance because that is the foundation. To know the lineage is the only
way to understand where these ideas came from and to understand that it is really *hard*
to have a new idea.

Difference between vintage and historical

It is common that people, especially those new to the field, do not fully understand the
value of the collectible object they are looking at, and they may even think they can find
it somewhere else for less, in other words, a vintage piece. And one must remember that
auction results do not always tell the full story, such as the condition of the piece and
other factors.

The value of a collectible is that it represents an idea, and only the benefit of hindsight
or history can tell you why it was important in its time, what else was made in the same
period or what has stood the test of time. For example, if you look at Bauhaus, even in
its day it represented new ideas and a new way of thinking, it was a transition from a

more decorative, Art Nouveau moment. And now 100 years later we can see in a bigger way how that influenced the rest of design history. So you have to consider the grand scheme of things and I think that's what is important when you look at a piece. Of course, some pieces are more important than others because they represent different things and ideas in a time line, but that is the verity that gives something its collector-ship value.

Her new clients

I would say, more and more, we have a different range of clients, but our newer clients are definitely coming from the art world. We have always had a strong base of decorative arts/design clients who collect only furniture, they do not collect art or anything else. Those people are still actively engaged.

But the whole landscape has changed in the last couple of years, and we have to adjust to the new players. Design collecting is unlike art collecting…it's a different thing. In art collecting, you usually have to know what you want and then figure out how to get it. With design collecting, you never know when and where you are going to find it – it's the hunt that's exciting. And the more you know, the more interesting it gets, and helps in deciding what to buy – is it a trophy, something to impress, do you like the way it looks, do you need a piece this big to fit in that room? Or is it okay to be awkward? Yes, with design you can be awkward – even if you don't need it or there is not an obvious place for it, you can rotate like everything else, and you buy it because you love it.

The future of design

Design just accelerated from zero to 60. It has been elevated in the last few years and will continue to do so at a rapid pace as collectorship grows and as collectors become better informed, dig deeper and go for fewer obvious choices. Just like anything else, the more you know, you want something more challenging. Emphasis on the historical aspect will grow, especially in discoveries of the later 20th century…there are so many places for the new collector to jump in. But it is a process, especially with the new group of collectors who are coming from another set of criteria in the art market.

The design market has its own special variables. Prices today are relatively undervalued, but the market still needs more buyers and more collectors to grow further.

Joseph-André Motte
Tripod chair, 1949, seat in rattan with central metal cross, 28 ⅜ x 29 ⅞ x 29 ⅞ in. (72 x 76 x 76 cm)

overleaf: **Wolfgang Laubersheimer / Pentagon**
Amazonas table, 1988, stone and steel, 29 ⅛ x 51 ⅛ x 27 ⅜ in. (74 x 130 x 70 cm). One of ten tables depicting shapes of rivers

Ulrich Fiedler

Dealer, Berlin

Berlin-based modernism expert Ulrich Fiedler has been sourcing early works by Gerrit Thomas Rietveld, Mies van der Rohe and Le Corbusier, among others, for over two decades. His gallery specialises in early 20th century pieces that are architectural and conceptual in their nature and form. He strongly represents that part of the design world which most approaches architecture, and his programme shuns anything that looks or feels like decor or stylistic embellishment.

Starting the business

I had already started collecting bentwood and steel furniture when I was studying art history back in the 1970s. My first piece was a Mies van der Rohe chair, which I found in a trash container. I saw it from my car, hit the brakes and nearly caused a crash. I found out that it was an original from 1928, and it was such a fascination for me because it looked so different from the common re-editions I had known before. I was already involved with modernism through my studies, but this original piece of furniture drew my life in a new direction.

Every weekend, I went at six o'clock in the morning to the flea markets in the area where I lived, first Cologne, then Düsseldorf, Dortmund, and then on to the next city...I tried to be everywhere. I made the acquaintance of all the dealers, and then I started getting the phone calls – we have this, we have that – and suddenly I found myself out of money. I had to try to find ways to make some, and that's how I started the business, without having any idea of becoming a gallerist.

I had to begin trading and selling pieces to continue. I spent a lot of time searching and researching, and through this I came across a lot of commercial decorative Art Deco furniture, which I sold to dealers so I could afford to keep the modernist pieces I liked. Next to the tubular steel chairs, I had a huge interest in bentwood furniture at this time. I worked on it with Alexander von Vegesack, later the director of the Vitra Design Museum, who became a close friend of mine. He was an important collector of bentwood furniture and I learned a lot from him about building up a collection in a professional and academic way.

Hans and Wassili Luckhardt
Chair, 1931–1932, bent chromed tubular steel frame, ebony-stained plywood, 34 ½ x 17 ¾ x 21 ⅝ in. (88 x 45 x 55 cm)

The technology of bending wood had allowed an industrial production of furniture. This was the origin of furniture design as a profession. Before that, the carpenter made the chair the way he wanted to make it, as he had learned from tradition, from his father and grandfather and so on. Now suddenly there was the possibility for somebody outside the workshop, an artist or another creative person – what we call "designer" today – to develop something, along with an industry that could produce it in multiples.

Defining his programme

I am looking for pieces that are important in how they bring, or have brought, forward the development of modern design; objects which were ahead of their time. Sometimes I say I am looking for the remains of a lost Utopia…the relics of a utopian ideal which had no chance to be realised, especially in the Germany of the 1930s. The objects I deal with are communicating ideas and ideals of the avant-garde art movements of their time.

The most fascinating period for me is when the 1920s artists, architects and designers abandoned all traditions to create a new world. The avant-garde of this period believed in the idea that a newly designed environment could improve the behaviour of human beings.

Much of the furniture of this time was designed to be mass-produced, to be affordable for everybody. But this only happened in the 1960s, when re-editions of the then-called modern classics came into fashion. Only a few pieces were sold before World War II, mainly to friends and members of the cognoscenti.

The first production of tubular steel furniture by Marcel Breuer, for instance, was not done in a big factory; the pieces were made by hand by a few craftsmen, but they had the intended appearance of an industrial product when finished. Also, the Bauhaus work-shops did not use any machines. In the metal workshop, where Marianne Brandt and Wilhelm Wagenfeld made their famous designs for lamps and tableware, the hammer was the most common tool. At the end, they polished the objects to cover all the tracks of handcraft to make them industrial look-alikes. It was a kind of laboratory to produce prototypes for later mass-production, which never happened.

"I am looking for... the relics of a utopian ideal which had no chance to be realised."

I do not consider our pieces as decorative objects to furnish a home; my clients collect them like art and buy when something fits the concept or idea of the collection they want to build up. It can be a very creative act that reflects one's own personality and image. This does not mean that you cannot use these pieces, but that is not the first motive for buying. In fact, I have sold important chairs which should not be sat upon if the buyer wants to keep them in their original condition, especially when an old fabric is involved.

I try to avoid any restoration. That means I have to be very critical in any acquisition, because I want to offer my clients authentic objects. Any later alteration, like a new chroming on a tubular steel chair, can destroy its aura and fascination. So I only conserve what is original, and a restorer treats the materials only to avoid further abrasion or oxidation. In some instances, I have refused a sale because the client asked me to re-chrome a chair or replace the original fabric. For this reason, it is also difficult for me to work with some decorators whose approach to the object is sometimes very different from mine.

From socialist relics to bourgeois collectibles

There is no conflict in my selling these relics. Most of them have gone to a museum so they are visible for the public, and if I sell some to collectors, most of them will ultimately give their collection to an institution, or create a museum with their collection, like Rolf Fehlbaum from Vitra did in Basel. In the beginning, I could not part with these pieces, but then I learned to do it. I am happy to have owned them once, and I have formed three or four very huge collections, each being one I would have chosen for myself if I had been a millionaire. Finally, I am happy because I am still very close to all the pieces I have handled, since all the buyers are friends whom I visit frequently. I have access to them organizing loans for exhibitions, and sometimes they come back to me because I buy them back, or trade them.

Marcel Breuer
Isokon lounge, 1935, molded plywood
in one piece, bent plywood frame,
31 ½ x 23 ½ x 52 ⅜ in. (80 x 60 x 133 cm)

On Marcel Breuer

There is one fact in Breuer's career that is little known; he made all his furniture designs in the first ten years of his career, when he was twenty to thirty. He was very young when he joined the Bauhaus and then made all his important designs, the wooden Lath Chair, then the Wassily chair. He is considered the person who invented the use of tubular steel for furniture.

Then he switched over to aluminium – his famous furniture that he made for the company Wohnbedarf in Switzerland. There was a big international competition in 1933 for the aluminium industry, which wanted to promote this material, and Breuer won all the first prizes. By the mid-1930s, he followed Walter Gropius to England and there he developed furniture in plywood together with the Isokon Company, which

> "When good design ... is born, it does not matter if it is aluminium or gold, for me it has the same value."

manufactured it and brought it to market. Those pieces, which were plywood versions of his earlier metal designs, also did not succeed and only a few were sold. Then he moved to the United States and started his career as architect. Up to that point, he had built really nothing. He was in furniture for only those ten years and almost everything he designed was during that period. In the years following, there were a few designs, but nothing important any more. What was, and is, important after that are his buildings.

Gerrit Rietveld

Rietveld is the man who reinvented the chair with his famous Red and Blue Chair. It was radical because he threw away all the traditions of furniture building and started anew. With this design, he neglected all conventional joints and all tradition. It had great impact, and everything that followed was based on it; it was equivalent to the development that Mondrian gave to the world of art through his radical abstraction.

I think that fewer than 20 original examples of the Red and Blue Chair have survived, and most of them are in museum collections. A Red and Blue Chair must have a full history and provenance because, you know, nearly every architect in the world has built one in his life just as a study. In original condition, I think today an exemplar is worth somewhere around $400,000–$500,000.

A historic perspective on the design market

I think that the development of prices for contemporary design pieces, and maybe also some French mid-century designs, occurred a little too fast and went too high; on the other hand, the development of more classic, modernist pieces was very regular; the prices grew more naturally and never had a crash. I doubt that today's prices for contemporary design are sustainable. I do not doubt the importance of Marc Newson or Ron Arad, but they went up too quickly. This is the same phenomenon that happened to contemporary artists.

Gerrit Thomas Rietveld
Zig-Zag chair, 1934, stained pine wood
mounted with iron nuts and bolts,
29 ¼ x 13 x 16 ⅜ in. (74.7 x 33 x 41.5 cm)

The Prouvé market

Prouvé's dealers bought an incredible number of pieces and stocked them in their warehouses. Then they started promoting them because they had a supply on hand to create a demand in the design scene, plus the ability to deliver the pieces, so that the prices grew instantly. If you have only one existing example and you sell it, there is no other chance for it. So with a rare item, you sometimes cannot create a market the way you can with material when you have 50 pieces in stock, like the Mexique or the Tunisia shelves of Prouvé/Perriand, where you sell the first one, and then the next one more expensively, and the next one higher and so on; thus you create a market and develop it. So we are left with this contradiction in that a piece that is not rare can bring a much higher price than a piece which may be unique.

Dealing in Eileen Gray chairs

Eileen Gray had two very different periods in her career. One was a decorative period at the beginning, with all the precious lacquer furniture, which today is very, very expensive. Then she met the modern architects of her time and she started her relation with Jean Badovici. He was the publisher of an important architectural magazine in Paris and very connected with the world of International Style. Through all those people, she changed fundamentally to a functional, but very personal functional style. This is the period I am interested in.

Her furniture was made mainly for her own homes, many pieces were built-in and integrated in the architecture. She was not interested in making the universal piece of furniture that would work in every flat in the world. She designed for special places. The most important piece I ever had from her was the S-Chair – it's a chair that you can fold together and it stands on a wall. It went to a museum in Germany for a six-figure price. I would consider the chair today would be worth at least $2 million.

Marcel Breuer
Side Table B18, 1928–1929, bent nickeled tubular steel frame, glass top, 28 ¾ x 22 x 30 in. (73 x 56 x 76 cm)

Exhibiting Jasper Morrison

I saw Jasper Morrison's first pieces at the Cologne furniture fair and one year later I made his first gallery exhibition with his early ready-made-like works. I like him, because he designed sympathetic, useful things on a

Paolo Pallucco and Mireille Rivier
Tankette coffee table, 1987, steel frame with rolling mechanism, aluminium plates, black lacquer, 13 ¾ x 30 ½ x 49 ½ in. (35 x 77.5 x 126 cm)

human scale. He is not trying to catch your attention with spectacular forms and shiny surfaces. Often, you recognize the quality of Jasper's designs on the second viewing. After post-modernism, it was refreshing to see his return to more classic design principles.

His personal aesthetic

Abstraction, constructivism and minimalism have great impact on my aesthetics. The unity of form and function makes a good design. If, then, an ingenious artistic language invades a useful object of everyday life, this piece can be as valuable as an important work of art.

Form is crucial; good craftsmanship or precious materials are secondary. When good design or a brilliant new idea is born, it does not matter if it is aluminium or gold, for me it has the same value. I also look for architectural elements in furniture – the tectonics of a chair, the tectonics of a wardrobe – that is very relevant.

I am not dogmatic in this, I also have an emotional approach to objects. I admire, for instance, the eccentric work of Carlo Mollino or the magical psychedelic light fixtures of the Italian 1970s.

Ultimately, I do not sell decoration, I am selling ideas. It is an ideological thing. I am behind what I do, I want to follow it, I am defending it and I will do it all my life, I am sure. I will not change my profile anywhere, anytime.

Barry Friedman

Dealer, New York

Barry Friedman has been an institution in the New York design field for decades, and has shown decorative arts from throughout the 20th century. Today, in three different spaces, he is involved in Deco, Mid-century as well as Contemporary.

Beginnings

This is my 41st year as an art and antique dealer. I began to buy and sell works on a small scale in the 1960s in order to finance my passion for collecting.

In 1969, I opened my first antiques shop at the 53rd Street Antique Center, where many dealers got their start. Then I was able to move to Madison Avenue and open a gallery called Primavera specializing in Art Deco. When I divorced in 1973, my wife took over the gallery. Eventually I moved into a large space in a brownstone on 82nd Street, between Madison and Fifth Avenues, very near the Metropolitan Museum of Art.

It was there that I began dealing in Symbolist and Pre-Raphaelite paintings and working with the best of design from the turn of the 20th century, like that of architects Charles Rennie Mackintosh, Josef Hoffmann and other artists of the Wiener Werkstätte. I was fortunate enough to discover this field at a very early stage. At that time I was also dealing in fine Art Deco pieces by Emile-Jacques Ruhlmann, as well as Art Nouveau furniture, in particular the work of Hector Guimard.

In the late 1970s and early 1980s, I started collecting furniture by architects, which eventually culminated in a 1984 exhibition, *Mackintosh to Mollino: Fifty Years of Chair Design.* The show was reviewed from here to Tokyo and everywhere between, with a major article with photos in *The New York Times.* We exhibited furniture by architects like Hector Guimard, Antonio Gaudi, Henry van de Velde, Josef Maria Olbrich, Peter Behrens, Richard Riemerschmid, Adolf Loos, Otto Wagner and Frank Lloyd Wright, all from the turn of the 20th century. Also featured were works from the 1920s and 1930s by architects and designers like Ruhlmann, Pierre Chareau, Jean-Michel Frank, Le Corbusier, Marcel Breuer and Alvar Aalto. From the 1950s, we showed Charles and Ray Eames, Eero Saarinen, as well as Jean Prouvé and Carlo Mollino (both probably shown for the first time at an American gallery).

Ron Arad
Oh-Void "No Solution No Problem", 2006,
silicone and steel, 25 ¼ x 47 x 24 in.
(64.1 x 119.4 x 61 cm)

I had discovered Jean Prouvé in Paris around 1980. At the same time, I met the grandson of Steph Simon (producer of Prouvé, also of Serge Mouille). I purchased between 50 and 70 pieces through the grandson at that time. Both artists were hardly known in America, and so it was very difficult to sell their work here. I donated some of the pieces to museums, put others in storage and sold a large number of pieces to a dealer [DeLorenzo] for his gallery and a restaurant that he had opened on West Broadway.

My next design exhibition in 1988, *The Bauhaus: Masters and Students,* included approximately 150 pieces from all phases of the Bauhaus. Many of the

> "I do not make distinctions between the decorative arts and fine arts, works made of glass, oil on canvas, or a piece of wood – what interests me most is whether the piece is captivating."

pieces found homes in major museums, and an extensive catalogue was published. Six months later, I put together another show, *Gerrit Rietveld: A Centenary Exhibition,* which travelled to two American museums. For both the Bauhaus and the Rietveld exhibitions, I spent approximately five years or more collecting the works.

Research and discovery

I feel that my expertise has been in discovering different fields and different artists, largely through research and travel. It is always a thrill for me to find a new artist, or rediscover a forgotten artist or movement that has relevance today. I enjoy the research aspect of the business very much and over the years have compiled an extensive

Forrest Myers
Parker, 2006, steel wire with black oxidised patina, 37 x 27 x 22 in. (94 x 68.6 x 55.9 cm)

library of books and catalogues on various subjects and movements.

Today, I have three galleries: The first one is Barry Friedman Ltd. in Chelsea, where we specialise in paintings, works on paper and photography as well as design. We have works as early as the 1880s through today, specialising more and more in contemporary art. We represent the new designs of Wendell Castle and the bronze furniture by the French sculptor Ingrid Donat. We also work with some of the best contemporary decorative artists in glass, ceramics and silver.

My second gallery, Friedman & Vallois, was founded together with my partners Cheska and Bob Vallois from Paris and is located on 67th Street and Madison Avenue. The gallery specialises in high-end Art Deco pieces by such artists as Ruhlmann, Jean-Michel Frank and Paul Dupré-Lafon. We also have major works by Diego Giacometti.

Ettore Sottsass with Poltronova
Elledue bed from Mobili Grigio series, 1969–1970, fibreglass, 38 x 96 x 84 in. (96.5 x 243.8 x 213.4 cm)

My third and most recent gallery is Friedman Benda, also located in Chelsea, which specialises in more cutting-edge art. My partner, Marc Benda, had worked for me for five years and was a director at Barry Friedman Ltd. Marc is one of the most

Shiro Kuramata
Glass Chair, 1976, glass, 35 ½ x 34 x 24 in.
(90.2 x 86.4 x 61 cm)

knowledgeable specialists of contemporary design. He has helped bring Ron Arad and Ettore Sottsass to the gallery as well as Joris Laarman, Marcel Wanders, Forrest Myers and Shiro Kuramata.

Dealing with personal taste

I do not like to make comparisons between art and design. As for the difference between the decorative arts, fine art and design...everybody is asking this question today. Speaking for myself, whether it is a painting, photography, a unique piece of glass made by Emile Gallé himself or a sculpture by Ron Arad, if it's great, I consider it to be great art. I do not make distinctions between the decorative arts and fine arts, works made of glass, oil on canvas or a piece of wood – what interests me most is whether the piece is captivating.

Ettore Sottsass
Cabinet no. 76, 2006, ebonised pear wood,
acrylic, birch burl and anodised red aluminum,
78 ¾ x 84 ⅝ x 19 ¾ in. (200 x 215 x 50 cm)

overleaf: **Ron Arad**
Big Easy vol. 2 for 2 sofa, ca.1989,
polished stainless steel, 40 x 83 ⅜ x 41 in.
(101.6 x 211.8 x 104.1 cm)

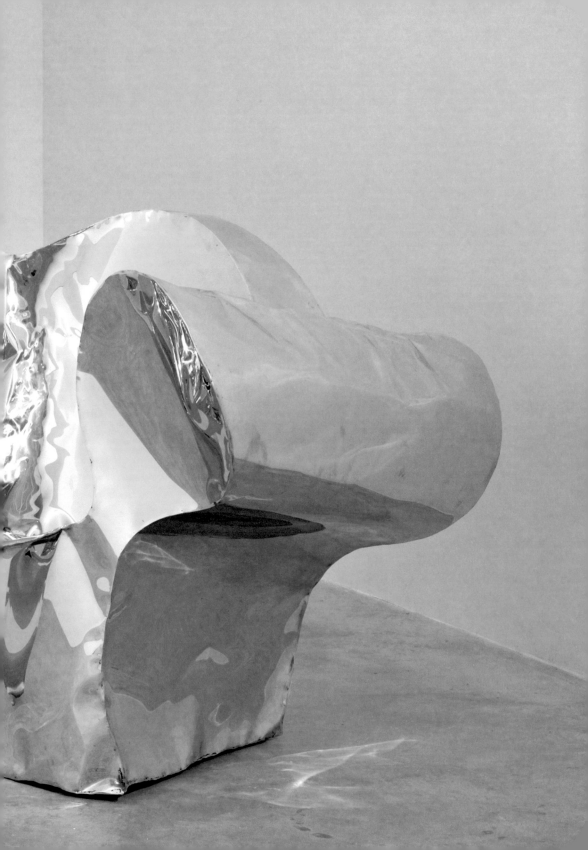

Didier and Clémence Krzentowski

Dealers, Paris

Didier and Clémence Krzentowski have been producing and exhibiting contemporary designers from their Galerie Kreo in Paris for a decade. Having launched the production of limited editions for several now-famous designers, Kreo today is synonymous with collectible and valuable contemporary design.

How they started

Didier: We opened our gallery ten years ago. Before that, my family and I were business partners with the great French ski champion Jean-Claude Killy. Our company created a very fashionable line of ski clothes, licensing Killy's name. My wife, Clémence, was also the manager of the Olympic flame for the Albertville Olympics Committee. We sold the Killy ski company in 1991, and I was trying to think of what to do next.

I had no ideas at the time, but I was a collector of contemporary art. I started mainly with photography, Nan Goldin – which then was about $300 a photograph – along with works of Cindy Sherman and Louise Lawler. I was also obsessed with collecting furniture, specifically design furniture of the 1960s, and then into the 1970s with designers like Pierre Paulin, and lighting starting from the 1950s with designers like Gino Sarfatti and Joe Colombo.

Clémence: My first interesting collaboration was when we got Philippe Starck to create the torch for the 1992 Albertville Olympics, and a commission for Martin Szekely to design the podium of the Olympic Games.

Our idea was to create an agency that would represent designers and get commissions for them vis-à-vis industrial companies. In the same way that Mark McCormack (International Management Group) represented athletes, we were going to take designers like Pierre Charpin, Marc Newson, Martin Szekely and represent them to industrial clients. This was our approach at the beginning.

Didier: When I met Marc Newson in the 1990s, he was quite unknown. I found his work amazing...especially considering that I do not think there can be more than a handful of top designers in the world at any given time.

Philippe Starck
Albertville Olympic torch, 1992, aluminium,
16.5 x max. ø 2 ⅜ in. (42 x max. ø 6 cm)

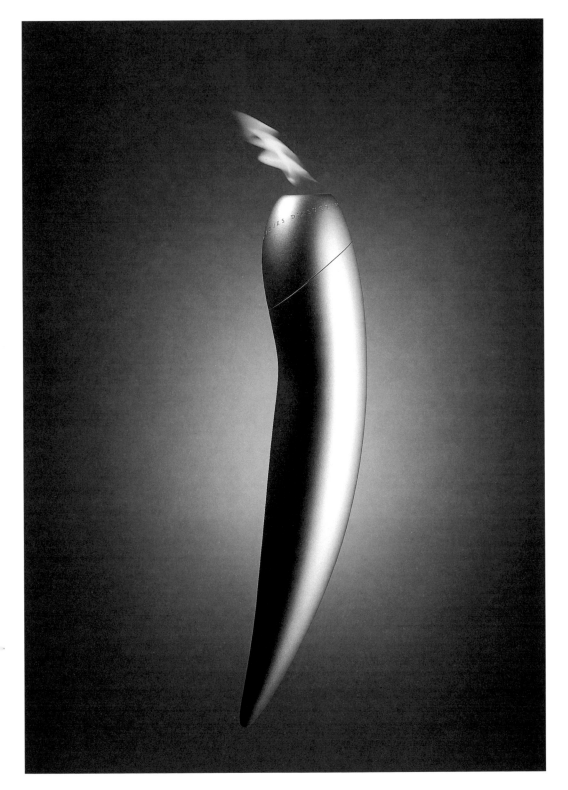

Galerie Kreo's philosophy

Clémence: We opened the gallery in 1999, and our first show was of works from our own collection – pieces by Joe Colombo, lamps by Verner Panton. Our early shows were held at Emmanuel Perrotin's gallery and at the Purple Institute before we even had our own space. Our first real designer show was with Ron Arad in 1999...since then we have had more than 60 shows. The late 1990s were a good time to open a design gallery, we were very lucky. Contemporary art collectors were beginning to take furniture seriously, which hadn't been the case up until then. This enabled us

> "Designers want to work with us because we give them several years to study and do the needed production. No one else is about to do that... other people just want to sell."

immediately to access funds for research. On the one hand, you had designers who were really interested in doing this type of research, and on the other, you had buyers who were interested in pieces like these. It was the perfect combination.

We have been pioneers in offering limited edition design pieces. We started by producing editions of eight pieces, plus two APs (artist's proofs) and two prototypes. The reason is quite simple. We began to collect contemporary art in the 1980s. At that time, the principle of a limited edition of twelve pieces already existed in sculpture. We applied the same numbering principle to design.

We do it this way because Galerie Kreo is a kind of "research laboratory" for designers. When we team up with a designer, we have no idea of how long it will take to produce the piece, or when we will be able to have the exhibition, so there is no rationale for determining its price. One of our main ideas was to leave designers free to create on their own schedule, as they wish, with no constraints – it is quite different from industrial projects like Marc

Martin Szekeley
Albertville Olympic Games podium,
1992, wood, 32 ⅝ x 137 ⅜ x 81 ¾ in.
(83 x 349 x 208 cm)

Ronan and Erwan Bouroullec
Assemblage 4, 2004, orange lacquered-metal light box and ceiling light, frame in black tubing, seaweed, white Corian stand, 71 x 100 ¾ x 78 ¾ in. (180 x 256 x 200 cm)

Newson's Ikepod watch company, where you know what your costs will be and what your marketing budget is.

However, in doing limited editions, one must realise that the process is long…it can take up to two years to produce the exhibit pieces and, sometimes, two more to finish the 12th and final piece. So in furniture design shows, our prices are higher than those of a furniture company because we've given the designer total freedom in the creative process. This, in turn, relates to the limited edition – we feel that at gallery price levels, we must be able to tell the client how many pieces were produced. When you are buying this kind of piece, you want to know how many of them exist out there.

Didier: The designers we work with today are those we represent worldwide, and we represent them exclusively – except Marc Newson. Currently, they are Ronan and Erwan Bouroullec, Pierre Charpin, Naoto Fukasawa, Konstantin Grcic, Hella Jongerius, Jasper Morrison, Jerszy Seymour and Martin Szekely among others.

How they choose designers

Didier: I have an extensive collection of books on design from the 1950s to today and, as I am an insomniac, I read all night long, trying to find designers who do not compromise.

Clémence: For designers who wish to challenge themselves artistically and creatively, our place is a great place to do it. We have an in-depth relationship with our designers. We produce books with them and we are also preparing the catalogues raisonnés of Ronan and Erwan Bouroullec, Marc Newson and Martin Szekely.

What makes a good gallery

Didier: A good gallery is one that chooses to defend and support its creators and their markets.

For example, Demisch Danant: they represent mainly French designers from the 1970s whom they believe in and support, showing the work in a respectful way, with pieces that are relevant. That is not easy, especially when exhibiting French furniture from the 1970s, which is still relatively unknown, not researched and poorly understood. They have chosen a period of furniture design history and they stand behind it, defend it, and are creating a market for it.

One must remember that for almost 20 years, Philippe Jousse, Patrick Seguin and François Laffanour had a very, very hard time launching Jean Prouvé and Charlotte Perriand, as well as Pierre Jeanneret and the market for French mid-century furniture and design. They did not need to do that, they could have done something else. It took that long for the public to understand how important the work was.

For contemporary art, we can also mention Pierre Marie Giraud and his work with ceramics. These are people who really believe in what they present. This is how I believe work for a gallery should be.

Hella Jongerius
Swatch coffee table, 2008, American walnut wood marquetry, table top of multicolored resin blocks, matte and glossy finishing, 13 ¾ x 63 ¾ x 33 ½ in. (35 x 162 x 85 cm)

Why Marc Newson's work is so important

Didier: His life is part of his work. He creates things that are ultimately for himself. In a way, his relationship to surfing, or his relationship

Gino Sarfatti
Ceiling light no. 2109/12, 1962, black lacquered aluminum, twelve globes in transparent glass, 23 ⅝ to 43 ¼ x ø 31 ½ in. (60 to 110 x ø 80 cm), globes: ø 5 ½ in. (ø 14 cm)

to the music industry in creating sound studios for his friends in Japan, or his lifestyle of globetrotting all over the world – represent his generation of the late 1980s and 1990s. All of that feeling, his environment and the whole mood can be felt in his work.

Clémence: For instance, with the Ikepod watch, you have two elements that are really characteristic of Marc's work – from the outside they seem to be incredibly simple, but on the inside, they are highly technical and complicated to make and produce. His watch looks sober and minimal, and extremely simple in its hemispheric, organic shape, but in reality it is a highly complex Swiss machine that completes all these complications.

Didier: When you review the body of his work in gallery shows, he has actually created very little. There are the aluminium pieces he did in the early 1990s that are very

Marc Newson
Event Horizon table, 1992, aluminium
and enamel, 31 ⅞ x 71 ¼ x 37 ⅜ in.
(81 x 181.4 x 94.9 cm)

important. The aluminium furniture has its history, going back to when Marc was a classic car fanatic. He loved the Aston Martin DB4 and bought one that needed repairs. While repairing his car, he became friendly with someone who had worked in the Aston Martin factory, doing bodywork. So from this guy's knowledge, combined with Marc's dream of the world of Aston Martin, came all the aluminium furniture. After that came another progression, with the pieces in marble for the Gagosian gallery.

Thinking about the risks of Marc Newson and other designers defecting to art galleries

Didier: First of all, I have not lost Marc Newson, as we are doing his catalogue raisonné for all his limited editions. We also make an exhibition every two or three years.

Designers like Konstantin Grcic, Jasper Morrison or Martin Szekely want to work with us because we say "yes", and give them several years to study and do the needed production. No one else is about to do that…other people just want to sell. During several years of working with Jasper Morrison, I got nothing from him – it took four years of work to finalise his first project; and in fact he had two exhibitions in a row.

In the future, if any of my designers wants to produce a bigger project, like creating a boat, or something that we cannot handle within the confines of this gallery, I have no problem teaming up with other galleries or organisations to turn out more ambitious works than we are capable of doing today. At the moment, we are not able to invest $5 million in the production of a single piece that we find interesting.

Konstantin Grcic
Karbon long chair, 2008, carbon fibre,
23 x 80 x 19 ¾ in. (63.5 x 180 x 50 cm)

Their goal

Didier: My goal is that in 40 or 50 years, the gallery will be one that people are still talking about: "Wow, what a difference they made, look at what they produced and see how they contributed to design history."

For example, Jasper Morrison has done both of his two gallery shows with us. For me, the excitement is when we do not know where we are going or how it will end. That is innovation in design, creating something new.

Konstantin Grcic has been working for years with sports technology, especially carbon fibre. It took months of elaboration to create a new long chair, and here we are, the Karbon long chair is in the gallery at this moment, in our new

"We sell a great work to someone who wants a great work. We never tell our clients that they are going to make money."

space at rue Dauphine, in Saint Germain des Prés.

With Martin Szekely, we worked with Lafarge, a company leader in the world of concrete, and we applied that technology to produce new tables with Ductal©, the new fibre concrete. Martin did a study to see how thin it could be made, and hopefully, this will spawn new innovations and new impacts elsewhere.

The designers we work with have chosen to study and research, and test new production, rather than to solely make pieces for the market. It is a personal choice.

Are there enough good new designers to sustain a contemporary design market?

Clémence: There are a few good new designers worldwide. We have to give them and their designs some time. Just as the contemporary art market took time to mature, I feel the same phenomenon is happening to design.

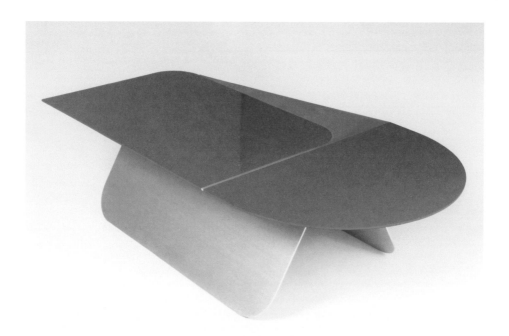

Pierre Charpin
Medium T coffee table, 2006, brushed and lacquered aluminium in water blue, 13 ¾ x 32 x 55 in. (35 x 81 x 140 cm)

Design as investment

Clémence: I think that design definitely can be an investment, but it is *a posteriori,* after the fact. When you study the truly great designers and what you are able to collect, there are not that many works available compared to the art world. One can find hundreds of artists and thousands of pieces of art, but there are considerably fewer designers, and for the same or less money, you can own some of their major works and some *chefs d'oeuvre.*

Didier: Buying design is the same as buying art. You need to seek out galleries with whom you share a spirit, a vision. We have a certain approach to the design world and our clients share that vision. Ultimately, the way we sell our design, whether it's Marc Newson or anyone else, is not as an investment. We sell a great work to someone who wants a great work. We never tell our clients that they are going to make money. That was never the purpose of this endeavour.

Marc Newson
Carbon ladder, 2008, carbon fibre and silicon, 79 ⅜ in. (201.5 cm) high, base width: 19 in. (48 cm)

overleaf: **Jasper Morrison**
Carrara Tables, Variation #13, 2005, Carrara marble, honeycomb aluminum, white nylon, 22 ½ x 101 x 15 in. (57 x 259 x 38.5 cm)

Zesty Meyers and Evan Snyderman

Dealers, New York

Zesty Meyers and Evan Snyderman started out working as professional glass blowers and won a Tiffany grant. Their design business, R 20th Century Design, grew from their collecting hobby, which led to selling at a New York flea market in the early 1990s. Today, R 20th Century is known for curating shows of Poul Kjærholm, Joaquim Tenreiro and vintage Wendell Castle, among others.

How they started

Very early on, we realised that there was a big gap in the design business between what was already famous and being marketed and what had yet to be researched, edited and discussed. We saw an opportunity to carve out our own niche. We set out to curate exhibitions, print books and establish ourselves as the experts in a field yet to be defined. Our goal, without knowing it at the time, was to create our own markets.

Their perspective

We began by seeking out information on the history of pieces, and what set us apart is that we like to share what we learned. That made it interesting for us; it was not about buying and selling furniture. We wanted to tell a story and to curate exhibitions. Museums were not yet doing it for 20th century design, and in many cases they still are not.

During World War II, new technologies were created for the war effort, which wedded new materials like molded plywood and aluminium to bring about modern design. Historically, it takes 100 to 150 years for furniture design movements to change significantly, meaning if modernism started in 1945, we are only half way through it today. In essence, the field of dealing in, and collecting modernism is still in the early stages of development.

How much new design is really different? An object can be made in carbon fibre or other new materials, but does that constitute a new and valuable idea? Only a handful of people create great designs. The design world is like the music industry – most people end up as one-hit wonders.

Verner Panton
Exhibition view, R 20th Century,
New York 2001. Seen through
Panton-designed textile:
Fun ceiling lamps, 1964, capiz shells,
Relaxer 2 rocker, ca. 1974,
in the background: *S chair,* ca. 1967

We represent design from four continents: South America, North America, Asia and Europe. We try to explore where, how, when and what it came from. How were people influenced at the time? The world was already global in 1945, with communications and world's fairs that introduced new and amazing things, along with great museums and periodicals that were showcasing design. The international exchange and energy of that era inspired us as we created our program here.

The work of Poul Kjærholm

After World War II, metal was an extremely difficult material to come by in Denmark, so working with it was like working with something the price of gold. Poul Kjærholm came up with a clear way of thinking about why, how and what he wanted to accomplish.

He was trained as a cabinetmaker in the traditional Danish mode of furniture making, and went through that school, working mostly with

> "In America, design has never really been an important subject. In Europe, it is part of everyday life."

wood – when we think of Denmark we think of woods like rosewood and teak. Then he wanted to become an interior architect; for him, the interior of a building was just as important as the exterior. But he was not an architect, he was a furniture maker and craftsman, and when he applied the crafts that are traditionally done in wood to metal, his work became really interesting.

Because of the quality of his craft and the cost of the materials, Kjærholm's work was always expensive. Compared to a designer like Jean Prouvé in the evolving collectors' market, Kjærholm required a more significant initial investment. Prouvé's work was, at one time, easier and cheaper to acquire because he predominantly designed for institutions and mass production.

Kjærholm's pieces have been in continuous production; some of them have already been produced for 50 years. A few items are more popular than others, so yes, perhaps 20,000 of certain pieces might have been sold – that is a high number for a single design. As Kjærholm collectors, what we look for is the earlier work; it stands apart in that more was made by hand in the craftsman's studio, the quality of materials was higher and the overall product has more character and elegance than we tend to see today.

The Kjærholm catalogue raisonné was published in 2008 [*The Furniture of Poul Kjærholm: Catalogue Raisonné* by Michael Sheridan, Gregory R. Miller & Co., New York] and we contributed time and effort to it because of the need to have an accurate source of information, to identify authentic pieces and help collectors refine their collections.

Defining design

The question is not what *is* design, but what is *good* design – because design is everywhere, in every aspect of your life. In America, design has never really been an important subject. In Europe, it is part of everyday life. Go to Copenhagen and you will see beautiful lamps in people's windows, at every socio-economic level. Design is widely appreciated in Europe, whereas in America it is limited to a smaller segment of the culture.

Because ours is a young country, we do not have the same wealth of history, nor have we ingrained, as yet, the respect for design and architecture into the fabric of our society. What makes American design so interesting is the interweaving of influences and history that came with the waves of immigration in the first half of the 20th century. Then there were people challenging the history of design, like Wendell Castle, who did not follow any rules and, in many cases, set out to break them.

About Joaquim Tenreiro

Tenreiro was originally from Portugal. He moved to Brazil as a young man, was trained as a woodworker and worked for a company that made copies of European furniture because the prevailing styles were either European or Portuguese colonialism. But Tenreiro emerged on his own – he broke away from the traditionalist style and formed the modern Brazilian concept of design. Oscar Niemeyer admired him and selected him to design furniture when he was building Brasilia, mostly between 1956 and 1961, so he created the identity of what Brazil would become when the history books were written.

Poul Kjærholm
Holscher chair, 1952, welded steel tube frame, natural halyard seat and back, 28 in. (71.5 cm) high

It is the sheer quality of the way things are made and the uniqueness of his designs that are remarkable. He was the master craftsman and an engineering genius. He developed his own

way of joining wood that no one else has ever achieved. Tenreiro did not have ergonomics machines. Somehow he could figure out the strength of the wood and how thin it could be carved; it was a challenge every day to make it better, more elegant, to push the material. In the sense of what he accomplished in wood and his technique, he is really one of the top five woodworkers and master craftsmen of the 20th century.

He started making his modernist furniture in the 1940s, and stopped by the early 1970s. He became too obsessed with detail and could make only art. Because he never looked at his furniture as design, he saw himself as an artist, so he devoted his later years to painting and sculpture.

People in America had not heard of Tenreiro five or six years ago, although in Brazil his work has been collected and exhibited for 30 years. Here, he did not exist in the public's eye, except to a handful of art collectors. So when we saw his work, we were just blown away by it. How could something this good slip through the cracks? His work is almost impossible to find in books except for an entry in rare Italian design overviews from the 1950s.

"People are just realizing...that design has real value. You can still buy one of the most important pieces by a 20th century designer for well under $100,000."

Single dining chairs range in price from $7,500 to $20,000 now, and certain chairs have seen an exponential increase in value. People who come in to buy Tenreiro are usually ahead of the curve – the tastemakers, as we would call them. They get it, they can see quality, they can see design, and they react, "How come I don't know about this...I have to have this," and they are always there first. People fall in love at first sight with Tenreiro's work.

How to justify a $300,000 Tenreiro chair

His iconic three-legged chair was made fewer than 50 times, and each of the 50 is unique and hand carved. Tenreiro never offered this chair for sale; he would make them as gifts for his best patrons and it became his most coveted design.

On Wendell Castle

When Wendell Castle came on the scene in 1959–1960 he broke all the preconceived notions of how furniture should

Wendell Castle
Two-seat sofa, 1967, walnut, 28 ¾ x 55 ½ x 28 in. (73 x 140.9 x 71.1 cm)

be used and made in the United States. He didn't come from a furniture background, he was a sculptor who studied industrial design and sculpture in school, in Kansas. When he moved to New York City, he came to realise that it was very difficult to make it there and he could not afford to continue working in bronze, which is what he had studied, so he decided to try his hand at designing in wood.

Being skilled with his hands, he made some furniture for his own apartment. Around this time, Castle was invited to enter a sculpture exhibition and it was here that he decided to challenge the conventions. Since furniture would not be considered for this exhibition, he thought of making a chair so radical that no one would know it was furniture. The piece was accepted as sculpture and went on the win the praise of many visitors.

Then he tried out for a furniture competition, but since he didn't know how to make standard furniture, he made a sculpture that looked somewhat like a chair. At that exhibit, a professor from the crafts school saw the sculpture and invited Castle to teach at the Rochester Institute of Technology where the School for American Craftsmen was well established. Up to that point, Castle had not made a single piece of conventional furniture!

Sculpting furniture

Now, as the professor of furniture making, Castle again decided to challenge the established rules. He saw an article in *Popular Mechanics* magazine, "How to Build a Duck Decoy". Why not apply this technique to furniture? So in the early 1960s, he developed a technique for stack lamination, which gave him the ability to achieve a greater volume in form. He was not proficient in joinery or dovetails – the essentials of traditional woodworking – so he started to glue blocks of wood together and carve them the way he carved sculpture. That set the furniture world on its

Oscar Niemeyer
Rio chaise lounge, 1978 (example ca. 2005), imbuia wood with woven cane seat, leather head-rest, 34 x 67 x 23 ½ in. (86.4 x 170.2 x 59.7 cm)

head because no one had ever thought to do something like this; they assumed it would never hold up. Wendell Castle's work was not about forming perfect joints, rather, it was organic and bulbous...he was creating sculpture in furniture. It was about form. In no time Castle, a fast learner, became one of the greatest craftsmen in the field.

Castle experimented with incredible, fanciful forms that have inspired generations of furniture makers. If you examine the history of the American Studio Craft Movement, it follows Wendell like a wave. When Wendell Castle does something, the whole furniture world follows. In the late 1960s, Castle became bored with everything in the colour brown and began to experiment with painting the wood. This was unsuccessful. His interest in cars inspired him to experiment with fibreglass, and things got really interesting. At this time, Castle could be considered the only American furniture maker working in plastic; he was following the trends of his European contemporaries like Joe Colombo and Verner Panton.

Wendell is a true artist and he is never satisfied with one success. His work of the 1980s and 1990s is completely different from that of the 1960s and 1970s. He moved more into Post-modernism in the early 1980s and produced really bizarre, radical stuff that even today is aesthetically challenging, in the same way that Memphis was. But now Memphis is collectible again. He has been referred to as the American version of Memphis, and before that he was the American version of radical Pop design going on in Europe. In the end, though,

Joaquim Tenreiro
Bookshelf, ca. 1954, jacaranda and reverse-painted glass, 65 ¼ x 79 x 14 ¾ in. (165.7 x 200.7 x 37.5 cm)

he is an anomaly; he is a unique American icon.

We have been handling Castle's vintage work for seven years now and have seen the market for his work grow tremendously in recent years. His work will continue to grow in value, although most of the world has yet to discover him. His collectors, traditionally, have been people who were more involved in the world of crafts. The art and design world is just now learning who Wendell Castle is.

In 1983, his work was shown at the Alexander Milliken Gallery in New York [*The Extraordinary Art of Wendell Castle*]. Alex commissioned him to do a desk for the exhibit, saying: "I want you to make the most outrageous desk, the most expensive thing you could ever imagine, let's just go for it." So Wendell made a desk with thousands of inlaid pieces of ivory and wood, an incredibly intense, gorgeous piece, and sent it to New York – this was in 1983 – indicating the selling price as $75,000. The gallery doubled it, because that is what galleries do. The desk was shown for $150,000 and sold right away to a major collector. Up to that point, no one had ever sold a piece of furniture for that kind of money.

People are just realising, since about the mid-1970s, that design has real value. You can still buy one of the most important pieces by a 20th century designer for well under $100,000. And only a handful of pieces from the era have broken the million-dollar mark.

Between the years 1960 and 1980, Castle produced about 350 works, all of them unique. His work was never inexpensive so the people who bought it had the means and, for the most part, still do. Many of the collectors I have talked to who own Castle pieces say they will never sell, they are going to die with them.

Joaquim Tenreiro
Three-legged chair, 1947, jacaranda from Mato Grosso and Bahia and peroba, 27 ½ in. (70 cm) high

Murray Moss

Dealer, New York

Murray Moss is a former fashion entrepreneur who started a retail concept featuring furniture and objects representing 20th century contemporary design. He was early in working with the Campana brothers, in producing the Maarten Baas *Where There's Smoke* series and now is producing large projects for Studio Job among other designers. Moss has evolved and grown with the market and has become more a gallery and exhibition space while focusing less and less on production furniture and industrial design.

How he started

I began the Moss shop on a very limited budget – basically a small, and therefore of necessity a highly "curated" collection of smaller industrial design objects. I did not want to have to fight the battle of going into a furniture ghetto, a design district with all the set presumptions it projects. I wanted people to look at my offerings with the proverbial fresh eyes, so I thought: "Where do people go with fresh, open eyes? Where do people go with the least fixed criteria? They go to look at art." So I decided to crash the SoHo art district (this was pre-Chelsea, remember), not because I wanted to position the work as art, but because I wanted the audience to come open-minded, looking for other readings, to see what was there. I wanted people to begin to see the duality of certain functional objects – certainly the functional aspects, but also the hidden agenda that some designers bring to their industrial brief, treating it simultaneously as a "canvas" with a much broader agenda.

If I had to characterise the business at that time, it was an industrial design store. I started with small objects at about seven dollars, and probably the most expensive thing I had was around $500.

Some of the pieces, even then, in the industrial offering, were what would now be called "limited editions" because, by definition, often what I chose from the industrial design sector had a very limited audience; they were generally unpopular to a wide audience, so as an industrial design store, I was, from the beginning, off-market. The pieces I preferred were usually those that had not been successful commercially for the manufacturer – that was the initial defining thing about

Maarten Baas
"Hey Chair Be a Bookshelf" with pitchfork, 2005, prototype, found items coated with polyurethane, approx. 83 in. (210.8 cm) high

Maarten Baas
*"Where There's Smoke…" Red-Blue chair burned
(Gerrit Rietveld),* 2004, beech marine plywood, burned,
finished with epoxy resin and polyurethane lacquer,
34 x 26 x 33 in. (86.4 x 66 x 83.8 cm)

Moss. Also, for instance, with the historical Italian producer Kartell, and many other producers I worked with, I was interested in the history of the company, so I would cull their stock, and found that they had "leftover stock", no longer in production, which of course is limited, but at that time was considered more as remains or dead stock. I would buy those pieces, usually at a discount, and offer them as historic pieces, giving detailed written information, but I did not say that they were limited or rarefied. In spite of the museum-like presentation, I was adamant about not being considered a gallery, but rather a shop.

Castiglioni and Pesce

I was first interested in the extraordinary work of these important industrial artists, and I was completely prejudiced towards Italian design and manufacturing because that is what I knew and where my base had been (for nine years I produced clothing in small factories in Italy). I was a passionate student of the Italian Industrial Post-War phenomenon – and I was enamoured of the problem-solving approach of certain designers who were using design to solve problems, that is, to get from A to B in the most elegant, clever, imaginative, interesting but convenient and no-nonsense way. That, for example, was the work of Achille Castiglioni. His Milan studio, now a museum, was a magical laboratory of almost child-like play married to highly sophisticated industrial processes.

For design artist Gaetano Pesce, who was born about 20 years later, times were a little better and the influences were different – the Italian economy was strengthening and Italy was beginning to emerge from the devastation of the War, so design could afford to respond to a political agenda, getting a little messier, not solving problems so quickly, letting the objects be somewhat more complex, richer, culturally responsive, expressive. This dual approach to design – Castiglioni's definitive problem-solving, and Pesce's broad socio-economic-cultural agenda – was my great interest, and the simultaneous presentation of those two generational approaches were what the store was first based on.

What is good design?

I could not describe to you, in absolute terms, good design or bad design. I do not believe such truths exist. What I can

Studio Job
Jewel safe from Robber Baron suite, 2006,
polished, patinated and painted cast bronze,
approx. 61 in. (154.9 cm) high

do is define a set, or sets, of criteria (ever changing!) I personally buy into and say: "If these points are what you accept as good, then this is good and that is not good." And by the way, I often am conflicted about what is good or bad, changing my mind as my experiences evolve. And why not? Aren't we supposed to grow? Aren't we supposed to evolve, to respond to new circumstances and new times?

Since I was already in my mid-40s, I was determined to use my new store as a context to play out my life, and to have it follow what I anticipated would be my

> "We each attribute value by making comparisons... This chair to me, today is certainly worth, for example, one month's stay in a small suite at the Ritz, Paris."

evolving interests; it was going to be completely autobiographical. I had no moral mission and acknowledged no obligations whatsoever, like trying to bring "good" design to the United States or offering a "balanced" selection of multi-national products or trying to present an absolutely accurate portrayal of "design today", or serving as an example for others. I have no set mission whatsoever, and my partner, Franklin Getchell, and I have never tried to freeze the brand. We acknowledge our offering at Moss to result from a passionate, personal journey, filled with personal biases, prejudices, and dramatically limited by our personal resources, including financial, intellectual and otherwise. We follow our passions.

Designing the business

I always imagined myself as the guy having the great little bistro in Paris, albeit world-famous, I admit. You go every day and sweep out front, you mend the curtains, cook the food, and in your tiny little shop you have twelve chairs, but it is considered the best restaurant in Paris. That is what I always wanted to be (read "control freak"). And without being too presumptuous, that is what I am trying to do with this store – to be local, particular,

Studio Job
Table from Robber Baron suite, 2006, polished and patinated cast bronze, approx. 30 x 78 ¾ x 39 in. (76.2 x 200 x 99.1 cm)

Studio Job

Perished bench (by Job Smeets and Nynke Tynagel),
2006, hand-crafted macassar ebony wood
with laser-cut inlays, relief imagery in cast bronze,
approx. 79 x 79 x 18 in. (200.7 x 200.7 x 45.7 cm)
with flaps closed, 134 in. (340.4 cm) with flaps open

autobiographical, and use the subject myself, not
the other way around.

How Moss has changed

Something big happened around 2003. The audience that previously did not exist for the objects and the subject that I was interested in – the hidden narrative within industrial design – this art audience that had been looking at a very narrow definition of what contemporary art is, suddenly, more or less on one day, showed up and said: "Where have you been my whole life?" And this new audience brought a different set of criteria to the work we represented – a set of criteria not solely defined by functional performance, as had previously been the norm.

Producing Maarten Baas

By 2004, Moss had dramatically evolved: the text was richer, and the time came when it could actually be fruitful to have a dialogue with artists/designers such as Maarten Baas. After seeing his graduation project from Design Academy Eindhoven, the Netherlands, I asked to meet him in Paris and said: "Please have lunch with me...I sense there is something in your student project that you are not done with, but I have the feeling that you believe you are done with it and I would like to talk to you about that." When we met, I laid out what I imagined I had seen in the work and said: "It looks to

Marcel Wanders
Crochet table, 2005, black cotton and epoxy
resin, 12 x 12 x 12 in. (30.5 x 30.5 x 30.5 cm)

me like *this* is what you are doing…is that it?" And he said: "Yes." Then I said: "Well, that deserves to be explored much more… you are not done yet."

Then we talked about it and I had the idea, which came from him, really, but I just helped articulate it, to burn his "education" – 24 pieces that were particularly important to him in his studies. To re-sculpt them, re-author them, to make transparent his heritage and take possession of it, using it as a base to go forward in finding his own voice.

Is Maarten Baas a good investment?
Of course I have to think of it that way, because I am the guy who has to put a price on it. I think it is expected and it's a fair question. And of course his work has increased in value, as has his recognition. But I do not articulate it, nor do I advertise it in that way, like "Buy this, it will go up in value," because that is not my motivation, or really under my control. Investment is not my first love and not why I'm doing it. But good work takes care of itself. Important collectors and museums acquire it, and of course that affects the value given the work.

How did a Campana brothers chair jump from $14,000 to $75,000 in one year?
Of course, there are factors other than Murray Moss! I can only take responsibility for what Murray does. We each attribute value by making comparisons. That's the age-old method: compare apples to oranges. "This chair, to me, today is certainly worth, for example, one month's stay in a small suite at the Ritz, Paris."
The new audience is now looking at these functional objects in the context of the broader definition of art. We are in this tenuous moment where the $45,000 Campana brothers' Sonia Diniz chair is an expensive side chair if evaluated only by the cost of its rubber-like materials, its ability to bear a person's weight, its comfort and durability and general suitability for dining…okay. But it is inexpensive if evaluated in a parallel universe, basically, as sculpture, as a canvas, as music, as film – so when other far more important qualities are considered, the next thing you know, it sells for $150,000.

What he collects
Unfortunately, at this moment, I cannot afford to personally own the greatest work of Carlo Mollino. But for quite a long time, beginning when I was a teenager, I would often bid at auction on the pieces I wanted, or buy from shops which, by the way, grew to cover a large spectrum of interests. My life/business partner Franklin Getchell and I do own personally some very

Tord Boontje
Night Blossom, 2003, jet black Swarovski crystal,
metal structure, blue LED light (100w total),
approx. 57 x 35 ½ x 65 in. (144.8 x 90.2 x 165.1 cm)

beautiful vintage pieces of Gio Ponti, and we had a great, though small collection of Armand-Albert Rateau bronze pieces, Art Deco, as well as an exceptional work by Jean Dunand. We've since sold many of them…in fact, the sale of one piece was used to finance the opening of the shop in 1994. Now we collect the work of the artists we represent.

Designers he shows now

It is easy to be "new", all one has to do is debut. It is very hard to have a truly new idea, or to build, over years, consistently, tenaciously, painfully on a previous idea. Today we show Maarten Baas, Studio Job and the Campana brothers, Hella Jongerius, Peter Marigold, Julien Carretero, Tom Dixon, Tomás Libertiny, Arik Levy and,

> **"I was adamant about not being considered a gallery, but rather a shop."**

of course, Gaetano Pesce. I am also very excited about the work being done in the new generation of 3-D printing using resins and nylon (stereolithograpy and selective laser sintering) by artists such as Patrick Jouin, working with the Belgian firm pioneering in this field, Materialise.

Gaetano Pesce is a person who continuously fascinates me because he has worked effectively in the same material (resin) since, say, the mid-1960s. It is easy to change materials. But it's sort of like a painter or a musician who stays with the same tools, the same instrument, and works them over and over, and of course the results are not the same at all. Who would say Giacometti did only one thing? Gaetano Pesce works this material so brilliantly and so differently, and it has evolved in so many subtle ways each time he uses it, for 40 years, that I have stayed with it because it is brilliant, always surprising and always new. It's been a tremendous personal privilege to know him.

Gaetano Pesce
Table Sansone 35401, 1980, polychrome polyester resin, 29 ½ x 76 ½ x 47 ⅝ in. (75 x 194 x 121 cm)

Marcel Wanders
White fishnet chair, 2006, aramid and carbon fibres, epoxy, 29 ½ x 33 x 14 in. (74.9 x 83.8 x 35.6 cm)

Are designers willing to be exclusive with the galleries?

You cannot own somebody, nor would I ever want to! We can give Maarten Baas, for example, everything we have, but we cannot speak for everybody, or be his only relationship, or be the only person Maarten is ever influenced by…it is the last thing that I would want in the world. When it comes to the marketplace and the work, say if Maarten creates a series, what I do feel is that we need reasonable exclusivities and, of course, there can be multiple exclusivities. We have exclusivity for Maarten Baas' studio work in the United States. But more specifically, we have global exclusivity for those particular unique or limited edition works that Moss originates, and produces or edits with Maarten Baas.

I believe that I have the ability to contribute a lot to an artist through long-term dialogue, and I hope that I am not wasting anybody's time, that when I speak to Maarten Baas or to Fernando and Humberto Campana, to Hella Jongerius or Tom Dixon or whomever, I hope that that conversation, other than being just friendly and nice, actually contributes something.

Patrick Seguin

Dealer, Paris

Patrick Seguin is an early supporter of several French mid-century masters, notably Jean Prouvé, Charlotte Perriand and Pierre Jeanneret. Along with Parisian dealers Philippe Jousse and François Laffanour, he pioneered and developed the international acclaim and market for French mid-century design. Seguin has curated design shows at the Sonnabend Gallery in New York as well as at Gagosian in Los Angeles, further advancing the design world's access to the top echelon clientele of the art world.

Beginnings

I started working in this business by chance. My first business was restaurants/nightclubs in the south of France where I come from. I arrived in Paris in 1986 and opened a restaurant with some childhood friends – we called it Le Distrito. It became popular quickly and that is where I met many important key figures such as the designer Christian Lacroix and the architect Jean Nouvel, who became my good friends (it was on behalf of our friendship that Jean Nouvel refurbished my gallery in 2003).

At the same time, I also opened a nightclub, one of these one-night-nightclubs that was soon very hot and animated. I did not ever go to bed before 7:00 am. During that period, I was collecting artworks by Hervé DiRosa and Robert Combas, artists of a French movement called La Figuration Libre, and a few pieces of design. Then I met my wife Laurence at the Bains Douches, a famous discotheque in Paris of that time. When Laurence became pregnant, I thought it was the right moment to change my life: my days should now start at 7:00 am and no longer end at 7:00 am.

I started collecting by buying at Drouot in Paris, one of the greatest French auction houses that fills up every day with all kinds of items, and where everything is sold by the end of the day – good, bad and indifferent. In 1989, I opened a gallery with Laurence but we were not really sure about what we wanted to show. Just before the opening, someone recommended that I meet a certain Philippe Jousse who worked at the well-known Paris flea market. We first met with our spouses in my restaurant and then went to my nightclub. The next day, the four of us signed together to become partners.

Jean Royère
Exhibition view, Sonnabend Gallery, New York 2008: *Ours Polaire sofa,* 1952, *Ours Polaire armchairs,* 1953, *Free-form oak table,* 1955, *Cabinet in straw marquetry,* 1959, *Sphère desk lamp,* 1960

This was the basis upon which we opened an art and design gallery with Philippe. Our business was founded on buying at Drouot or at the flea market, then selling it in the gallery. We worked that way during the eleven years of partnership with Philippe. Since then, we have split up but we are still very good friends as well as competitors.

Paris dealers in the 1990s

We were lucky enough to start up the gallery just a few months before the crisis of the early 1990s. Since there were very few clients, this allowed us to hold on to our inventory for several years until 1995–1996, when the business slowly picked up.

During all these years when Jean Prouvé, Charlotte Perriand and Jean Royère seemed so important to us, very few people were interested. Everybody was looking towards Gilbert Poillerat, Elizabeth Garouste and Mattia Bonetti and Tom Dixon, who did more decorative objects. At the flea market, some clients would fight over a sub-category of Art Deco pieces from the 1940s that had nothing to do with the great Emile-Jacques Ruhlmann, Jean-Michel Frank, Pierre Chareau or Paul Dupré-Lafon. For them, the furniture of Prouvé and Perriand, considering the simple materials that they used, metal and plain wood, was not very convincing.

Our idea was to develop and change the mentality of collectors so they would evolve from their conservative criteria to a more refined and modernist aesthetic. We were in competition with some furniture knock-offs of Ruhlmann or Dupré-Lafon, completely revarnished, renovated, shiny, decorative and easier to integrate into the flat of the average French collector than the more severe and rigid designs that we specialised in.

Charlotte Perriand / Ateliers Jean Prouvé
Bookcase, 1965, cherry wood and bent sheet steel, 4 ⅜ x 36 x 1 ⅛ ft. (133 x 1100 x 34 cm)

We started with a few Americans who had been alerted to our pieces by Anthony DeLorenzo in New York; he was already

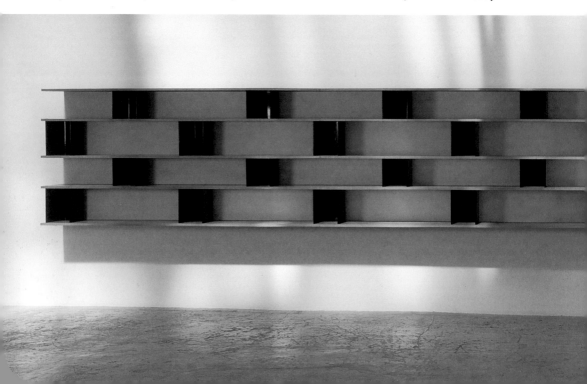

handling French furniture from the 1950s and had a very established clientele for Art Deco. The first collectors we saw coming to the gallery were people like Ileana Sonnabend and Antonio Homem – she used to come every time she was in Paris – or Peter Brant, Ronald Lauder, Larry Gagosian and Susie Tompkins, founder of the brand Esprit. From the younger generation, Maya Hoffmann and Philippe Segalot were our European pioneers.

Buying inventories from schools and government agencies

We were lucky because unlike many designers who are commissioned by private individuals, Prouvé and Perriand had a great number of public commissions from the French government. We arrived on the scene when the civil services needed to renew their furniture, so we were able to acquire large collections directly from these institutions.

> "Fifty years later, it took them 18 months to replace the façade that Prouvé had created in only five days in 1949. What progress!"

For instance, in 1992 we bought the entire collection of the University of Antony, about 20 kilometres outside of Paris. One of the buildings was a dormitory that provided about 86 rooms all laid out by Jean Prouvé. Each one was fully equipped with a bed, bookcase, desk, all by Prouvé, and a lamp by Serge Mouille. As for the dining hall, we bought the whole set of chairs, the famous Trapeze tables and the coat racks.

There was also the Cité Internationale Universitaire de Paris, where each represented country had commissioned an architect, some really famous, to construct a building to accommodate the foreign students. For instance, there was the Maison des Etats-Unis

Charlotte Perriand / Pierre Jeanneret
Desk and armchair, ca. 1946, blackened wood,
metal and leather, 28 ¾ x 88 ½ x 39 ⅜ in.
(73 x 225 x 100 cm)

(House of the United States), Maison du Brésil, as well as maisons for Switzerland, Mexico, Tunisia, Cambodia and many others. It is a large complex situated in a forest-covered park in the 14th district of Paris. Le Corbusier created the Maison de la Suisse in 1932 and the Maison du Brésil in 1956, and he and Perriand designed the furniture for both buildings. At the houses for Tunisia and Mexico, furnishings for the students' rooms as well as the community rooms were designed by Perriand and Prouvé.

We ended up buying all of the furniture of the Maison du Brésil in 1994. It wasn't that easy. You have to know that by the end of each academic year, new groups of students came in for summer classes, which meant that the rooms were occupied 365 days per year. It was impossible for the administration to foresee a public auction because that would leave the rooms empty for a lapse of time with no guarantee that the furniture would be sold. Therefore we made an offer of purchase, a cash advance, and only obtained the furniture a few months later, after it was replaced.

The rooms were built according to the Modulor principle developed by Le Corbusier, a system that applied human proportions to architecture and design, with a unit of measurement based on his own size (183 centimetres for his height and 226 centimetres for his height plus his arm raised up). It was through making additions, subtractions and multiplications of these two digits that Le Corbusier created his units. The length, height and width of the individual rooms and each piece of furniture came directly from this principle.

In each room was one multi-functional wardrobe by Le Corbusier-Perriand, one Perriand bed, a perforated steel lamp by Le Corbusier, a blackboard with its wall unit and there was the famous cube by Le Corbusier which was multi-purpose – it could be a stool, a bedside table or a step to reach something up high. The showers were made of pre-cast concrete done by Le Corbusier with doors in curved aluminium.

overleaf: **Jean Prouvé**
Service station,
1951, Azzedine Alaia
bedroom, Paris

Think about it, after 50 years of use in schools the urge to change this furniture was obvious. Most of the pieces were very damaged. The maintenance staff did their best to keep beds and desks in good shape, but this old stuff had been covered with layers of institutional paint. The beds had been broken, painted over, screwed back together etc. Out of 80 rooms, only 44 of the Le Corbusier cubes had survived and we found just 28 wall lights.

Two years before, at the same Cité Internationale Universitaire de Paris, we had bought all the furniture of the huge dining hall, which included 87 Compass tables of Prouvé, small and large, as well as 454 Standard chairs. Just as with the University of Antony furnishings, most of the pieces were damaged and so we had to restore, rehabilitate, clean and sometimes put all back together. It was a lot of work. Remember, in those days in my gallery, you could buy a Prouvé Standard chair for 1,000 francs. One thousand francs was about $150. Twenty years later, the same chair cost between 5,000 and 7,000 euros.

What makes Prouvé important

Prouvé was, above all, a brilliant creator and a totally committed citizen. Craftsman, workman, industrial constructor, engineer, architect, designer, he was as comfortable in designing and manufacturing a standard chair as a building. He would push the materials to their physical limits. Let us take steel plate for example – he bent, welded, almost tamed the material until its hollow body offered a new resistance that he could apply for the base of a chair or a building's structure.

Jean Prouvé
Central table, 1956, bent sheet steel and laminated wood, 28 ¾ x 130 x 27 ½ in. (73 x 330 x 70 cm).
From the Cité Universitaire, Antony

In 2003, I organised an exhibition on Jean Prouvé at the Sonnabend Gallery in New York, the first design and architecture exhibit in a contemporary art gallery. We showed 86 pieces, and there were even some in the courtyard: a pre-fabricated house and an incredible swing. Museums and institutions bought many items, particularly the MoMA [Museum of Modern Art].

It seemed to me that there was a true connection, interaction, crossover between contemporary art and this type of furniture. I think that Prouvé and Perriand's furniture interacts beautifully with contemporary art because of its rationality and refusal to get too decorative. The furniture I show coexists perfectly with the work of artists that I admire such as Andy Warhol, Jean-Michel Basquiat, Jeff Koons or Richard Prince, as well as younger artists.

At Larry Gagosian's invitation, I organised the exhibit *Jean Prouvé – Charlotte Perriand* in 2004 at the Gagosian Gallery in Los Angeles. It comprised 125 pieces and was an incredible show in this great gallery designed by Richard Meier. This exhibit, like the one we did at the Sonnabend Gallery, was commercial; everything was for sale except a few pieces which had come from private collections. That makes things much more difficult since it is much harder to gather and offer so many items for sale, rather than to simply choose here and there from private collections or museums.

I returned to the Sonnabend Gallery with another show in 2006, *Le Corbusier – Pierre Jeanneret,* and most recently, in collaboration with Jacques Lacoste, did an entire curated show in honour of the great French mid-century decorator Jean Royère. Both shows were very successful.

The market for Prouvé

There has never been a tremendous amount of speculation in Prouvé's furniture. The materials were not "noble", like Deco's ebony and bronze; instead he used enamel steel, plywood and Formica. We can say that Prouvé's market built progressively and slowly, but surely. I know many of these collectors…perhaps I am not familiar with some others because they buy in auction houses, or via interior decorators or art advisors. But our collector's base has kept growing, just as the contemporary art market has grown.

I find that Prouvé's market has really grown outside of any speculative spikes. How can you justify such a price for a chair when, at the beginning, people thought there might be hundreds of this type of chair? Of course, there were about 500 chairs at the Cité Internationale Universitaire, but they were all soaked up by the market. It takes a minor miracle, today, to be able to assemble a set of eight matching chairs to go with a table. For the commission of Lycée de Metz, about 40 beds were produced, but we have pieces that were made in very limited series and sometimes we just have the prototype (which is unique), so the supply is really not as great as people might have otherwise thought.

Can French Mid-century go out of fashion?

No, I don't think so. Prouvé and Perriand represent a breaking point in furniture's history, and because of this rupture, they are essential and historical. Prouvé has really been digested into our culture today and will continue to be part of it in the future. Many designers are, or will be, influenced by his work.

Jean Prouvé
Pair of doors, 1949, lacquered steel,
Plexiglas and fiberglass insulation,
116 x 37 ½ x 1 ⅞ in. (294.6 x 95.3 x 4.8 cm)

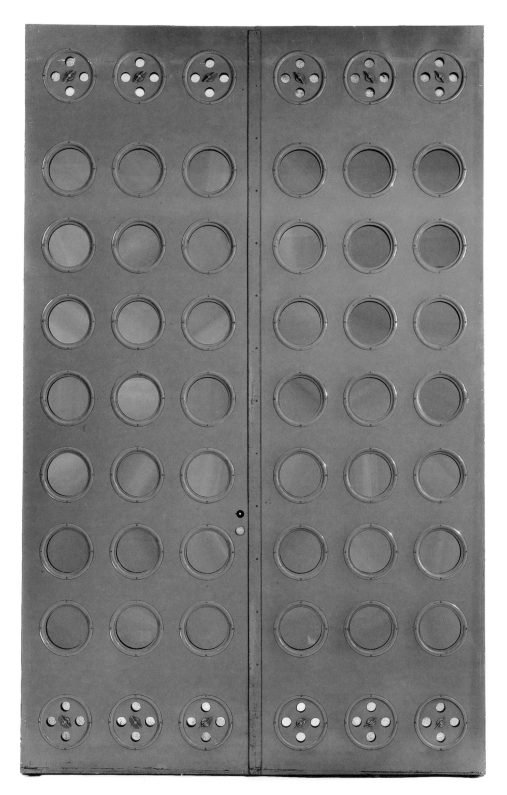

Obviously, if we see another financial crisis, an object that is worth ten could someday be worth nine, or even maybe seven, but then it will go back being worth ten and more. We cannot forget how difficult it is nowadays to find good pieces. It becomes harder and harder every day.

As I said, I got into this business by accident; I have no formal education in the worlds of art and design. Of course, there are other designers I could be interested in, like Mies van der Rohe and Carlo Mollino, or Marc Newson and Martin Szekely of today. But I have decided, and this has actually become like an identity for me, to focus on four names from design and architecture and one from the decorative arts. The gallery was founded on the postulate "French mid-20th century". From the beginning, we have represented Jean Prouvé, Charlotte Perriand, Le Corbusier, Pierre Jeanneret and Jean Royère.

The gallery, through the years, has published several books on design and architecture, notably on Jean Prouvé, the latest of which (620 pages, two volumes) was published in association with Sonnabend and has recently been released. We had previously published a book on Jean Prouvé in collaboration with Enrico Navarra in 1998 (270 pages); also in collaboration with Enrico Navarra, a monograph of Tadao Ando; and, for the Biennale d'Architecture de Venise in 2000, a book on Jean Prouvé's dismountable architectures.

Cité Cansado and Chandigarh

Our work involves research, and by flipping through magazines and books of the 1940s and 1950s, we discovered that there was a whole treasure trove of Perriand-Prouvé furniture in Mauritania, for instance. So after doing the homework, we then travelled to Mauritania (Africa).

There we went to a city called Cité Cansado, a mining town that had been basically exploited in the 1950s. The city was built by French architects. We learned that 18 of the apartments had been created for the managing team and the other supervisors. We found much of the furniture in situ or just spread all over town.

The same procedure led us to Chandigarh in India. Thanks to extensive documentation, we knew that Le Corbusier had built, at Nehru's request in 1951, a city that would become the political and administrative capital of this region in the north of India. Nehru gave full permission to Le Corbusier, asking him to be "expressive, experimental and not to be strangled by the traditions." Several years later, Oscar Niemeyer did quite the same global project in Brasilia.

Concerning Chandigarh, Pierre Jeanneret, who was Le Corbusier's cousin, created the major part of the furniture required for the administrative buildings: assembly, high court, secretariat. He stayed there for 15 years as the chief architect of the city. When he died in 1967, his ashes were scattered in Lake Sukhna in Chandigarh, according to his last wishes.

The furniture we found in India was broken and unfit for use. From the high court, we were able to buy, in auction, about 700 pieces – tables, chairs, desks, all broken, no longer in use, all piled up under the gigantic concrete archway of the roof. Unlike Prouvé's furniture which is metal, Jeanneret's furniture was in wood and wicker and really damaged. We then embarked on a long process of restoration and rehabilitation.

Heeding how times change

Prouvé once said that there is no difference between the "meuble", which means furniture in French, and an "immeuble", which means a building. So basically, for Prouvé, each piece of furniture, each design, embodied the architecture that one would find in an entire building.

Think about the building that Jean Prouvé did in Paris in 1949, called Fédération Française du Bâtiment. It exemplified ground-breaking technology with ribbed aluminium panel walls and the first aluminium curtain-wall. This idea revolutionised the traditional principles of construction. Prouvé claimed he could resolve the matter of traditional construction. The building had five levels, or five concrete floors, on

Pierre Jeanneret
Tronc table, ca. 1955, rosewood and metal, 17 ¾ x ø 33 ¼ in. (45 x ø 84.5 cm).
From Chandigarh, India

which Prouvé would apply his aluminium panels at the rate of one floor per day. Five floors, five days. The level of technology and forethought that went into the Fédération Française du Bâtiment was amazing.

In the 1990s, because the sound and heat insulation systems were outdated – and despite its historical importance – the whole aluminium facade was dismantled. As a twist of fate, this "Fedebat" building was the headquarters from which came all the decisions for urban planning and architecture since the end of the war. It would have been easier to dismantle the panels, to comply with standards and to save the facade. But things happened in a different way and the French government did nothing to save this masterpiece.

The facade by Jean Prouvé was dismantled without caring for one minute about rules of conservation. Fifty years later, it took them 18 months to replace the facade that Prouvé had created in only five days in 1949. What progress! The facade today pales in comparison to Prouvé's. How is it that no one understood the significance of this building which, like many others of that period, was ultimately destroyed.

When the facade was dismantled, we were able to save a small part. One of these precious pieces was shown in our Jean Prouvé exhibition at the Sonnabend Gallery; it now belongs to MoMA.

Alasdhair Willis

Dealer, London

Alasdhair Willis is the founder and CEO of Established & Sons, a London-based company which produces contemporary design as well as select limited-edition pieces. He has worked with several important architect/designers like Zaha Hadid and has also produced works by leading designers like Jasper Morrison and artist Richard Woods. He is focused on developing excitement for British design and regularly hosts celebrity-attended bashes with his wife, Stella McCartney.

The mission of Established & Sons

Established & Sons was launched in April 2005 to represent and work with British and British-based designers. I formed the company with Sebastian Wrong the designer, and Angad Paul who is the CEO of Caparo Industries – together we own the company. Caparo Industries is a British manufacturing company predominantly based in the automotive industry. Caparo supports us with a number of their manufacturing facilities as well.

We started off with a mandate, but it was always our intention that once we built the business and the brand up to a level that people became aware of Established & Sons overseas, we would then start working with overseas designers. I wanted to reverse the trend of what was being done in the UK where British designers or British-based designers had to go over to the continent to realise their ideas. The obvious example is an overseas manufacturer like Cappellini, where so many designers went to have their work produced.

On the other hand, designers I know and work with, like Ed Barber and Jay Osgerby, have formed what is now one of the strongest design studios in this country, called BarberOsgerby. I not only can represent them through the gallery on their editions and one-off pieces, but also through their production pieces as well.

There is a whole list of similar cases if you think of the big names like Jasper Morrison and Ron Arad and others. There was never anywhere within the UK where they had a platform to work with and a home. Our intention was to create one, and that's what we did, but we always took the long-term view. Having established this foundation, we now have expanded our range. So we are working with Ronan and Erwan Bouroullec,

Maarten Baas
Duuk, 2008, aluminium, rubber, plastic and stone, 56 ¾ x 53 x 49 ½ in. (144 x 135 x 126 cm)

also with Konstantin Grcic, and we had a show with Maarten Baas.

We work with a lot of British manufacturing, but I am not trying to ram the square peg in a round hole. I am not saying that we will use British at all costs. What I have done is to target those areas and manufacturing capabilities within our country, like automotive, where we are still strong and relevant in the world today.

An example would be a show that we did in the gallery called *Surface.* We had this four-metre table – its thinnest point is two millimetres thin – a carbon fibre table designed in a collaboration between Terence Woodgate, a British designer, and John Barnard, who is the ex-head of Ferrari Formula 1. There are two versions of the table, the four-metre version which is an edition of 25 pieces, and a three-metre version in an edition of 99. It is an incredible piece, it's pure, pure design…the large piece is £38,000, the small one is £25,000.

In 2005 when I launched in Milan, I started right away with a Zaha Hadid Aqua table, an edition of 12 pieces at about £45,000. The prototype has since sold for about 300,000 dollars.

What he's working on

I am working on pieces with Jeff Koons and some star artists which I am very excited about. As I said, we're working on pieces with Konstantin Grcic and the Bouroullecs, and they are really interesting.

Having these two aspects to the company – from the production pieces that we now sell in 50 countries, right the way through to the edition pieces within the gallery – allows us to have that level of experimentation which I think is absolutely necessary within design, to really push things and take risks and be open to failure and which until fairly recently, has not really existed.

> "In five years time, I would really hope that we are the leading design company and have the world's best design gallery as well."

Working with Maarten Baas

The Chankley Bore is taken from an Edward Lear poem, a nonsense poem. Chankley Bore was this made-up, fantasyland kingdom. Maarten Baas read the poem and was moved and intrigued by it.

I gave him the opportunity and freedom to work and, in a sense, I took him out of his studio. Apart from his chair, his pieces with Moooi, all his work comes out of his studio. And I said: "Look, let's take you somewhere else. Let's take you into a different area...I want you to go to a place you find uncomfortable."

So these pieces are editions...I mean, they have to be editions. Twelve in the edition, and there are six pieces. That's it. There are no different colours coming out, no different material finishes, you know, it's not going to be an extended family. That is the end of the collection. And that's very important.

The future of his company

There are numerous areas and directions we can take, but our thrust is as a design company. We already have a design consultancy where we work with and consult with

Amanda Levete
East, 2008, Nero Marquina marble corner desk, 112 ½ x 32 ½ x 32 in. (286 x 83 x 81.5 cm)

a number of property developers and hotels and so forth – that's a different part of the business. But the core business is the furniture and the design, and I really want to continue to push the envelope with designers. I would also like to have a platform in a few of the other markets…in five years time, I would really hope that we are the leading design company and have the world's best design gallery as well.

Where is our world going in the next five years? I think we have to get through the next twelve to 24 months of the economy. Regardless of what anyone says about it – "everything's fine, everything's fine" – there is a slowdown at the top end.

I think, in a strange kind of way, that is actually going to help the business, because it will weed out some of the chaff and we will see the quality come through. At the end of it, we should have a situation where the pieces that I'm referring to – the sub-standard pieces that are out there – will hopefully disappear and we'll be left with some quality that we can build on. So I think that the future is strong, but I do come back to this level of responsibility.

BarberOsgerby
Iris 1300, 2008, anodised aluminium table, glass top, 15 ¾ x ø 51 in. (40 x ø 130 cm)

overleaf: **Zaha Hadid**
Aqua table, 2005, gloss black laminated polyurethane resin and white silicone, 165 ¼ x 57 x 29 ½ in. (420 x 145 x 75 cm)

THE TASTE

Whereas the art world has its plethora of consultants, some of whom are extremely influential, there really is no such thing in the design world. I have created another category of participants for those who influence the design market but do not fit into any of the other groups. For example, the two superstar interior designers included here are indeed advising their clients on what and where to buy, as well as how much to pay. But once the house or apartment is finished, the relationship ends, and so the market influence can be significant but may be short-lived.

Celebrity fashion designers have long been tastemakers in the field and thus they are good reference points. Certain hoteliers can also launch trends, as can architects and other celebrities. The

MAKER

design market is more fickle than the contemporary art world, and just one or two sales at auction, either high or low, can create severe swings in the value of a work.

The discovery of forgotten and untapped fields of design, whether it be Memphis, Italian or French Pop, is something the tastemakers will be following. In design, even if you have chosen your style and your field of interest, it's always good to keep an eye on what everyone else in the market is doing, and the conversations in this section will shed a light on how trends get started and how they affect values in the market.

Jacques Grange

Tastemaker, Paris

Jacques Grange is one of Paris' best known and most established interior designers. His glamorous career includes working for Yves Saint Laurent in the 1970s all the way up to the recent conversion of the Mark Hotel/Condominium in New York. One of the most worldly and sophisticated connoisseurs of the worlds of art and design, he qualifies as an eminence grise in the field.

How he began

I started studying design and art, thanks to my mother, at École Boulle and École Camondo. When I was 20 years old, I began my decorator work with Henri Samuel for two years, and then I joined the Didier Aaron Design office in 1968. During that time, I met with Marie-Laure de Noailles, extraordinary art patron and art collector, who opened my eyes and played an important role in encouraging me and shaping my career through her keen intelligence and sense of judgment. In Paris in the early 1970s she received guests in a famously harmonious setting that reflected a lively savoir faire, an innate taste and sense of freedom that was not merely lavish, but absolutely right. I was also able to meet and become good friends with people like Yves Saint Laurent and Pierre Cardin, as well as others in New York like Andy Warhol and Paloma Picasso. These were the years when I learned and developed a taste for design, as well as for Art Deco and contemporary work.

> "I will never use a copy because that, for me, is something really unpleasant and even somewhat offensive."

It was also when I developed my taste for exoticism, travel, Morocco, and this is why, although I am not a designer, I am known for developing interiors that involve elements of traditional design and a sense of colour, as well as the history of French craftsmanship, while all the while incorporating a taste for contemporary art as well as contemporary design. Therefore, someone like me is never interested in curtains or interiors of that kind. I am interested in the interior only if there is an artistic element that I can bring to it.

Pierre Cardin
Mushroom commode, 1979,
lacquered wood, 59 x 17 ¾ x 45 ¼ in.
(150 x 45 x 115 cm)

The difference between interior design and architecture

I never studied formal architecture and I do not create buildings; I have always focused on creating the scenario of the interior spaces. The first work I did on my own was to design an interior for the twin sister of the Shah of Iran. I did her apartment in Paris as well as her home in the south of France.

The next projects for which I am best known are the interiors I did for Yves Saint Laurent and Pierre Bergé – their apartment in Paris as well as their house in Deauville. Then I also did their house in Marrakesh in Morocco. With Yves Saint Laurent and Pierre Bergé, we explored our mutual tastes and such diverse fields as Art Deco, as well as symbolism, the use of bronzes and the use of orientalism. In Marrakesh we did something that was mostly based on an interest in orientalism, whereas in Paris we focused more on the work of Jean-Michel Frank and creating an Art Deco feeling. Then in Deauville we were really thinking about the work of Marcel Proust, so the entire Deauville country house was done with a 19th century sensibility.

We took these concepts all the way through to the gardens, and in Deauville we even built a Russian dacha as a kind of a folly house.

I work as though I were directing a film, so I create a scene and setting based on the theme and concept that we have decided upon. Different jobs come from different perspectives, for example, that of creating a scene, a scenario, or a look. In other instances we would take the approach of a collector, particularly in Paris with Art Deco furniture for Yves Saint Laurent and Pierre Bergé – so in the Paris apartment we used Jean-Michel Frank, Eileen Gray, Emile-Jacques Ruhlmann, Jean Dunand, as well as Armand Rateau.

It is interesting for me because I knew many of the designers personally, including Jean Prouvé and Diego Giacometti – I used to go Giacometti's studio and order the work directly from him.

Reflections on decorators and the history of interior design

I believe I am also quite well known for focusing on and bringing back to the public eye the impressive work of the Deco interior designer Jean-Michel Frank, who is famous for the Palace de Noailles as well as other works he did in places as far distant as Argentina. In a way I feel that his career is quite similar to mine; he worked in Europe, he worked in South America, he worked all over the

Jean-Michel Frank
Flower stand, ca. 1930, black patinated wrought iron and terracotta

Elizabeth Garouste and Mattia Bonetti
Tripod occasional table, 1995, gilt metal and silver leaf
over ceramic top, 28 ¾ in. (73 cm) high

world, as have I. But when you think of the leading designers of our time, I think there are very few. I appreciate in particular the design dealer Pierre Passebon whose taste I find very heterogeneous.

In a way, decorating is a strange kind of work because you develop a very intimate and close relationship with your client during the time that you are on the commission. I also did François Pinault's apartment in New York, and for that interior we used some Diego Giacometti furniture, some Jean-Michel Frank, and I designed the rest of the furniture myself. Although I do not design furniture for production, I have designed furniture for installation and for specific apartments in the classic style.

I have also worked for the Niarchos family, so I perform a little bit as a doctor – the patient comes in and the patient may be sick, and I direct him to beautiful objects, beautiful furniture, beautiful interiors, and try to resolve the problem. Part of my goal in this work is to discover beautiful objects for my clients, and then I direct them to buy and to furnish with these things.

When I work in this manner I do not really obey any rules, I like to mix different periods, different designs, beautiful things as much as possible. But once again, of course, for a recent commission I did in New York City for collectors, I went back to Jean Dunand and Jean-Michel Frank. I will never, ever use, in any of my interiors, something in-the-style-of, or after-the-design-of someone else. So I will never use a copy because that, for me, is something really unpleasant and even somewhat offensive. I would rather use something that is creative in plastic, than to use a piece of metal furniture that is a copy of the original.

How he buys

When I buy for clients I never buy with an investment concept. The first thing that comes to mind is a love of beautiful things. It is really about discovering what you fall in love with. Buying has now become an investment because, with time, these objects have become more and more rare, and therefore more and

Gio Ponti
Coffee table, ca. 1953, white and polychrome metal lacquer, blackened brass legs, 15 x ø 35 ⅜ in. (38 x ø 90 cm)

more expensive. But initially, the collecting that I did with my clients never started as an investment proposition.

I am all about developing a taste for what I call "the creator". For example, think of Jean Royère – I was one of his first supporters and am part of the rediscovery of his work in France. I was also one of the champions of Jean-Michel Frank's work and, at the time, we bought all types of furniture by him for nothing. Now, a piece of Jean-Michel Frank is quite expensive, but in the beginning this was not the case.

"Today, if you have bought great works of art but you do not have great design, this is just a sign that you have not really understood the full picture."

For me, it was really about discovering the design that mattered. In other words, this was strictly an aesthetic exercise, not an investment exercise. Therefore, I will buy something even when it becomes extremely expensive if it is just so beautiful that I cannot help myself, but once again, I never look at it strictly as an investment. It is an emotional and aesthetic experience that has driven my work for all these years.

Design as investment

Do I believe that design is an investment? I think for the absolutely beautiful, beautiful pieces, yes, it is – because in this world, there are just fewer of them available on the

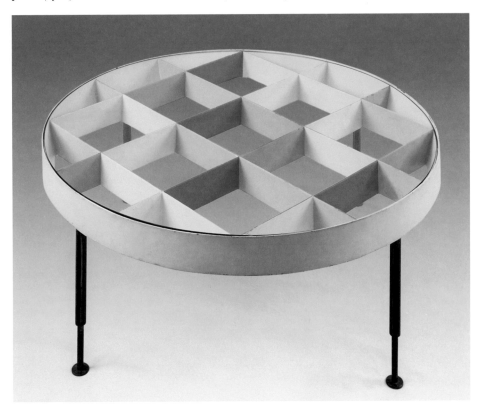

marketplace. Take Jean-Michel Frank, for instance, the main part of his work was created in the 1920s and 1930s, so there are fewer and fewer of his pieces – and remember, he died before the end of World War II. Looking at the work of someone like Jean Prouvé, his is a far more intellectual approach to design – this is work that was created after the war and I am less susceptible, less charmed, less infatuated with this type of intellectual approach.

Of course I do appreciate the industrial aesthetic and how it looks and feels very contemporary, but personally, I am not particularly motivated to collect this type of work at today's prices. In fact, I feel that some of the prices for it have actually become absurd. Of course, there is always the exceptional, absolutely rare piece that I would go for if I fell in love with it – but generally speaking, this more intellectual work that started in the 1950s is not really my thing.

Overall, both art and the decorative arts have become financial markets, therefore we have to think in terms of the art market as well as the market for design. This is quite a disturbing phenomenon for me because collecting started as a pleasure, and

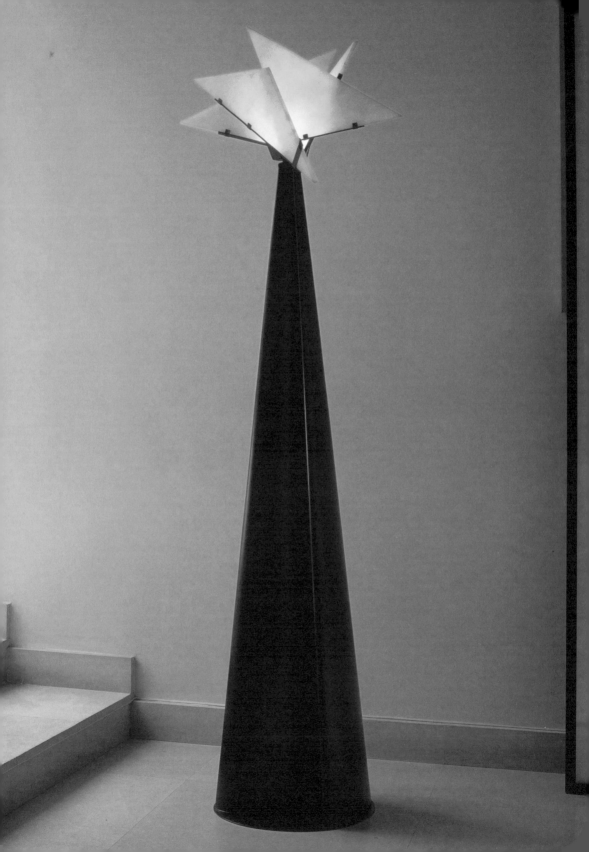

not as a method of investment. Of course, when I advise my clients now, I need to keep in mind the financial characteristics of these aesthetic choices, and say: "Yes, this will also be a good investment." But the problem is that if the client thinks exclusively about making good investments, they will be making a mistake, and they will be investing poorly when it comes to art and design.

To have a great collection

To have a great design collection in your home is not only a pleasure, but a form of social status – that is, it is also a way of being recognised socially. Therefore, if you are hanging a painting by Damien Hirst, you also want to have a piece of furniture by Prouvé. This is what defines you as a member of the cultural elite. This creates the code, and the code is something which is immediately and easily understood by those in the know, and

Jean Royère
Armchair, ca. 1950, metal tube frame in lacquered vermillion, 26 ¾ x 22 ⅝ x 29 ⅞ in. (68 x 57.5 x 76 cm)

Jean Royère
Commode croisillons, ca. 1950, wood,
metal tubing, mirror drawer knobs,
33 ½ x 44 ½ x 18 ⅞ in. (85 x 113 x 48 cm)

is completely opaque to those outside of the cultural loop.

If you think about other fields like Art Deco, for example, there are very few wonderful pieces that appear on the market any more, and if they do, the values are at a whole different level. Looking at contemporary design, the design of today is also extremely expensive. Work that does not seem to be that tremendously valued right now is from the designers of the 1970s. And even mid-century Italian is not that expensive right now – providing we exclude Carlo Mollino, and you can still find many beautiful things by Gio Ponti, his work is still somewhat affordable. I also think the work of Ico Parisi is quite beautiful.

Today, if you have bought great works of art but you do not have great design, this is just a sign that you have not really understood the full picture. It also means that you now need to travel to the right places, in the right way, and spend time with the right artists and creators. This whole concept goes really far in the sense that we are defining an entire lifestyle and not just ownership of a specific thing.

Marc Jacobs

Tastemaker, New York

Marc Jacobs is the creative director of Louis Vuitton and also designs his own line under his name. Jacobs has successfully brought art into the fashion world by inviting guests such as Takashi Murakami and Richard Prince to design handbags and accessories, and has successfully brought a highly original and fresh eye to one of the world's top luxury brands. He is a seasoned collector of contemporary art and design.

Fashion and Design

I think furniture and clothes are probably the same, meaning there is form and function to both. Clothing performs a function but it also can be a very beautiful thing, and the same with furniture. There will always be people who blur those lines. Take somebody like Rei Kawakubo, whose fashion is so sculptural and sort of abstract that you think it was probably conceived of more as an artistic creation. The fact that it covers a body is second to the form. Most designers think first of clothing the body…and how the outcome is also beautiful is somewhat second to the function. There are people who design furniture or a sculpture that you can sit on, but there are others who probably design a

chair to be attractive or interesting. I'm looking at so much furniture these days, and that is what I see.

His first apartment

My old apartment was all Jean Prouvé and Charlotte Perriand, and that's when I felt like I lived in a gallery. This was about eleven years ago...I had first moved to Paris and I walked into a gallery completely by chance, I don't know what drove me there but the gallery was Jousse-Seguin.

I went in and saw a chair by Prouvé. I had never heard of Jean Prouvé and did not know who he was. I saw the chair and a desk, and then I saw the Serge Mouille lamp and the Perriand piece and I said: "I like that, I like that, I like that...can I have that?" And Patrick Seguin said, "Sure," and he started teaching me about it. But I wasn't interested in learning. I told him I did not want the long story, and that "I am not interested in what the designer built, or who he is, or anything." You see, I looked around the place as though it was a furniture store...it was a gallery, but that didn't mean anything to me, I just knew that I was attracted to a piece and I bought it. Then, sure enough, I went back and started buying the Georges Jouve, the Alexandre Noll, and all of a sudden I was shopping at Jousse-Seguin all the time – that was when they were still partners.

Alexandre Noll
Sculpture, ca. 1950s, mahogany,
47 ¼ x 29 ½ x 18 ¾ in. (120 x 75 x 47.6 cm)

Why he sold his Mid-century collection

I filled an apartment with Prouvé, Perriand, Alexandre Noll and such, everything including the library, the dining room table, the bar, was from these designers. Suddenly, before I knew it, I felt like I was living in a furniture store because it was all that, there was nothing else. There was no art – just all this Mid-century furniture.

Then when I did this new place with my friend Paul Fortune, my first thought was that I want this home to have a different vibe, I want it to be warm, to be comfortable, to have fabrics and upholstery...and Prouvé was not really about that. I would say I sold 75 percent of it. I kept some of the bridge chairs, a couple of the little wooden stools.

What he lives with now

Now I've got this eclectic mix of Mid-century stuff, some French, American, and some Scandinavian. It feels really comfortable. Anybody who comes to the house always says: "It feels very nice to be here."

At the same time, you don't get a sense that it is designed; one doesn't get the feeling – very unlike the last apartment – which

Maria Pergay
Flying Carpet daybed, 1968,
stainless steel, 11 ¾ x 118 ⅛ x 39 ⅜ in.
(30 x 300 x 100 cm)

was: "Oh my God, you're really into Prouvé and Perriand." That one was really graphic, everything was red, blue, white, black, it was very *done*, the library, the desk, the dining room, right down to the lamps and ceramics. There was no kind of mix, it was one-note and very flat.

This new house is really a collection of things; everything is simple but nothing stands out, it all disappears to form a pleasant ambiance. The colour palette is very similar, the rooms have much more fabric, with pieces that I upholstered in plums and olives and ochres.

My most expensive piece, probably, is a very beautiful Dominique table which I bought from the Yves Gastou gallery in Paris. There is Poul Kjærholm. I bought a lot of things from Nilufar, an excellent gallery in Milan. I also bought beautiful rugs from the 1930s that are in all the rooms.

Then I started buying some Giacometti lamps and pieces. There's a lot of French, like the Arbus and Quinet chairs and tables – as I said, it's really a mix. I went to galleries and bought things and then started to learn about them. You would not walk through the house and identify it as: "Oh it's this style, or that style." At the same time, the rooms do not look like a Bohemian hodge-podge…everything just blends and disappears.

It is not a grand house at all, but it has a garden. Anyone who has ever been to that area in Paris would know that the great thing about it is that I have an amazing view of the Eiffel Tower, it is literally in my back yard. So I've put this big, Paul McCarthy Pinocchio sculpture in the garden…you look out and see the Pinocchio and then you see the Eiffel Tower, and it's just very funny. It is beautiful.

Paul Evans
Hanging sideboard, ca. 1964, gilt and enameled steel, painted wood and slate, 21 ⅝ x 96 x 22 ¼ in. (54.9 x 243.8 x 56.5 cm). From the Sculpted Front series

The Ado Chale lamp he did not buy
I loved the Ado Chale lamp, but when I introduced the idea of the lamp to Paul Fortune,

he said: "No, it's not really the right style for what we have in Paris." I feel like Paris is done, it's really done. I am pretty much happy with the way it looks and I am not shopping for it any more. There is not a wall that does not have a painting on it and there is no place for this lamp. The only option would be if I decided to change something.

> "Only five years ago, everything I wanted had to be wood...textures of velvets and satins and silks. Now, all I want is bronze, nickel, silver, chrome and gold."

Now, this new townhouse in New York that I am working on is a new beginning, so let's see if the Chale lamp will fit into it. Part of me is really insecure, and so there are things I have bought in the past that people could try to talk me out of. But there is no way in the world you could talk me out of Paul McCarthy's Pinocchio if your life depended on it, because I wanted it so badly, and in my mind I saw it sitting in the garden...I could just see it.

When I am really sure of something, I cannot be talked out of it. If I make a mistake, so be it. However, I do not believe there is any such thing as a mistake when you really want something.

On hiring a decorator

I have a terrible sense of designing and decorating a room. I am really bad with proportions. If somebody shows me blueprints or a floor plan, I have no sense of how much furniture would fit into it. You give me the measurements of the table and I do not know what that means. I have no visual perception of size, or scale, or proportions.

What he is buying now

I like old furniture, I think I like the patina. I love 1970s stuff right now, that is what I have been looking at lately…I like Paul Evans.

What happened was – and this is an example of how it works with me – a couple of years ago, a catalogue arrived in my office in Paris, from Nilufar, and on the cover was a detail shot of one of the Cityscape series of Paul Evans. I looked at it, I don't know how many times – inside was a section that was all Paul Evans – and I put it away. A year passed, two years passed, and I said to my assistant in Paris: "Where is that Nilufar catalogue with the silver graphic cover?" She pulled it out, and it was Paul Evans. I kept looking at his work in other catalogues that came in. Then I thought: I must be having this 1970s kind of glamour moment,

> "I do not want to buy something when it's trendy. I will buy when it feels right for me, not when it feels right for the market, because I am not doing it as an investment."

I just love the way it looks. It looks super-modern, but although it has all the modern materials and the patina, it is not modern like something that was made today.

The work is not woody, it is not warm; it has these metallic surfaces, the textures, and the crystal. I love the opulence of it, yet it looks modern, and the forms are modern. It is not ornate, what stands out are these glossy, glamorous textures. That's what I think is really, really appealing. I saw all this and said: "Wow!"

I find myself responding to designers of the same period – the 1970s – one of them is French, Maria Pergay, one is American, Paul Evans, and the other is Belgian, Ado Chale. It's all coming together now, and I wonder: why is it that only five years ago, everything I wanted had to be woody; there had to be textures of velvets and satins and silks, and why was everything within this kind of earthy colour palette? Now, all I want is bronze, nickel, silver, chrome and gold.

Georges Jouve
Low table, ca. 1954, enameled ceramic, 12 ½ x 42 x 12 in. (32 x 106.7 x 30.5 cm)

Why, I don't know. I am not like Karl Lagerfeld. He goes through a stage when everything is Marc Newson, or every-thing is Memphis. He is notorious for that. Lagerfeld will do

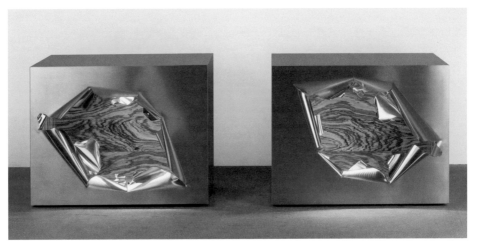

Maria Pergay
Broken Cubes end tables, 2010, stainless steel, snakewood interior, 21 ⅝ x 21 ⅝ x 29 ½ in. (55 x 55 x 75 cm)

a house in Memphis and then say: "Memphis is finished." Period.

That is not my thing. I do not understand how I got to where I am, but there is a process I go through. As you said, things do come back. Looking at Marc Newson's furniture, I don't want it now – I love it, I think what he does is amazing, but I do not want it. What I do want are these late 1960s and early 1970s versions of futurism or modernism…I want it to have the patina, like an old-fashioned take on what was modern back then.

Maybe that makes it a little more romantic than the stuff that is done today. All I know is that I had never seen Maria Pergay's Flying Carpet until I looked on the internet last night. Literally, it was last night that I saw it for the first time, and I thought: "This is so great!" All that stuff is very appealing to me right now.

I come into things slowly and I get there in my own time. I am obsessed with that Ado Chale lamp – which I have been for a while – but now it feels like it could happen. It was a few years ago that I first learned the name of Paul Evans, and was able to associate it with a style of furniture. Now I am obsessed with actually having it, now I *want* it, now it is not just something that *looks* attractive, I want to live with it.

His method

There are trends, but I am oblivious to them. I do not want to buy something when it's trendy. I want to buy either before or after the trend. I will buy when it feels right for *me,* not when it feels right for the market, because I am not doing it as an investment. So the fact that I have discovered Ado Chale – I don't care if it was "the thing" to have ten years ago. Who cares? I'm not doing it to be in fashion. I know that if I have it, it will be perfect. I am not worried about that.

Karl Lagerfeld
Tastemaker, Paris

Karl Lagerfeld, widely recognised as an influential designer of our time, is best known for his work as the chief designer for Chanel. When not busy with shows all over the world, he has decorated and collected design for his Paris residence among others. His style is to amass large quantities of a particular design or period and then sell the entire collection through auction or private galleries.

Discovering Prouvé

You know, I bought Jean Prouvé 20 years ago, when nobody wanted him. These chairs I own were made for a school. I also have a set of 40 chairs and ten tables from his first known public work, for the Credit Lyonnais bank. I bought them for nearly nothing from a very good dealer, Anne-Sophie Duval, who unfortunately just died. Now people ask me for a chair, and I give them as gifts.

Why he is not a collector

I am a fashion person. I change clothes, furniture, houses, collections. Life is about change. There is a moment when things cannot become any better; then you change. There is no feeling of home in my house. I do not have those feelings. I am utterly free, European, free-minded, and I have no sense of possession. But to have no sense of possession is easier if you have owned a lot.

However, I can keep things like a joke – the furniture of my childhood home, for example. I have kept the pieces, but I don't use them. They are too tiny for me. It's a very beautiful set of Biedermeier furniture – the desk where I learned how to write and how to sketch, even the paintings my mother put there that weren't good enough for her, the leftovers, the German Romantic paintings.

New York apartment

I will do the new New York apartment in the style of the Deutscher Werkbund, the architectural movement that had designers like Bruno Paul, Hermann Muthesius and Peter Behrens, who taught Walter Gropius and Le Corbusier.

Marc Newson
Pod of Drawers no. MN-12PDB, 1987, fibreglass and riveted sheet aluminium, 50 ⅜ x 27 ½ x 17 ¼ in. (128 x 69.8 x 43.8 cm)

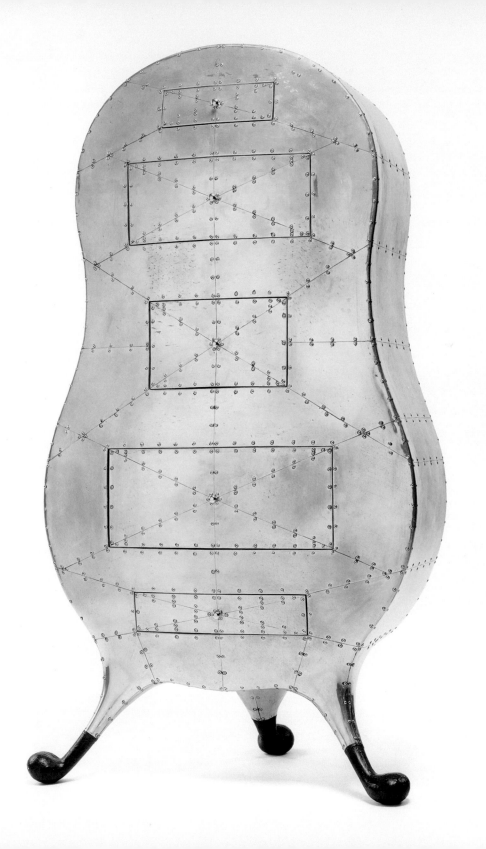

They did modern things differently in 1910, before the Bauhaus. I have a collection of furniture bought 20 years ago that is stunning, very colourful, in bright red, yellow, green and gold. Suddenly people are discovering Werkbund. Everyone knows Vienna Secession, but there is not much left. Werkbund is Germany for me, a Germany that I can identify with.

My apartment is in Gramercy Park. I like it because it's very German and very New York at the same time – the New York of E. B. White.

His current enthusiasm for contemporary design

I have known and followed it for years. I bought the first piece of furniture that Zaha Hadid ever made, for Sawaya & Moroni – a sofa 5.5 metres long – 20 years ago in Milan. If you ask me what genius is, I would say Zaha Hadid.

Most of the furniture in my Quai Voltaire apartment is from the well-made limited editions of the artists of Galerie Kreo: Marc Newson, the Bouroullec brothers (Erwan and Ronan) and Martin Szekely. Everything Martin does is great. The last thing I got from him is a real piece of art, a mirror made of a silicium-carbide-based ceramic that is more expensive than gold. For Quai Voltaire, he made two three-metre-long tables – one for writing, one for sketching – in white Corian with metal stripes. They face each other in the over-20-metre-long space that I made from three rooms.

There is also a huge sofa by Amanda Levete and two of the most beautiful coffee tables

Jasper Morrison
Wing-nut chair, 1985, hardboard, piano hinges and wing-nut connectors, 31 ⅞ in. (81 cm) high

I've seen in years, from Established & Sons, the British-based design company that Stella McCartney's clever husband Alasdhair Willis heads. He does expensive limited editions like Kreo but also cheaper versions. One version of Amanda's sofa costs £80,000, the other £10,000, and they are both beautiful. And I have chairs by the English designer Tom Dixon, two sofas by the French designer Jean-Marie Massaud and my favourite statue, *Serenity,* by Elie Nadelman.

"I change clothes, furniture, houses, collections. Life is about change."

How he chooses

We live in a period of revivals – post Bauhaus, post 1970s, post 1960s, post whatever. What I like about the things I have bought from Galerie Kreo is that they have a voice only from now. The art that I think is genius is conceptual art, Land art. My favourite artist is James Turrell, and that is not for the living room.

I love contemporary art, but not at home. At home I want only books. Not even photography. In my home in Paris, there are no walls, just glass walls, glass windows, glass doors. It is a glass box. You push one button and 50 doors – 25 on each side – open at the same time and you have the library. On one side there are reading books, on the other side art books. It is like a flawless spaceship flying over

Ronan and Erwan Bouroullec
Lit Clos, 2000, lacquered polyester resin, wood and metal, with futon and tatami, 71 x 100 ¾ x 78 ¾ in. (180 x 256 x 200 cm)

Paris, because at the end you have these big windows with a view of the Seine, the boats and the Louvre. It's a very strange feeling, like life is short and the day is nothing because it is so enchanting. You get dressed and undressed and the day is over.

Love of books

Art is something you feel. You don't have to own it. But I am a slave to my books. I am not a bibliophile. It is the inside that is interesting to me.

> "There is no feeling of home in my house… I am utterly free, European, free-minded, and I have no sense of possession."

I keep them at my apartment and elsewhere. I have a huge photography studio next door, on the Rue de Lille, with a bookshop in the front part (stocked with beautiful books on art, fashion, design, decoration, photography and gardens plus a selection of international art magazines) that is doing very well.

Actually I have three houses – I mean, I have three houses right around the Quai Voltaire, and other houses elsewhere. I turned a nine-room apartment into a huge suite

Martin Szekely
Concrete table, 2009, concrete,
29 ½ x 110 ¼ x 56 ½ in.
(75 x 280 x 143.5 cm)

only for me, with a kitchen to warm up things that people can bring when I call. I have no servants in when I am home. Nobody. I want to be alone, like Garbo.

My studio next door is a huge place, and there is an apartment over there for guests. My library there has almost 60,000 books. When I leave my apartment where I stay for the night, I have a townhouse for lunch and guests, and books next door. All these places are three minutes from one another.

In fact, I am a guest in my own house. I hate the smell of cooking. And in this little townhouse, you know what I am doing with the décor? It's called the French house because I am mixing 18th-century furniture with French Art Deco by Louis Sue and André Mare.

Martin Szekely
Stoleru sofa, ca. 1987, alcantara upholstery
and wood, 32 ⅛ x 43 ⅛ x 34 ½ in.
(81.6 x 109.5 x 87.6 cm)

Peter Marino

Tastemaker, New York

Peter Marino is a brand name in super high-end interior design, and is perhaps best known for his luxurious residential projects and his successful retail designs for iconic names in the fashion world including Fendi, Valentino, Chanel, Louis Vuitton and more. His work for private clients includes furnishing with everything from Dupré-Lafon to the Lalannes and his choices are known to broadly influence the markets.

Start of his career

I worked for Andy Warhol and then I worked for Arman, over 25 years ago, so my career has been with artists from the very start. Andy is the one who put me into business at the beginning of my career. I did the Factory, which was located on the north side of Union Square, and then I did his house on 66th Street. That was 1978, my first year of business.

Then I did Fred Hughes' house on Lexington Avenue, which was the house where Andy and his mother had lived for 20 years when they came to New York. Fred Hughes was Andy's business manager and the person who seriously made Andy into a business – the art machine that he became, the Silver Factory and all that – because Andy was not that until after Fred got hold of him. Luckily for me, I let Fred get hold of me too, and that's how I met the Agnellis, the Rothschilds and all the others, because they were all going to the Factory to have their portraits done.

Guess how I was paid back then? Paintings. Today, the eleven Warhols on my walls are all from that time; the ones you see in the reception area are all signed "to Peter" on the backs. It did not cost him a thing.

The best part of the story is that I had said to him: "But Andy, you know, I need some money." I was just starting off and I had to pay my rent and I said: "I can't just take *art,* I mean, I've got to eat, I've got to…" So he gave me a check for $100 for expenses and as he signed the check, he said: "Peter, if I were you I wouldn't cash that check, some day my signature is going to be worth a lot more than this check." And I thought, "You're such a scam artist, screw you," and I ran to the bank to cash the $100 and went out to eat. And of course he was right because the check written to "Peter

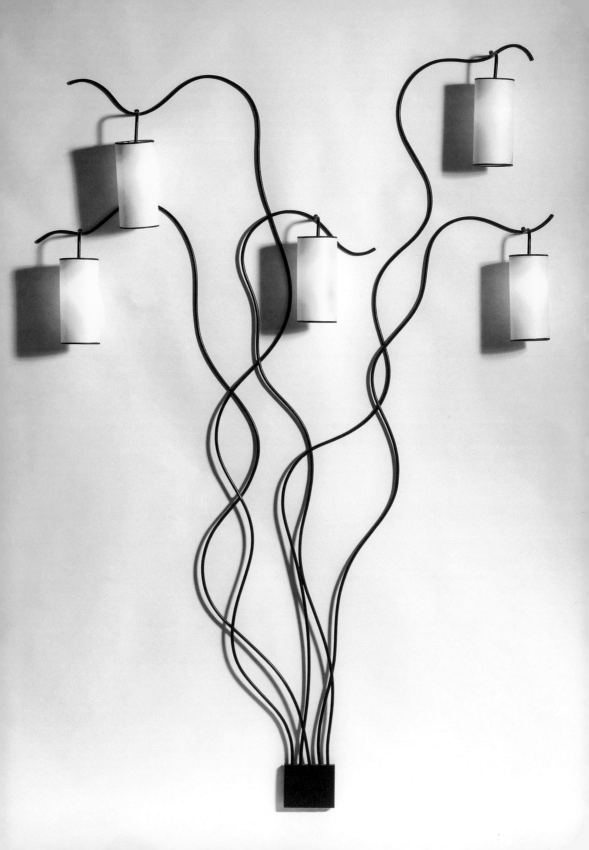

Marino, Architect, Andy Warhol" would have been worth thousands, it would have been worth a lot to me even now…it's so funny.

Warhol collected furniture the way he collected everything – for trading; he was the original Trader Vic. He had works of Cy Twombly and Roy Lichtenstein and Frank Stella and so many others, and it was all through trades. The artists in those days, in the 1960s and 1970s would trade, so his painting collection was spectacular, and he would trade whatever he could with all the dealers, too.

> "Those gorgeous veneers from the 1930s do not exist, even if you stand on your head and spit million-dollar bills."

The design boom

Definitely, the trend that is great right now is that the separate worlds of decorative arts and fine arts are overlapping. We see it with designers who are having gallery shows, although a lot of it started in the late 1980s, with Michael Graves and others doing teapots and dishes.

In fact, architects always did these things, so I view it now that we are simply returning to the way it was in 1900. For example, Wiener Werkstätte did everything – vases, silverware, knives and forks, they did buildings, chairs, anything that people used in their daily lives. Because of America's strength in technology and engineering in World War II, there was an enormous breach when architecture took the deep swing towards engineering, and the breach was between architects doing engineering, and others doing work like designing a chair. I always considered interior architecture as valid as exterior architecture – it is all architecture, I do not make the distinction.

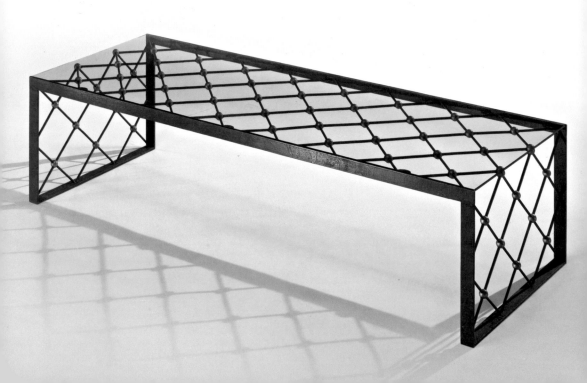

Marc Newson
Medium lathed table, 2006, white Carrara marble, 30 ¼ x 47 ¼ ø in. (77 x 119.9 ø cm)

The principles of design apply to everything; in fact, architecture was known as one of the "applied arts", which is a very interesting term. As I said, after World War II engineering went off in one direction and the art niche got left to a few people doing curtains. It was really awful. There was such a gulf that it led to a huge rise in non-architects, now known as "interior designers", doing interiors and furniture, and these designers ended up doing things that didn't exist before. So I think it's a really good trend that architects today are again being asked to deal with everyday items, they are taking furniture and interiors more seriously.

On the other hand, not everybody is good at everything. There are some dress designers who can do anything, like Karl Lagerfeld, and there are other dress designers who should really stick to doing dresses. Different people have different ranges of talent, of course. My point is simply that today's public is more open to architects working in areas other than traditional architecture.

Comparing new and old

When it comes to contemporary designers, the rule of fashion enters the picture. They are *in* fashion at the moment. If you ask for a $200,000 piece from Ron Arad and then ask me about a signed piece of Martin Carlin furniture, why would that go for only $1 million? Martin Carlin was the great French furniture designer from the 1770s and 1780s, so if the Carlin piece is worth $1 million, then the Ron Arad piece is not bad at $200,000.

Jean Royère
Tour Eiffel coffee table, ca. 1947, steel, bronze and glass, 13 ¼ x 51 ⅛ x 21 ¾ in. (35 x 130 x 55.3 cm)

Looking at a scale of the last 300 years, one sees a nice kind of calibration there. If today's pieces are great works of art that you *think* will last forever, that you are truly interested in, okay. If, as I fear, some of them have become so trendy and symbolic only of the time in which they live – a very narrow period, where you say that this design defines the 1990s – yes, that will have value but, between you and me, it will not carry forward for hundreds of years.

There is a difference between a very trendy piece of design for which one pays a great deal of money because so many people are trying to be trendy at the moment, versus a piece of design like those of the great French furniture makers, who were trying to make pieces of furniture that would look good and endure for a thousand years. There is a difference in the basic *goal*. And the market at the moment has a trendy fervour to it that I do not think will last.

When the design bubble will burst

I think that we are seeing one bubble of many bubbles, and another one will go higher. This particular trend is here, and even if the bubble does not burst, another bubble will appear because the trendy world, by definition, must change.

I do not think the Marc Newsons and Ron Arads ten years from now will be as hot as they are now, because by its very nature, the trendiest, hottest guy at the moment is not going to be that person ten years later. It does not work in fashion, it does not work in architecture – you know, Frank Gehry is already surpassed by Herzog & de Meuron. Everybody gets surpassed if you are very strong at your moment, so he or she is a bubble...I am not saying it is going to burst, but I think other bubbles will fly higher because of the essential *trendiness* of their designs. And further, I do not think their goal is really to create something timeless.

Jean Royère
Red chair, 1946, French oak frame tinted brown with covering of red velour, 37 x 16 ½ x 15 ⅜ in. (94 x 42 x 39 cm)

American versus European collectors

There is an interesting split between the way Americans think and how Europeans think, and half or more of our business is European. If I put a great furniture collection together, or a very good painting collection together – and I have done many collections – Europeans look at it as spending money.

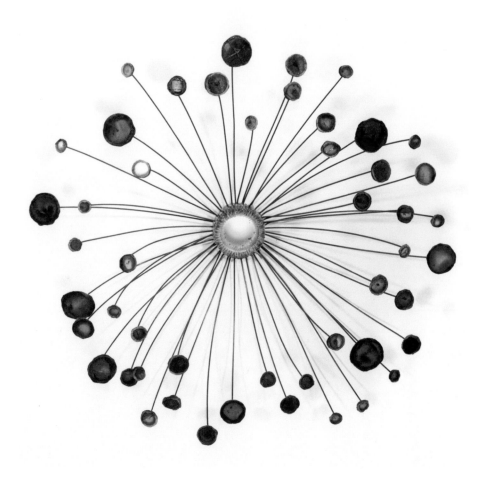

Line Vautrin
Ombelle convex mirror, ca. 1964,
Talosel resin, glass and brass,
ø 15 ¾ in. (40 cm)

When I was a young kid in this business, I would come on very "American" in recommending a piece: "This is a great investment, $200,000 for this desk, it is a great investment." And the European client would look at me and say: "Peter, you don't even know what an investment *is*. You may tell us that this is a great way to spend money, but it is not a great investment because I am not buying this to sell, I am buying this to *have*."

I won't cite too many names, but I work for many big American bankers and, when deciding on a piece, they all want to know if it is a good investment. "I'm buying this Paul Dupré-Lafon desk for $250,000 – is it a good investment, is it going up?" And I chuckle because the answer is that it depends on your point of view.

If you were European, you would think of it as spending money, not as an investment. So when you ask me whether it is

overleaf: **Emile-Jacques Ruhlmann**
Berger dining set, designed 1923, built 1927–1928, red lacquer finish, table top closed: 29 x 159 ½ in. (73.5 x 405 cm), chairs: 40 ⅛ x 17 ⅜ x 23 ⅞ in. (102 x 44 x 60.5 cm)

an asset class, I do not know the answer to that. There are two ways of looking at it. Americans look at their possessions as assets; Europeans do not, they really don't.

How he defines collectible design

It is a combination of many elements, one of which is: what is in fashion *now*. Think of a designer like Jean Royère – 25 years ago you couldn't *give* away his furniture, I mean that for $100 it could not be sold at auction. Now it cannot be bought for 100 times that.

I am a big admirer of Royère, although I am not a big collector of French 1940s and 1950s designs. Generally, what I collect is work up to World War II and the end of hand-made furniture. Once furniture became machine-made, its values became somewhat less for me because those pieces are ultimately very reproducible.

I do not believe that anything that can be made brand-new, as fantastic as the design might be, is something that ultimately is worth a great deal of money...yes, it is worth *some*thing, but my point is that there are no work-

> "Americans look at their possessions as assets; Europeans do not."

men who can make that great piece of Emile-Jacques Ruhlmann because those crafts-men are gone. It was made by hand, and though you might try, those gorgeous veneers from the 1930s do not exist, even if you stand on your head and spit million-dollar bills.

On Nakashima

I used George Nakashima for a house in the Hamptons 20 years ago. I love his work because it is sculptural but, although it has a place, it is not what I would call mixer-

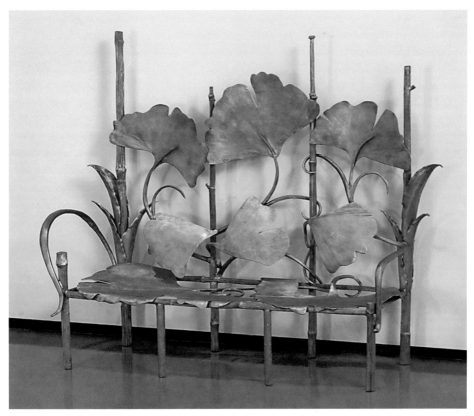

Claude Lalanne
Les Grandes Berces bench, 2000, bronze,
71 x 71 x 26 in. (180 x 180 x 66.6 cm)

friendly. A little bit of George Nakashima goes a long way because it's so strong, you cannot mix it with too many things. It is hand-made and ultimately it will be only slightly more valuable than machine-made furniture, in my opinion.

The importance of connoisseurship

The buyer has to be just as careful about furniture as with art. Because of the auction houses, paintings at the moment are more liquid, but if you want to buy furniture well, meaning signed pieces that are real, you need just as much help in buying furniture as you do in paintings. With paintings, a clever person certainly gets a condition report, and – unless you are hyper-professional – a little coaching if you're investing a great deal of money, so you learn about linings and what this painting has gone through and details of its history.

In the case of furniture, a good furniture expert will always give you what I call the shocking truth, and your reaction is: "You mean three quarters of the bronzes have been replaced?" Yes, it is legal; under Italian law only 25 percent of the piece must be original to be called antique. The potential buyer also needs more knowledge about collecting the "applied arts". You look at a piece and then buy it for $100,000 and one day you decide to sell it and Sotheby's tells you that three quarters of the

Emile-Jacques Ruhlmann
Tardieu desk, 1929, metal and lacquer,
30 x 107 x 62 in. (76.2 x 271.8 x 157.5 cm).
For the Salon des Artistes Décorateurs

bronzes are fake, the veneer is patched ABC, and there is more. You have to be aware of the pitfalls, which is why I always say: "Get good advice."

At my firm, we are scrupulous about having experts look at pieces before we pass anything off to clients, which is why I think I've ended up with the most serious clients in the world. I take this very seriously. I am going to be there for my clients when they are selling that million-dollar commode and make sure they will recover their $1 million as well as a profit. If I think it is good and right, it usually is.

We have more than 15 billionaire clients, and that is a lot. Why? Because we are *extremely* serious about their money. It takes a lot to buy the applied arts; it requires a vast amount of knowledge and most people don't realise that. They think that buying a desk is buying a desk and that an auction house would never sell anything that's not worthy.

Why he won't attend an auction

I have not personally attended auctions for over ten years because I cannot. It is actually horrible, I can't even walk through the auction house now; I go on private viewings only because people follow me through the auction house. I can't even say, "That's a nice piece," or six people start to register interest... I mean, I cannot. So I am very aware of it, and I am hyperaware that if dealers realise that I have chosen something, they are going to start

Paul Dupré-Lafon
Desk and chair, 1940s, parchment, oak, maple, patinated bronze, leather, 28 ¾ x 71 x 38 ⅝ in. (73 x 180.2 x 98 cm)

supplying me. It is not as much fun now as when I was younger…then I could do things without being noticed.

As to what I buy, I can put a great piece from any period in a room; if it is beautifully designed and beautifully executed I do not care what era it comes from. For example, I am one of the biggest proponents of certain Victorian furniture because some of it is so well done and so well made – I don't mean a piece that is entirely a copy of something else, which bores me to tears.

On the other hand, when people today build homes like Colonial Williamsburg houses, I think it's moronic, there is nothing between their ears. I mean, do these people wear wigs and breeches? Why would they want a house that looks like it was built 300 years ago? When people come to me and request this, I ask what's wrong with them.

Is design an investment?

I subscribe to the European view, that what I buy is spending money. In light of that, my homes are not investments for me, they are my homes, and the objects I own are not investments for me, they are what I spend to have a wonderful life. The investments of money that I have in funds and financial interests are a separate category. I do not look at money spent on buying something as an investment.

For example, I would never buy a thousand pieces of furniture and stick them in a warehouse and hope that they will go up in value. No, that does not interest me, that is not my business. My business is in guiding people towards that one piece that I have compared to 30 others and I decide: "That's really the good one." That is what is so great about working with people who appreciate fine things. It is connoisseurship that I admire.

My best clients are so terrific that I can point out a desk and tell them: "That is great." They do not ask why anymore, they come, they look through six books, they show me the 28 examples and say: "You are right, that's the good one, get it." I mean, that's why I live, to work for people like that. They say: "I see, it's the best one of its type. Get it!"

Robert Rubin

Tastemaker, New York

Robert Rubin, former Wall Street commodities trader, has redefined what it means to be a patron of 20th century design. He quit his day job to do a PhD on Jean Prouvé at Columbia. He financed the rescue and restoration of Prouvé's Maison Tropicale which he donated to the Centre Pompidou Foundation. He bought and restored Chareau's fabled Maison de Verre in Paris and he turned his Bridgehampton racetrack into a golf course replete with contemporary design and joke paintings by Richard Prince.

How he started collecting

My interest in design started with my interest in automobiles. There really isn't much of a difference between a race car and the Tropical House or the Maison de Verre. They are all artisan prototypes meant for eventual mass production. Even the Maison de Verre, which is a very high-end, custom-built house, deals with the industrialisation of architecture, just in poetic rather than practical terms.

After I made some money, I started buying old racing cars, fixing them up and going vintage racing. I really loved finding lost cars – for example Grand Prix cars from the 1930s and 1950s that were sent to "the colonies" at the end of the year's racing calendar so they could be offloaded to the locals. You start with whatever factory records you can get your hands on – other than the Germans no one kept very good records – and you end up in Brazil, New Zealand or, once, even Angola. I took two cars out of South Africa in the 1980s that were rebodied Grand Prix Maseratis from the 1920s! I paid $30,000 for a two-page contract between Maserati and Tazio Nuvolari that proved that Nuvolari had won the Belgian Grand Prix in it. It completed the file.

When I was living in Paris in the early 1990s, I went to an auction and saw some furniture by Ettore Bugatti made from Bugatti car parts. Not Carlo Bugatti, the brother who makes the Syrian-looking parchment furniture, but the famous car guy. The owner was selling it from an incredible collection of 20th century furniture in order to finance the restoration of a Romanesque church that he had bought. I said to myself: "My kind of guy..." I was outbid on the Bugatti furniture.

Pierre Chareau
Maison de Verre, Paris 1928–1932, glass and glass blocks, iron, steel, duralumin, natural rubber. In collaboration with Bernard Bijvoet. Restored by Robert Rubin

Pierre Chareau
Nesting table model no. MB 106, ca. 1924, walnut, 21 ¾ x 24 ¼ x 15 in. (55.2 x 62.8 x 38.1 cm), extended: 31 ¼ in. (79.3 cm)

But it was there that I discovered Pierre Chareau and, shortly after that, Jean Prouvé. Up until then, I had been collecting 18th century American furniture, pieces from Philadelphia and Boston like ball and claw foot tables, and American silver. I love Paul Revere. Revere had a great press agent: Henry Wadsworth Longfellow. The others, like Meyer Myers, toiled in comparative obscurity, but made even better silver. American silver is fascinating because, like a race car, it is crafted for beauty and pleasure but it relates to function.

In fact, any time an object can't be pigeonholed as either purely functional or aesthetic, it becomes interesting to me. The functionality of the object creates limits, and limits are good for the creative process; if you give a guy a blank slate, or a blank check, it doesn't work. For me there need to be some constraints. The Maison de Verre is better because they had to insert it into an existing 18th century house. The Tropical House needs to go in an airplane hold to Africa for dry assembly. A race car needs to be light and go fast without falling apart.

I am not a big fan of high-end fabrication art, where the art is in the production process. For example, I think Jeff Koons' three basketballs [*Three Ball Total Equilibrium Tank* from 1985] is better than the huge train that is planned for the plaza of the Los Angeles County Museum of Art because the train is too much about a feat of engineering fabrication, whereas the basketball sculptures are just as resonant, and they do not have all this scale and finish for the sake of scale and finish.

Why he sold his collection

I sold most of my Prouvé furniture when I got the Tropical House and started to restore it. We had a single-owner sale at Sotheby's in 2002. I'm very proud of the scholarship in that catalogue. I don't buy or sell because I think something is going up or down, I buy what I like as prudently as I can, and sell when I need money, or when I'm getting something in the same vein that makes what I am selling redundant.

Even though I am a retired commodities trader, I do not take a traderly approach to design and architecture. On the contrary, these projects of mine take forever. The repatriation and restoration of the Tropical House started as an idea in the late 1990s and there is still work going on around it. The Maison de Verre of Pierre Chareau is a project for a lifetime. And the golf course in Bridgehampton – the Bridge – I bought that in the early 1980s as a racetrack, now it's a golf course and I am still working on that.

I realised the Tropical House was the quintessential Prouvé object and I did not need all this other stuff. I assumed at the time that whatever money I put into the Tropical House was gone, one way or another, because the operation of resurrecting the house was not economically viable. If you look at what happened, the Paris dealers went to Africa, they took out all the furniture and left the house. Next step would have been to take the doors. It was worth more dead than alive.

Buying Prouvé's Maison Tropicale

I loved the idea of taking some of the money I had made and launching what seemed like an uneconomic operation at the time: to bring this house from Africa without any sense of whether it had any value. It was one of two houses that had been shipped there in 1951, designed by Prouvé as prototypes for inexpensive, mass-produced housing.

I financed Eric Touchaleaume, a French antiques dealer, to go there and bring the houses back, which he did. I took mine, he took his, and we went our separate ways. Contrary to what I often hear, though, he did *not* hack them out of the darkest jungle. The houses were in the war zone in the Congo, but that was downtown Brazzaville. They were widely known in architecture and preservation circles since pictures of the houses by Bernard Renoux had been published in a book put out by the French government in 1995 or 1996. Then Patrick Seguin and Philippe Jousse put out their catalogue on Prouvé in 1998, which contained more photographs of the houses in situ.

Pierre Chareau
Desk model no. MB 744, ca. 1927, steel and ebonised wood, 38 ½ x 51 ½ x 18 in. (97.8 x 130.8 x 45.7 cm)

The two houses are the same. One is slightly larger than the other, but they are both assembled from elements of the same building system. There is a big difference in the way they are

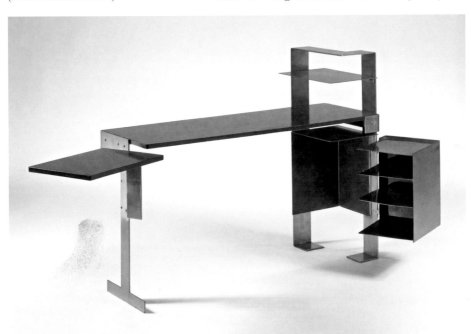

restored, but they are two iterations of the same prefabricated system. I wanted to get one house, restore it and demonstrate to people that Jean Prouvé was not decorator fodder, but rather a master maker of architecture.

Prouvé buildings were being torn down and cannibalized – "chopped" for parts. People were using fragments in high-end residences. I sold a pair of doors for about $600,000 at Sotheby's. The Tropical House had the problem all surviving modernist buildings have – in spades. The real value is always in the land. The building is just an inconvenience to real estate development.

> "The Tropical House is an 'edition of three' because Prouvé couldn't make any more... He wanted to make thousands of them, just couldn't find the financial backing."

I thought: "Rather than kit it out in pieces, I'm going to restore it intact to present this legacy that is being dissipated by the ravages of time...and decorators." I never imagined in my wildest dreams that the other tropical house would one day sell for $5 million. I thought I was flushing money down the toilet. It's funny because the Tropical Houses were originally meant for low-cost housing. Now they are more expensive than high-end Manhattan real estate.

On the second Maison Tropicale selling for $5 million

It is a complicated subject. On the theory that all publicity is good publicity, it's good that people understand who Prouvé was, but it is not without its ironies. Prouvé, Charlotte Perriand and others like them resurfaced via their furniture, which has been purchased by contemporary art collectors because it looks good with contemporary art. But that is a post-modernisation of Prouvé. In reality, Prouvé was a hard-ass, card-carrying modernist with deeply held, left-leaning socialist views. He was not a Communist, but he was not an abject capitalist either. He was interested in building. He sold furniture to finance his experimental constructive systems.

He was quite an experimental guy. He even gave stock to his workers. The labour unions hated him, the other factory owners hated him, he pissed off everybody, it was part of his charm. I think this Post-modern appropriation of Prouvé has deracinated him a little. He's no Philippe Starck. Prouvé has a particular meaning in his time and place and people have appropriated him into the 21st century in a way that is different.

I am not critical of André Balazs (the buyer of the other Maison Tropicale at auction). I think he runs a great hotel business, some of my favourite hotels in the world: the Chateau Marmont, the Mercer. If he turns around and puts it up for sale for $20 million next year, I'll have a different view, but for the moment I think you preserve things in the way you can. Show me a museum that has $5 million to buy this house and put it up. So I think if he has chosen to buy this object and exploit it in the context of the hospitality business, it could be worse. I have more of a problem with Eric Touchaleaume's restoration, it's overly refabricated and finished – restored to within an inch of its life. Now it's a garden folly.

Sometimes, this use of Prouvé as fashionable décor bothers me but if that were the standard for judging the creative output of the past, think of all the artists who would be

rolling over in their graves if they saw where their paintings are today, who owns them and how they are being displayed. You cannot think that way.

Why he gave his Tropical House to the Pompidou Museum

Originally, I actually thought I would use it at the Bridge golf club for a halfway house, and then as I got more and more involved in it, I realised that the Tropical House had to be more than just a place to stop and have a cheeseburger between the front nine and the back nine.

Displaying the Tropical House completely empty

The house is more important as an exemplar of a constructive system of endless possibilities than any single house. The genius of the house is the way it can be assembled and how the pieces go together; by leaving it open without walls and by leaving pieces off, one can understand the constructive logic of the house. That is how an architect today, or somebody interested in design, should be looking at it.

The idea is to present the Maison Tropicale or the Maison de Verre in a way that makes people in the 21st century think differently about architecture. Not pedantically, but with intent to stimulate. Isn't the real question: "What is the relevance of all this history to the practice of architecture today?"

Jean Prouvé
La Maison Tropicale, 1951, aluminium, steel, Plexiglas, 1500 sq.ft. (139.4 sq.m.). Restored by Robert Rubin and donated to the Centre Pompidou Foundation

Two kinds of Prouvé

To finish up on the subject, there are two kinds of Prouvé: large lot jobs for universities, for

Jean Prouvé
Compass dining table, ca. 1950, lacquered steel
and oak, 28 x 77 ½ x 31 ½ in. (71.1 x 197 x 80 cm).
From Electricité de France

example, several thousand desks and chairs, and then his special-order prototype work which, for its rarity, may be more interesting from a collector's standpoint, although not necessarily from a historical standpoint.

In fact, when I curated my first show at Columbia, I specifically chose, as the co-curator, an architect who I thought was Prouvé-esque in spirit, but who had no clue about Prouvé historically. He didn't collect anything except parking tickets. So I took my collection, from $500 chairs to $100,000 desks, I spread them all out and said: "Make the show out of this. Use what appeals to your architect's eye without regard to what the market considers choice or rare." I wanted to get outside the collector's mentality. A collector looks at the value of things in a certain way, which is not the same way an architect or a scholar or anybody else looks at the same object.

I don't like to focus too much on a market-based analysis, because the market often gets in the way of appreciating something. Collectors have a way of over-valuing certain things because they are attractive and work decoratively, and under-valuing the more difficult and less accessible thing even though it may be the artist's work that resonates the most.

As to prices that are in the hundreds of thousands of dollars for works that were meant to be made by machine – I would say this is the difference between an explicit limited edition and an inadvertent limited edition. The Tropical House is an "edition of three" because Prouvé couldn't make any more, not because his gallerist told him to make eight plus two artist's proofs. He wanted to make thousands of them, just couldn't find the financial backing. Is a Kangourou chair that much more beautiful than a Standard chair? I could argue that the Standard chair is to his furniture what the Tropical House is to his buildings: the pinnacle. He just managed to make thousands of them in his lifetime because they were so useful and beautiful and economical. The Kangourou chair looks great today next to a Basquiat but there was little demand for it in its time.

Pierre Chareau's Maison de Verre

I had put the Tropical House up in France before it was shipped to Yale. One of my professors from Columbia was there. He had written a book about Chareau and was friendly with the family that owned the house. He saw what I had done with the Tropical House, thought it was great and said that my wife and I ought to buy the Maison de Verre. I thought he was kidding.

Chareau, an interior designer who had built little, ran with the Paris avant-garde and collaborated with a Dutch architect and a French artisan metal worker on the Maison de Verre. The result was amazing. He did another very important house with Robert Motherwell, a project in East Hampton, which was torn down in 1985. In 1985, nobody cared about these things.

It's interesting that he is thought of as an Art Deco designer because there is a certain visual confusion in people's minds about him. In one respect, I think it's because the few pictures that people see over and over again of the Maison de Verre show a lot of Chareau furniture that was made well before the house; it belonged to the original owners and they brought it with them. If you came to the house now with all that out of the way, you would see it much more as a cubist/constructivist space – Braque meets El Lissitsky.

We have about 1,000 people a year visiting it and we make it available for scholars who are working on various related projects – one woman is doing a PhD on the plumbing. Its high level of intactness makes it a wonderful case study. There is a little furniture and a lot of built-ins; the house is basically an aggregation of built-ins – furniture as architecture – the moving walls, shelves and screens are what sculpt the space and transform it.

My wife and I live in it a couple of months a year, as our children grow older we will spend more and more time there. We've done an enormous amount of work on it already, rewiring and the like. The real challenge will be to live in it as our principal residence some day. Our goal is to provide for the long-term protection of the house after we are gone, which was probably the goal of the Vellay family in selling us the house. I believe they chose us because they understood that we were interested in acquiring the house to live in it and preserve it.

Ian Schrager

Tastemaker, New York

Ian Schrager and business partner Steve Rubell founded the epic and historic Studio 54 nightclub in the 1970s, and Schrager, on his own, opened Morgans Hotel in 1984, pioneering the concept of the "boutique hotel". He created the Royalton and the Paramount as well as the Gramercy Park Hotel. He has hired breakthrough designers from Philippe Starck to architects Herzog & de Meuron and has also used artist Julian Schnabel for interiors. He is largely responsible for making contemporary design synonymous with excitement and trendsetting cachet.

Designing Studio 54

In a way, Studio 54 was a design concept because it turned a nightclub into a stage, and so people were dancing on stage rather than in the old, underground club rooms. One of the things that Studio 54 accomplished was to take a nightclub up a notch…not paint it black etc. Instead, we put a little glamour into the design and some sophistication into how it looked. Combining the club with a theatrical concept is one of the reasons why I think it became truly combustible and took off from there.

The nightclub business, although this may sound unexpected, gave me the opportunity to be involved with many creative disciplines, because there was no structure. It demanded attention to design, architecture, film, video, theatrical staging, theatrical sets, lighting, music, video, fashion and, in a very undisciplined way, really gave me a foundation that whet my appetite for design – because I realised what a difference it made. We used to do parties that were actually design-centered because, after all, we had the same music and the same liquor that everybody else had, so we had to distinguish ourselves from others by the experience that we created.

Since then I have used this approach in all of my design projects. In the beginning, one of the reasons I started working with European rather than American designers was that I was looking for a heightened experience, something different. I wanted something that was not readily available, somebody who would take a kind of different approach. And I did not know I loved design.

I remember when Steve Rubell and I opened our first nightclub in Queens – on the first night, Steve went down

Philippe Starck
Pair of J. (Série Lang) lounge chairs, 1986, aluminium and leather upholstery,
33 x 24 x 27 in. (84 x 61 x 68.6 cm)

Philippe Starck
Bar stools, 1988, cast aluminium and upholstery, 29 x ø 14 in. (73.7 x ø 35.6 cm). Originally designed for the Royalton Hotel

with the kids at the bar and I went up to the DJ and the lights, and that night set the tone of what we both did...a natural division of responsibility. We borrowed money to put the concept together along with the visuals, and we started working.

A very sophisticated designer, and the first we ever worked with, was Andrée Putman from Paris. She was a great stylist and was largely inspired by Jean-Michel Frank. She had done the apartments of Karl Lagerfeld, Yves Saint Laurent, and was very much into the Paris fashion scene. We were very much into the New York fashion scene, so we hired her. We came with no preconceived notions except that we wanted to do a hotel, and not the type that our parents liked – not that I rejected their tastes, but I wanted something that was about my own culture. Andrée Putman came in and we did a hotel that did not really look like a hotel; it broke all the rules and that process was almost like a utopian experience. I got completely smitten by it.

Philippe Starck
Pair of Len Niggelman lounge chairs, 1986, cast aluminium, cloth and velvet upholstery, 26 x 27 x 32 ½ in. (66 x 68.6 x 82.6 cm). From the Schrager residence

Choosing designers and architects

I have a good window on the popular culture through magazines and books. It's possible to sit in a chair in your living room and see everything that's going on with a careful selection of magazines and books. I read everything I can get my hands on.

I saw a work of Philippe Starck in Paris – it was a traditional French brasserie but updated and modernised, so it had the essence of a French brasserie, but unlike anything I had ever seen, and it was modern. The bathrooms had a sense of wit and irony about them; people would go into the bathrooms and not even know how to use them. So when I saw how he reinvented a French brasserie and how he took a lavatory and made it a platform for amusement – I thought, that is what I want to do with a hotel, to refigure and reinvent it, especially because Morgans, the first hotel I had done with Andrée, was really more about style. Now I wanted to use some really original furniture, original creations, which is why I went to Philippe Starck when we did the Royalton.

But in terms of Starck's furniture, whoever would have known that some of the pieces that were done in the 1920s, 1930s, 1940s, 1950s would become collectibles? True, they were done with a functional purpose in mind, but they are unique. This type of furniture is art, but a different kind of art. Ordinarily, the only purpose of art – and I am not really a student of this, it's just what I feel – is to lift the spirits and make some sort of emotional connection, captured on canvas in the way a poet might write a poem. Furniture,

> "I would have to be an idiot not to realize I should have bought more Lockheed Lounges."

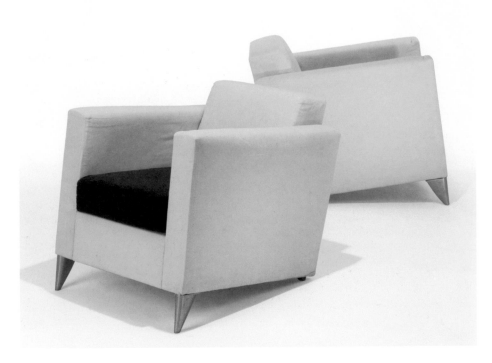

on the other hand, has that quality, but it also serves a functional purpose. It has another dimension but to me it is just as much art.

Destroying Philippe Starck's interior of the Royalton Hotel

The Morgans Hotel group bought the Royalton. I cannot second-guess their redecorating, they must have had their reasons, they are smart guys. But I think what they did was wrong. I have moved on, so I do not have that kind of emotional attachment to the hotel. It seems to me, though, that it can sometimes be a burden to deal with an icon of design, and perhaps the design is no longer relevant and the place is not successful, but people still want to retain the design.

I think that books on the Royalton will be published and talked about even ten, 20, 50 years hence, and I love that. It is my work and I love it. When I take on a project and try to create something that is really well designed, even if it is trendy or provocative and edgy, does not mean that it cannot be a classic and stand the test of time. This is ultimately more important to me than anything because it is my work, my life, and if the public embraces it, then it's wonderful.

David Adjaye
Monoforms 1 (type II Petra), 2007,
Hassan green granite, four elements: each
15 ¾ x 15 ¾ x 15 ¾ in. (40 x 40 x 40 cm)

His Phillipe Starck-designed apartment
The apartment was on Central Park West and it was like a little jewel box, it was really great.

Starck was a real talent and he came to it in an undisciplined kind of way, his was more of an attitude and approach, and he had a great sense of style. He was not bound by the normal rules, he did not follow a logical progression the way designers usually do. He broke all the rules and what he did had a certain buoyancy about it, a sense of wit and humour, an irreverence and whimsy that people responded to. All the kinds of feelings that people perhaps experience when they look at a painting, they got from his interiors.

In the end I sold the apartment with everything in it. The people who bought it sold the furniture; they put my name on it at the time, I guess to increase the value. The buyer was a really nice man and had a family, and I think he probably sold it because he wanted to go on and do his own thing.

I am now moving into the penthouse at 40 Bond, the building I have just built, designed by Herzog & De Meuron, it's really spectacular, really great. They had designed certain aspects of the penthouse but I was not sure that they would be able to devote the time and energy to do an individual apartment. There are so many considerations: What about the rugs? What about the stitching on the sheets? I was not sure that they would not run out of patience.

So I hired British architect John Pawson who is known as a minimalist, although I did not want a minimalist apartment. I wanted an envelope, a clean envelope that took advantage of light and worked spatially. Of course, people asked: "Why would you hire

John Pawson, one of the most famous minimalists in the world?" Because I want a modern, clean envelope, and I think he will be good at it. He may also design some pieces of furniture, but I intend to look around and buy a lot of collectible pieces.

Design as investment

Of course, I do believe that design is a good investment. The only thing one must be careful about is if it is easily reproduced, because the quantity of a piece could impact its potential increase in value. However, when someone like Zaha Hadid produces a desk for £170,000, that does not apply, it would be a one-off piece in the same way that a painting is one-off. That is not the part I like, though.

What I do like is when a piece of furniture is made to do something, and because it is so unique and so well designed, it becomes a collectible. That is more interesting to me than setting out to create a desk that sells for £170,000 because it is one of a kind. That is very obvious to me. What really interests me is if someone signs a chair, even a far less expensive chair, and then it gets into a big market because it is so well designed and 50 years later it looks just as good as when it was created and it becomes a collectible. Why? Because it reflects the society of its time. It's sort of like the time capsule. That is one of the reasons we like painting and why we like furniture.

I do not buy a piece because someone says: "Let's hold the market down, let's limit the supply…let's make it very, very expensive…it is only one of 10, it's an edition." No. That is relevant, of course, but what interests me is that Le Corbusier designed a chair and then 50 or 60 years later it is so great that it is collectible. It is unique. That, to me, has

more attraction than a piece of furniture selling for £200,000 or £300,000 because it is one of seven pieces.

Today's architects and planning form over function

Today's architects exemplify the opposite of "form follows function". If function follows form, I have no problem with it except that it has to function. If it does not function, it is not successful. In the categories of art, architecture and furniture, the art has no purpose other than to elicit a response. But architecture and the furniture must serve a dual purpose – they have to be functional. If not, the object is not successful, and the producer/creator should go out and paint or do something else. I think that's where the difference lies.

Design by an artist, the Gramercy Park Hotel by Julian Schnabel

For the Gramercy Park, I wanted to reinvent and rethink every step along the way, to depart from anything I had done in the past. I wanted to capture the aesthetic of an artist or his studio where no rules are followed; the ambiance can't be categorised or defined, extraordinary and ordinary things are put side by side and traditional vocabulary is mixed with edgy ideas in furniture design.

The result is so individual, so original and quirky it is unlike anything you have ever seen before. When you visit an artist's studio, it may look chaotic but there is a certain organised chaos to it, and it looks spectacular. It's the same with an artist's home. I did not want to do anything that had a "look" that could be defined as Art Deco or Art Nouveau – no, I wanted to do something that was solely itself.

Julian Schnabel created the art for the space, with some works in the style of Picasso, and certain people were offended. But from my point of view we were not doing an art gallery. We were doing something intended to be irreverent and having some fun; it was not meant to be disrespectful, obviously, it was supposed to reflect a little bit of irony and irreverence. Julian has designed a number of things for the hotel. He designed a couple of end tables that are very Giacometti-ish in appearance, the curtain rods, door handles, lamps in the lobby, the fireplaces and irons, lamps in the rooms...any number of pieces.

This time, I own the works in the hotel, because I would have to be an idiot not to realise I should have bought more Lockheed Lounges.

Philippe Starck
Custom booth and table, 1999, leather,
marble, matte chrome-plated steel, mahogany,
46 x 84 x 60 in. (116.8 x 213.4 x 152.4 cm).
From the Schrager residence

Axel Vervoordt

Tastemaker, Antwerp

Axel Vervoordt is widely regarded as an original and eclectic collector, dealer and interior designer known for his sophisticated taste. He created *Artempo* at the Palazzo Fortuny during the 2007 Venice Biennale and his arrangements of antiques, classical sculpture and Asian art, mixed with sculptures by Anish Kapoor and James Turrell, were a landmark in the recent history of the design world. The following year he produced *Academia* and, in 2009, his show entitled *In-finitum* completed the trilogy.

How he works

I like people very much and I like to make them happy. I am not a decorator who wants to put his own style everywhere and then people have to live in it. For me, doing an interior is like making a portrait of someone and finding the right objects to suit the individual. My clients have become very great friends and I want to lead them to know themselves even better – by looking at art and discovering things they haven't seen before. And when their house is finished, it's like they have been living there all their lives – that is the feeling they need to have. It is a total love of conception rather than mere decoration. I have always liked things that are timeless, and understated.

It makes no sense to me when people take a contemporary picture like a Rothko, just because it's expensive, and hang it above a very expensive marquetry French commode. I do not care for it. I think Arte Povera, or a Mark Rothko or Lucio Fontana painting go much better with the very pure furniture made by a shepherd in the mountains – even when it has little monetary value – because they belong more naturally together in spirit.

Starting out

I think my great international success came in 1982 with my first biennale in Paris. By then I had a good inventory, including fabulous pieces of royal collections, and my stand was located right at the entrance to the fair, thanks to Didier Aaron, who was

Edina Altara
Mirrored Wall, 1950, five hand-painted, reverse-decorated and scorched mirror-glass panels, applied to a door and two unpainted panels, door-mounted panels: 79 ¼ x 23 ¼ in. (201.5 x 59 cm), 49 ½ x 34 ¼ in. (126 x 87 cm), 49 ¾ x 34 ¼ in. (126.5 x 87 cm), 49 ½ x 34 in. (126 x 86.5 cm), 49 ½ x 11 ½ in. (126 x 29 cm), unpainted panels: 79 ½ x 3 ⅜ in. (202 x 8.5 cm)

211

Le Corbusier
Stool from Maison du Brésil, Cité Universitaire,
Paris, ca. 1956, oak, 17 x 13 ⅛ x 10 ⅛ in.
(43.2 x 33.3 x 25.8 cm)

my godfather there and helped to get me in.

He liked me and he encouraged me to get a big booth. I arrived in Paris with everything I had prepared, and when I looked around, the booths of all the other exhibitors were like palaces with beautiful arches, niches and interesting construction. I was so depressed, I thought that my booth was going to be terrible because, after all, I had not done all that work. I was so tired and feeling miserable, I went outside the Grand Palais and fell asleep on the grass for two hours.

When I woke up and returned to my booth, the surroundings had changed...the exhibitors had added even more elaboration, faux marble, faux papier, and it all looked so boring, so bourgeois. Since the others had done everything, I decided to do nothing. I left the Grand Palais as it was, even the concrete floor, and within that open space I created a display by mixing everything I had.

I grouped the contemporary art, the Asian and the baroque pieces in an interesting way, as one would see them in a large artist's studio. This was very new because the idea of a loft and that kind of mix – almost nobody did anything like that in 1982. At the end, it was almost sold out. Then I met important clients like Valentino, the Labèque sisters, Leo Daly, Hubert de Givenchy...Rudolf Nureyev, Yves Saint Laurent and Pierre Bergé, they all became clients.

About his *Artempo* exhibition at the Palazzo Fortuny in 2007

Artempo's message was about recognising the differences between objects and putting them all together to create one harmony. Think of many people sitting around one table, having a fabulous dinner while, at the same time, each one keeps his own personality. With all of them together, the result is stronger than each one separately.

I never expected *Artempo* to be such a big success because it was a very personal story, it reflected my own passion and was something I wanted to express and communicate. I thought that nobody would understand it, but it was a greater success than I could ever imagine.

The theme of *Artempo* was "Where Time Becomes Art". My point was that time itself is art, that time changes things the way it changes the facades of Venetian houses, which are totally cracked, but they then become like abstract painting. Or take a stone which I included with several of the Picasso and Giacometti pieces. It was a simple, found stone but its shape was so amazing that people thought it was created by an artist. I told them, "I found

Scott Burton
Rock chair, 1981, Sierra granite,
32 x 50 x 52 in. (81.2 x 127 x 132 cm)

it in the street." It was made by nature and time, over millions of years. For me, that is the primary message of art…to make us see in a different way, to open our eyes. That is why contemporary art is so important, and so valuable and expensive.

His view of contemporary design

We design furniture ourselves (the Axel Vervoordt Home Collection) because I do not find what I like in the market today. I like furniture to be very discreet, very comfortable and beautiful; it should age well and get better as it is used.

Many of the furniture pieces made today are easily damaged – you scratch it and that's the end. For me, the more scratched, the more used, the more I prefer it. Some of the current design furniture is very interesting to look at, but often uncomfortable to touch or to sit in.

> "I want things that are used, with patina. Once they are restored, they lose all their value and authenticity."

I feel that many of today's architects and designers are creating pieces for their own pleasure. They are producing designs that are very personal, but they do not realise, or do not know, that people have to *live* in it. We see the most fabulous shapes in plastic, but you touch the surface and hurt yourself, or you damage the piece and it is ruined.

However, I am not against contemporary design. I am against nothing, I think everything is important. Everyone who wants to create a piece should have the freedom to make it.

Max Ingrand
Chandelier, ca. 1955, crystal, gilt brass,
15 ½ x ø 22 in. (39.4 x ø 55.9 cm)

Accepting things as they are

I very much like the use of humble or poor material in rich proportions, like the stools made by Le Corbusier. When you see them, they are aged, the paint is off and you feel they have some life. That is a total way of looking at furniture and why I want things that are used, with patina. Once they are restored, they lose all their value and authenticity. I think you have to accept things as they are, and that was a key message of *In-finitum,* where we called it, "As-it-is-ness".

His foundation

There are things I will never sell, and they are protected by the Vervoordt Foundation because they form the basis of an idea. Eventually, they will go to the museum which we are building on our property called the Kanaal – it was once an abandoned factory along the Albert canal outside of Antwerp. My son Dick and his team are working on this huge project where there will be apartments, offices, showrooms and shops. At the centre of it will be the Vervoordt Foundation. When it is complete, we will be able to share the collection with many more people, and organize exhibitions around the artists we like.

The architects collaborating on this project are Stéphane Beel, Coussée & Goris and Bogdan & Van Broeck. Our vision for the museum is very human and universal and it is felt by those working on it. Just as a very good painter thinks about himself while using his brush to express a cosmic feeling, I hope that the museum will function as the brush of a great feeling. I do not want this collection to be a portrait of myself...rather, it reflects a universal thinking and that is why I want to share it.

In-finitum: completing a trilogy

My goal was to do an exhibition trilogy. After the *Artempo* show in 2007 came *Academia, qui es-tu?* in Paris in 2008, which was more about the artist questioning himself, as well as the onlookers questioning themselves. The last of the series was *In-finitum* in 2009, the Latin word which means both infinity and unfinished.

It seems to me that we, as human beings, can never think of something as perfect. We can try to achieve perfection but there is always an essence that we can never achieve – like a void or the infinity, and it is also the non-finished. Simply put, in the non-finished is infinity. You see this when you look at an old work of art that has never been completed because the artist decided to leave it in an unfinished state, or because he died during its creation, or whatever the reason.

Unfinished works of the 19th century did not sell well, so naturally when dealers discovered such pieces, they finished them themselves. They added arms and repainted them. It is just awful! I want to take it all off and bring them back to their unfinished state – because you will see infinity in the empty spaces. Artists like Degas and Derain and Cézanne often left works unfinished, and so did Picasso.

His personal philosophy

I never bother worrying about a good business decision because if you work well in a very personal and honest way, success comes automatically.

In the life of a fly, which is only one day, ten minutes is a lot. In the life of a star spanning millions of years, one hundred years is nothing. I feel as though five hundred years or one thousand years could be yesterday. I do not want to see the difference between yesterday or today, or one hundred or five thousand years ago. For me, everything blends together because there is a message of peace and harmony, interest and intellect, initiation and creativity in all the pieces. Yet they all keep their individual personality and live together like one soul, one expression.

Advice for the new collector

Follow as much as you can your personal feelings, deep feelings in the stomach without thinking, but be guided by a very good dealer. It is unfortunate that too many people build their collections only at auction sales and buy only what everybody else buys.

If you look at all the great collections in history, you will find that they were made by two people, the collector who had the money, and the dealer beside him who was the adviser. I think that keeping an open and very trustful relationship with a good dealer is very well worth it. That way, your collection will have unity and you have somebody behind you who is knowledgeable and responsible, because buying only in auction sales is dangerous.

Good collections need to have an underlying spirit…there should be a message, an extra dimension. You should discover and buy works that fit your vision, and buy what other people are not yet buying.

THE AUCTIC
HOUSE

20th-century design at auction has come from somewhat humble beginnings. Whereas Deco was able to carve out its own market niche in the 1980s, historically, antiques had always made the big prices at auction. American Empire designs by names like Duncan Phyfe and French Empire by Georges Jacob had always made good money in public sales. The somewhat secondary grouping of less valuable things was called XXth Century Decorative Arts; here we found Tiffany lamps, Lalique vases, Gustav Stickley furniture, an occasional chair by Frank Lloyd Wright with some Art Nouveau.

Most of the design shown in this book would not have raised an eyebrow only 20 years ago, and would have fallen into the "decorative arts" grouping, but times and tastes have changed. About ten

N

EXPERT

years ago, things really took off and Phillips de Pury pushed forth some really new and exciting 20th century pieces, positioning them as valuable collectibles and no longer merely vintage furniture. In time, the market for top pieces from the 1920s through the 1960s really took off, as did the secondary market for contemporary designers. Recently, Newson's Lockheed Lounge traded hands for over $2 million and the Dragons armchair by Eileen Gray made $27.8 million, so today 20th century design is the most expensive furniture in the market.

Auction prices can be lumpy with some results flying high, and other things going unsold, so serious collectors do their homework before they bid.

Gerti Draxler

Auction expert – Dorotheum, Vienna

Dr. Gerti Draxler is head of the design department of the Dorotheum, Vienna's historic auction house founded more than 300 years ago. Since 1996, her commitment and enthusiasm have contributed to the resounding success of the bi-annual design auctions in which she juxtaposes historical design with contemporary works. She has taught at the Akademie der Bildenden Künste Wien, worked at the Neue Galerie contemporary art museum in Graz and written for various publications.

A global perspective

Dorotheum has been holding design auctions since 1996, twice a year. During this period of time, we have shipped some 9,000 design objects to Vienna which, after the sales, have again come to be scattered around the globe. Vienna had no substantial domestic market in the design field – and this, by the way, also holds true for modern art.

Vienna's major design collections were created around 1900 by the Jewish bourgeoisie. The vacuum that emerged after World War II has never been filled and therefore still exists today. We have always seen ourselves as a meeting point to present novelties and offer a forum for discussion. Unlike seeing the pieces in museums, you can touch and try out all the objects exhibited during our public viewings, thereby learning a great deal about condition and authenticity.

We have been operating profitably from the very outset. And it is gratifying that our previews have taken on the character of a temporary "design museum."

Eighty percent of our sales go to international collectors, dealers, interior designers and museums, with the United States in first place – over the years, it has remained unchallenged as our most important market segment. Top lots also find buyers on the Asian market and in the Eastern European countries. Here we benefit from our historical role as a link to the East. Our Asian and Eastern European clients' focus is on the contemporary sector where Zaha Hadid, Johanna Grawunder, Philip Michael Wolfson and Ron Arad are currently making the most prominent appearances.

Their demand for historical design is much lower and concentrates on pioneering works by Adolf Loos and Koloman Moser, or French Art Déco.

Eduard Wimmer-Wisgrill
Two-tier cabinet, 1933, pinewood,
55 x 52 ½ x 21 ¼ in. (140 x 133 x 54 cm).
Made by Wiener Werkstätte

Dorotheum specials

It would never have occurred to me to restrict the concept of design to a limited period of time. When I make my selection, I always ask myself about the merits of an object, where it is located within the history of design, and what conceptual background makes it special. That means that, essentially, each auction spans from several examples from the early 19th century to the present day, although considerable shifts in focus have taken place over the past 15 years.

Also, I have always been interested in early solutions, several aspects of which sometimes amount to trailblazing accom-

> "Where do we run into a special Gerrit Rietveld, Marcel Breuer or Koloman Moser? It is easier to find a Picasso, which costs many times as much."

plishments. In 2002, we auctioned what appears to have been the earliest laminated wood chair, a model by the Belgian cabinetmaker Jean-Joseph Chapuis from 1805 for the Château de Laeken in Brussels. The chair featured a neo-classical design, but was highly innovative in terms of the material that was used.

Looking for great works

It may not come as a surprise that we have always been looking for early Thonet objects, the Thonet company having been a pioneer in serial mass production and marketing.

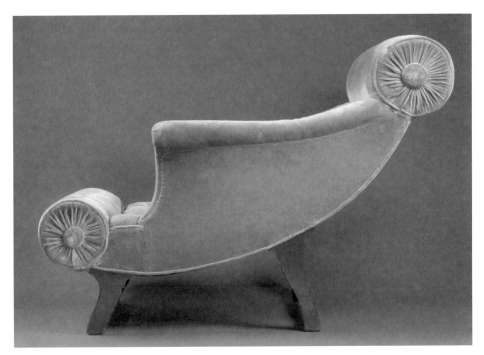

Adolf Loos
Knieschwimmer armchair, ca. 1906, wood
with velvet upholstery, 31 x 27 ½ x 13 ½ in.
(79 x 70 x 34 cm)

However, it has become increasingly difficult
to get hold of a Model No 14 chair from 1859
(also known as the "bistro chair") or its pre-
cursor, the Boppard chair, from 1835–1840. They are all preserved in museums or collections and are rarely available for sale.

The same goes for custom-made furniture from the period of the Vienna Secession
which, because of its radical formal rigor, is highly modern. As a Viennese auctioneer,
it is more or less a must for us to carry it in our range. In an auction catalogue from
Vienna, people expect to come across Josef Hoffmann, Adolf Loos, Otto Wagner and
Koloman Moser. Recently, minimalist tables and stools, which are frequently painted in
black and white and often cannot be attributed with certainty, have increasingly come
to appeal to collectors of contemporary design, for these models combine perfectly with
the latter. Another typical example is the Austrian architect Josef Frank. Having emi-
grated to Sweden in 1934, he exercised a great impact on Scandinavian design with the
furniture company Svenskt Tenn. It seems natural for us to offer works from Frank's
Viennese period.

Josef Hoffmann
Dining room set, ca. 1901–1902, extendable table,
six armchairs, wall paneling and storage units, cabinets
and wardrobe, pitch pine with marquetry of South
American satin wood with copper mounts, wall storage
system: 59 x 124 ¾ x 23 ¼ in. (149.5 x 317 x 59 cm),
wall paneling: 58 x 197 in. (147 x 500 cm),
table: 30 x ø 55 in. (76 x ø 140 cm), armchairs:
37 ½ x 21 ¾ x 21 ¾ in. (95 x 55 x 55 cm)

Design-art crossover

During the past years we have seen an approxima-
tion between art and design that takes place on a
mutual basis and has brought about both a multi-
farious exchange between the two disciplines
and various hybrid forms. It is exciting to observe
how artists approach the subject of design. A chair

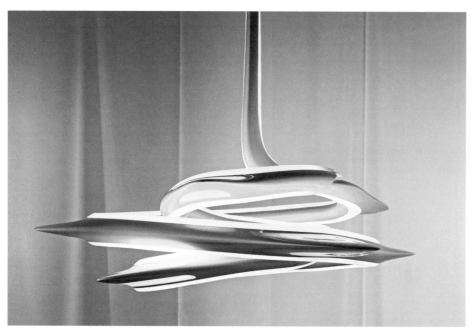

Zaha Hadid and Patrik Schumacher
VorteXX chandelier, 2005, fibreglass-reinforced
polyester, LED modules, 59 ½ x 57 ½ x 65 ¾ in.
(151 x 146 x 167 cm)

by Franz West or Heimo Zobernig is never purely design, but always also a conceptual exploration that embraces the question of how the chair can function as art. Conversely, designers cross over into the aura of the art object – an approach that holds all the market-stimulating promises we are currently witnessing. The artist-designer seeks to attract the interest of art dealers rather than furniture manufacturers and is soon ennobled through museum exhibitions, with auctions becoming forums of price policy.

Where design is going

In the years to come, we will experience a sustained interest in contemporary design, in part because it is easier to find. Today, outstanding vintage design is extremely rare. Frequently it is a unique object, or one that was produced as a limited series, or was custom-made for a specific ambience. Where do we run into a special Gerrit Rietveld, Marcel Breuer or Koloman Moser? It is easier to find a Picasso, which costs many times as much. Compared to the visual arts, significant vintage design is still extremely underrated and has a high potential in terms of value increase.

But in my view, contemporary design production is a wide and exciting field, with countless peripheries still to be discovered. What I have in mind here is the creative reservoir of Africa or Israel, or new ideas originating from wherever, that are conceived through global exchange. In terms of content, I believe we are moving in a conceptual direction, with sociological and ecological issues being addressed to an increasing extent.

Adolf Loos
Tea table, ca. 1905, mahogany,
24 ¾ x ø 27 ½ in. (63 x ø 70 cm)

Philippe Garner

Auction expert – Christie's, London

Philippe Garner is the international head of 20th Century Decorative Art & Design at Christie's. In 1970, fresh out of college, he joined Sotheby's and stayed for over 31 years with a brief two-year interlude at Phillips de Pury. He is broadly recognised as an eminence grise in the field.

Launching the Deco market

Europe was a series of countries with rigid trade borders in 1975 when Sotheby's initiated high-profile auctions in Monaco; the principality would serve as a centre through which we could offer works of art gathered from all over Europe, and indeed beyond, and sell them without the tax liabilities that we would have encountered at the international borders. So it was, effectively, a free-port situation. I realised, early on, that if my sales were to be rich and interesting, they had to have a significant component of great French decorative arts because at that time – and this remains true today – it was French material that dominated the market, and I was determined that my sales should occupy a key place in that market. So Monaco was the site from which I could really take a position in the French as well as the international marketplace.

I had started in the auction business in 1970 and gravitated straight away towards the 20th century. The market was in its infancy. Art Nouveau was still as much in demand as Art Deco. The 1920s had a small though committed following; prices were modest by today's standards and scholarship was fairly scant – we simply did not have all the monographs, the research and back-up data that we all use today.

But there were great enthusiasts – Yves Saint Laurent and Pierre Bergé, for instance, who were already collecting. They bought selected pieces in the historic 1972 sale in Paris of furniture and works of art from the collection of Jacques Doucet. This was the last opportunity to compete for pieces from the great collector's estate – a provenance regarded as magical. That sale set a new standard for Art Deco; it really put it on the map and gave it the credibility it had not enjoyed before then.

Koloman Moser
Die verwunschenen Prinzessinnen (The Enchanted Princesses), 1900, inlaid and applied cabinet, doors with carved green glass teardrops, ebonised interior, 67 ½ x 21 x 12 ⅞ in. (171.3 x 53.3 x 32.8 cm)

Eileen Gray
Dragons armchair, ca. 1917–1919,
leather upholstery, 24 x 35 ¾ x 26 ⅜ in.
(61 x 91 x 67 cm)

On Yves Saint Laurent and Pierre Bergé

Saint Laurent and Bergé shared a profound regard for the tradition of creativity associated with Paris. They appreciated the richness and importance of the city's culture, particularly in the years just before World War I and through the 1920s, and they decided to build a comprehensive collection of fine and applied art that reflected their love and respect for everything that Paris represented. So that was the starting point – and they were inspired by their admiration for certain collectors and patrons who had gone before them, perhaps most notably Marie-Laure de Noailles, a wonderfully independent and adventurous art collector whose taste embraced Picasso, Goya, Burne-Jones, and who became a great patron of Jean-Michel Frank. So Saint Laurent and Bergé set off on their collecting with sophisticated role models in mind.

Why Deco is hot and Art Nouveau is not

Deco is still very hot. Why has Art Nouveau really fallen out of fashion? It's a good question and I wish I knew the answer. I think there are extraordinary objects from the Art Nouveau era, and wonderful object lessons in design. And yet, to get your head around the Art Nouveau period, you have to situate those works in a broad and quite complex background of Symbolist art, Symbolist poetry, the utopian ideals that were coming out in Belgium, for instance, through Victor Horta, Henry van de Velde and others – there's so much social, political, artistic, literary background that you need to understand in order to position the objects. And I fear that, as the decades move on, the period becomes much more remote and, therefore, more difficult for younger generations to get to know and appreciate.

For the modern eye, a lot of Art Nouveau can seem highly decorative, perhaps over-decorative, over-elaborated. The tendency today is to look for clarity of form and concept, whereas Art Nouveau is the opposite of that, it tends towards the sumptuous, extravagant and decadent.

One needs to take a little time to analyse and deconstruct these objects as examples of design, but I think their very decorative strengths tend to overwhelm, and people don't always easily see the design element. They might more easily see it in work, say, by Hector Guimard, who created those wonderful Paris Metro entrances, or in his furniture and objects which are such pure sculptures. The idea of applying the principles of organic growth to design is so eloquently expressed in Guimard's work that it somehow transcends

Diego Giacometti
De chasseurs table, ca. 1963, patinated bronze with deer and dogs, glass top, 17 ¼ x 27 ¾ x 21 ⅞ in. (43.8 x 70.2 x 55.5 cm)

its era. But to many contemporary eyes, too much Art Nouveau is locked in its time, and many find it hard to pluck out individual pieces and make sense of them in a modern context.

Regarding the 20 million euros paid for a chair by Eileen Gray

The Dragons armchair by Eileen Gray caught the imagination of certain collectors and made just over 20 million euros. I suppose it sets a benchmark and a reference point. It doesn't mean that the great pieces are worth 20 million each, but what it does mean is that people will have more courage to pay one million or two, or perhaps a little more, for pieces of comparable rarity, quality and importance. I think it inevitably gives confidence.

Let's turn the clock back to the Doucet sale 1972, and an Eileen Gray screen

> "Why has Art Nouveau really fallen out of fashion? It's a good question and I wish I knew the answer."

titled Le Destin – a lacquered screen with stylized symbolist figures on one side, and an abstract linear motif on the other. This was knocked down for 170,000 French francs which was, at the time, 36,000 U.S. dollars.

That was a world record for Art Deco...it made the front pages of the newspapers. The buyer was Robert Walker, an American collector-dealer in Paris who was instrumental in putting the spotlight back on Eileen Gray. It's interesting to realise that the first truly significant auction price for Art Deco was for that Eileen Gray screen in 1972. Eileen Gray's production was so small and special that it is somehow fitting that she should reclaim her place at the top of the market through the Saint Laurent sale, because she represents a perfect combination of extraordinary vision and true creativity. Her output is important from the historical perspective, but from a market perspective, there is also the factor of incredible rarity associated with everything she made.

I read recently through Gray's day books of her Galerie Jean Désert. When she opened her own retail outlet in Paris, months went by without a single piece of furniture being sold. You have the sense that if she hadn't been turning over carpets with reasonable regularity – the sales of carpets constituted the core of the business – the venture would have been regarded as a disaster. It was hardly a success. Without the carpets, there would have been virtually no trading at that gallery. She was a visionary ahead of her time.

About Mackintosh

One of the highlights I have most enjoyed was to bring wonderful works by Charles Rennie Mackintosh to the market. I've sold some of the great pieces over the years, superb examples.

Mackintosh's creations were virtually always made for specific commissions. There was no retail production, so everything is documented and can be provenanced down to a very specific context. It was a very limited production.

The great years extended little more than a decade, from his 1897 commission for the Argyle Street Tea Rooms.

Emile-Jacques Ruhlmann
Table lamp, before 1925, bronze, lampshade curtain of glass pearls, 39 ⅜ in. (105 cm) high

Consider the influence that British design, and particularly Scottish design, had in Europe. There was a great exchange of ideas between Mackintosh and his contemporaries and the emerging avant-garde in Vienna, in Darmstadt. Those European schools, which were the crucible of design that unfolded into the Bauhaus and other crucial landmarks of 20th century design, all have a debt to pay to Charles Rennie Mackintosh. I would agree, one might call him a maverick designer, but so many of the creators, designers, artists – call them what you will – who acquire a high status in the history books, and with collectors, do so precisely because they break the mold, because they have a distinct vision...and in some cases, they may be prophets without honour to their contemporaries. Being prophets without honour, they are misunderstood; they have a vision but they don't take a broad audience with them...they are ahead of the curve.

Personal experiences

I met Eileen Gray in Paris in the early 1970s and felt very privileged, a few years later, to be invited to handle the sale of her estate through my acquaintance with her niece and executor, Prunella Clough. Such connections bring me close to the story. I met

Charlotte Perriand all those years ago, so to be able to sell a great piece of Charlotte Perriand, created by someone I have encountered, is very exciting for me. Just as I love the opportunity today to meet a Ron Arad or a Marc Newson and to hear these people talk, to see history unfolding and, in my professional capacity, to help put the spotlight on works that reflect outstanding creativity and imagination through the decades.

What I certainly don't want to encourage through our auctions, because I think it would shift the balance in an unhealthy way, is to create a situation where, effectively, we become retailers, primary market makers for work that has gained fashionable kudos but may not have staying power. I prefer, in that respect, to keep just enough distance so that we – as influential secondary market players – try to present works at auction that are already on the way to establishing what the French would call their *lettres de noblesse,* works that have gained and sustained credibility. Now, that credibility must be reflected in peer recognition, not just in the eyes of ambitious dealers and hungry art collectors, but with the endorsement of historians and curators. In the end, appreciation needs to be multi-faceted to situate a career in the pantheon of design history.

Edgar Brandt
Lantern, ca. 1925, patinated wrought-iron and glass, 25 x 10 ⅛ x 10 ⅛ in. (63.5 x 25.7 x 25.7 cm)

The contemporary design bubble

I feel that the heat has gone out of the contemporary design bubble, but there is absolutely a place for the best design work to be recognised and celebrated in the marketplace. There always has been, and always will be, the money factor. In our consumer culture, vulgar as it may be, money has become to some extent a measure of recognition.

I've cited one or two historic designers who did not have much of an audience in their day. I think the contemporary situation is very different because we live in an age of extraordinary, speedy communication. Ideas can be zapped around the world in a millisecond; we know what's going on in every city; we can download reports on what's happening virtually instantaneously; knowledge is shared, ideas disseminated so much more rapidly than ever before. There is an incredible level of awareness of current trends, of what is being made, what is being offered into the

Warren McArthur
Lounge chair, ca. 1930s, aluminium, curved tubular frame, upholstered in deep rust, 27 ½ x 21 x 49 in. (69.8 x 53.3 x 124.5 cm)

marketplace. The danger that goes with that is that we have come to expect design creativity to be subject to an accelerated turnover period, as if it were high fashion. I do not think product design should be quite that seasonal.

On Zaha Hadid

The name Zaha Hadid springs to mind as an architect who has a powerful signature approach, an ongoing appetite to engage with new technology, new materials and new possibilities; I see in her furniture and object designs the wonderful kind of bravura energy of form and line as well as the technical and structural characteristics that one sees in her architecture. She is an outstanding example of the mature designer who truly deserves credit. She has come a long way. She has been working for decades, finding her visual language, so to speak, and that impresses me so much more than the next hot young designer, fresh out of art college, who feels entitled to be picked out and to make an immediate mark, find patronage and market support.

Looking to the future

I feel that the turning of the millennium has had a significant impact on the psychology of all of us who look at history, and who are interested in the art and design of the past. The 20th century is now closed. It has become a slice of history. And I think that little distance – we're only a decade on – does subconsciously create a position from which to take stock. The high points of the 20th century can be discussed, researched and traded with the kind of historical detachment that might apply to our interest in the 18th or 19th centuries or any other era.

There is a consciousness that *now* is very different from *then*. We evolved through the second half of the 20th century with one decade flowing into the next, into the beginning of a big new chapter of history. The extraordinary technological revolutions that we have experienced are also a defining part of the new culture, with a young generation that values the creations of its own time…so it is quite logical that there should be this celebration of "now".

Gio Ponti
Display cabinet, 1950, Ferrara root-walnut, painted wood, steel and brass, 71 x 94 ½ x 18 in. (180.5 x 240 x 46 cm)

top: **Gio Ponti**
Study Centre table, 1950, Ferrara root-walnut with brass stretcher and sabots, 30 x 71 x 31 ¼ in. (76.5 x 180.5 x 79.5 cm)

overleaf: **Gio Ponti**
Executive office, 1950, oak and glass pedestal deskwith brass sabots: 31 ½ x 79 x 29 ¾ in. (80 x 201 x 76 cm), dashboard with brass reading light, brass shelf and storage compartments, panel: 63 ¾ x 113 ¾ x 12 ½ in. (162 x 289 x 31 cm), oak and leather side chair: 35 ½ in. (90 cm) high

Peter and Shannon Loughrey

Auction experts – LAMA, Los Angeles

Peter Loughrey, founder and director of Los Angeles Modern Auctions (LAMA), and his wife Shannon Loughrey, who is managing director, together run an auction house that is committed to showcasing 20th century artists, designers and architects. LAMA has built a reputation for supporting the works of designers who reflect a "unique West Coast feel", like Paul Laszlo, Greta Grossman and Billy Haines, as well as modern icons like Charles and Ray Eames.

What makes LAMA different

As an auction house based in southern California, we have had important advantages in the field of modern art and design, primarily because of our close proximity to the great surge of original houses and businesses that were built in the post-World War II era. Indeed, the record-breaking boom in new building during that time virtually assures a large pool of original modern design and fine art for us to draw upon.

Back in 1992, when we first opened, we put works by Charles and Ray Eames, Eero Saarinen, George Nelson and Harry Bertoia in our sales, which surprised many people if only for the fact that these designers had yet to start bringing substantial prices (my favorite item from that sale was a unique, handmade wood bowl and nutcracker designed by Russel Wright for his own use and sold with an original letter of documentation from his famous Dragon Rock residence; estimate: $300–$400!). But perhaps the most cogent aspect of our first sale was the inclusion of contemporary design like Frank Gehry's Grandpa Beaver Chair, a design that was less than eight years old and, up to that moment, available only through art galleries. I firmly believe that my first auction was the very genesis of the now-popular trend towards "Design Art".

Los Angeles was a place where collectors were just beginning to buy and restore post-war homes. These houses were built for returning GIs, workers in the rapidly expanding aerospace, airline and entertainment industries. The market for sympathetic design to fill these new progressive houses would attract the attention of top designers like KEM Weber, Warren McArthur, Gilbert Rohde, Paul Frankl

F. F. Kern
Table lamp, 1951–1952, hand-carved mahogany, brass-plated hardware and custom-dyed rawhide shade, 50 in. (127 cm) high

background: **Paul Laszlo**
Woven wood drapes, 1952,
two panels: 8 x 17 ft. and 8 x 8 ft.
(243.8 x 518.2 cm and 243.8 x 243.8 cm)

and Charles Eames. Other Los Angeles designers are only recently becoming well known outside the area. Works by Greta Grossman, Dan Johnson, Milo Baughman and Sam Maloof are now regularly showing up in design auctions across the country.

The case of Paul Laszlo

Perhaps one of the most uniquely Californian design successes is Paul Laszlo. A Hungarian émigré, Laszlo quickly understood the opportunity to re-invent yourself in the American West. Having studied and successfully practiced architecture in the Vienna and Darmstadt Secessions, he immediately embraced the prevailing "international style" upon arriving in Los Angeles in 1939. However, unlike fellow émigrés Richard Neutra, Rudolph Schindler and Raphael Soriano, who excelled at creating avant-garde designs on a modest budget, Laszlo went after the wealthiest of clients. He demanded full artistic control and was known to design every detail of a client's residence, once including a dress for a client's wife in fabric exactly matching the wallpaper in an entrance hall. His client list trended to the self-made business man. There were department store moguls, timber barons, captains of industry. It is no wonder he met such clients; his office and showroom were on Rodeo Drive in Beverly Hills.

Paul Laszlo
Sideboard, ca. 1952, two red-lacquered cabinets with inlaid corrugated doors and Lucite hardware on a blue-black lacquered base, 41 ½ x 126 x 20 in. (105.4 x 320 x 50.8 cm)

Laszlo excelled in creating his own brand of luxury with a unique vocabulary. While other architects were reducing ornament and using simple, humble materials, Laszlo was covering furniture in exotic elephant-hide leather, old world lacquers, chenille and Lurex-adorned lampshades and reverse-painted glass murals. For a John Hudspeth commission in 1951, the cost of just the furnishings for the house was a staggering $150,000. In today's market, his work is highly sought by collectors who also buy

> "These designers were heavily influenced by the natural California surroundings."

Carlo Mollino, Gio Ponti, Samuel Marx and Billy Haines. His value has been steadily increasing and, recently, the Los Angeles County Museum of Art acquired a chair from a McCullough Chainsaws showroom commission for its permanent collection.

California interior design history

In a constant quest to show something new to the auction market, auctioneers return regularly to Californian design history. Christie's 1988 sale of the Billy Haines designs for Edie Goetz (the daughter of Louis B. Mayer) was an afterthought to her collection of Picassos, Modiglianis and Monets. However, in retrospect, it introduced Haines' work to a wider audience and offered a peek into the luxurious interiors of the elite social strata that ruled the Hollywood golden era. Haines' interiors for Jack Warner, Ronald

Reagan, Walter Annenberg and Betsy Bloomingdale were designed and executed with the level of detail and quality of any French decorator.

Haines, Laszlo and Samuel Marx's works in California represent some of the greatest interior projects of the 20th century. But in my opinion, these have yet to be properly put into context. Perhaps that's because many of them are still intact, relatively under-published and rarely exhibited – for 50 years some of Haines' best work has been almost completely un-documented. The recent world-record sale of Picasso's *Nude, Green Leaves and Bust* ($106.5 million, May 2010), owned by the late Sidney and Frances Brody, was surrounded by Haines' iconic "long and low" living room, again overshadowed by the Brodys' more valuable fine art collection. Mrs. Brody was famously private and never allowed the entirety of her home's interior to be properly documented. I once asked architectural photographer Tim Street-Porter if there was one interior he wished he could have shot, and he answered: "The Brody residence."

Paul Laszlo

Lamp, 1952, hand-painted glass mural, 43 in. (109.2 cm) high, hand-woven shade of chenille, metallic Lurex, jute and thin wood strips by Maria Kipp

More recently, the designs of Greta Magnusson Grossman have caught the eyes of auctioneers, dealers and collectors. Grossman arrived in Beverly Hills from Sweden in 1940 and began delivering designs to local furniture manufacturers like Barker Brothers, Brown-Saltman and Glenn of California. However, it is her lighting design that has developed a wide market of collectors. Over the last ten years her Grasshopper floor lamp produced for local manufacturer Ralph O. Smith has increased in value from a few hundred dollars to nearly $10,000. The design is at once simple and sophisticated and will find itself at home next to Jean Royère or Marc Newson. Its spun metal, bullet-shaped shade and slender, bent tubular-steel frame epitomise the mid-century American aesthetic of doing the most with the least.

Paul Laszlo

Fish-shaped table, 1952, solid wood with dark 'teakwood' finish and applied blue-green seashells, brass-tipped base, 26 x 63 x 35 ½ in. (66 x 160 x 90 cm)

Pair of curved benches, 1952, solid wood with dark 'teakwood' finish, 31 x 66 x 35 in. (78.7 x 167.6 x 88.9 cm)

Craftsmen vs. mass production

By the 1970s, mass-production companies like Herman Miller and Knoll were moving on from home furnishings to office and contract systems. This created a void in the market

that coincided with a distinctly Californian trend of casual production. Designers like Sam Maloof, Jocko Johnson, Arthur Espenet Carpenter, John Nyquist and many others were finding a very dedicated following for craftsman-designed and produced furniture. These designers were heavily influenced by the natural California surroundings and each had independently developed a simple, unadorned, rounded-off style. They and hundreds of others were showcased in an annual exhibition called *California Design,* held at the Pasadena Art Museum from 1958 to 1976. The market for their work is still establishing itself with very few examples surfacing at major auctions. However, quality pieces have already topped the $100,000 mark and will, I believe, continue to increase in value as the work continues to surface from original owners.

The work of J. B. Blunk, for example, has gone from zero to $250,000 in less than four years. It is now shown in galleries like Blum & Poe in Los Angeles. Blunk's pieces have turned up at every major design auction and have been sold at Art Basel, Design Miami and other major design fairs. The success of his work has happened almost too fast, but it indicates that there are still many undiscovered artists from this period that will appeal to the collectors marketplace.

I believe that over the coming few years, and with the help of major museum shows like the groundbreaking exhibit planned by the Los Angeles Country Museum of Art in 2011, *California Design 1930–1965: Living in a Modern Way,* collectors will be offered many new names from California to consider. Some will become stars and some will not, but every design auction will be selling and promoting these names in the foreseeable future.

Charles and Ray Eames
Storage unit ESU 421-C, ca. 1951, walnut plywood, zinc, steel and masonite, 58 ½ x 47 x 17 in. (148.5 x 119.3 x 42.5 cm). Top left: back view

Alexander Payne

Auction expert – Phillips de Pury & Company, London

Alexander Payne is the worldwide director of design at Phillips de Pury & Company, and has pioneered several new concepts. With the support of his chairman Simon de Pury, he helped Phillips be the first to truly showcase contemporary design in the context of the contemporary art world. He has created beautiful glossy large-format catalogues and his auctions have generated numerous record prices.

The design business

The design market is one we all believe in at Phillips de Pury, particularly Simon de Pury, who has a great passion for the subject. Many years ago, when he and I started working together, he had the foresight and the vision to focus on design and to support the design department at Phillips – we are now reaping the benefits. This took many years and a great deal of energy; it required following the market as well as developing new ones.

The meaning of the term "design art"

We, at Phillips, first used the term "design art" in 2000. At the time, I realised there were facets of the market which were architecture-driven, crafts-driven, technology-led, and I thought the term aptly described how those works were breaking down boundaries between the applied arts and fine arts, thereby creating new areas of collecting.

I feel that many cutting-edge, contemporary design works express this tension between art, design and architecture – that's why we began using the term. It was a way to define works which were social, cultural and sculptural all at once; for example, works that were both functional pieces of furniture as well as artistic expressions.

As the market took off and as art fairs proliferated, more fine art collectors entered the field, new manufacturers appeared and suddenly everyone was throwing around the term design art. At the time, it served its purpose. Now I feel there must be a reclassification. I made the distinction then and started the debate, but now I'd like to move ahead to set new precedents, to think out of the box about how design, architecture, craft and decorative arts are perceived beyond labels.

Patrick Jouin
Prototype C1 chair from the Solid series, 2005,
rapid prototype stereo-lithography,
31 in. (78.7 cm) high

Is design a good investment today?

Design has many parallels to the contemporary art market. Like many art collectors, design collectors do what they do with love and passion and for the thrill of collecting. But there are also extensive opportunities for investment. Some very prominent designers have become highly, almost incredibly valued within a very short period of time. Those collectors who collected with their hearts and souls, who stuck their necks out and believed in visionary works, will see the greatest gains.

Designers to watch

I have a very exciting relationship with many contemporary designers: I've grown up with them, watched them develop and seen them graduate from various schools around the world. I like buying works by young designers. To be at the cutting edge of innovation, whether it involves re-imagined forms, materials, processes or typologies, is inspiring and full of possibilities for the collector.

> "Ten years from now I see collectors in design growing tenfold – I really do."

Gio Ponti
Chest of drawers, ca. 1953, walnut root-veneered wood and bronze,
32 x 39 ½ x 18 ½ in. (81.3 x 100.3 x 47 cm)

Today, designers of particular interest include the Campana brothers, Zaha Hadid, Marc Newson, Jurgen Bey, Martin Szekely, Maarten van Severen – all of whom have been successful at Phillips and many of whom we pioneered at auction.

At one point we were in danger of too much influence from the art market. Everyone was decidedly focused on the designs of today. We were forgetting icons like Ettore Sottsass, Joe Colombo and Pierre Paulin; it was foolhardy. You don't forget Mark Rothko or Jasper Johns. For a time we were in further danger because collectors were leaping over the 1970s and 1980s, very fertile decades, to concentrate only on very recent design. I am working very hard to show how important these earlier designers are, with good results thus far, because we have received great responses from collectors.

Contemporary design values vs. 1960s and 1970s design values

We must maintain the perspective of what we are doing now and what we are trying to do in future, and not to be overly influenced by contemporary art prices. In my opinion, great designers like Ron Arad or Zaha Hadid are still genuinely under-priced. Their markets are still very young, I really believe that. I have been in this business over 16 years. I used to sell Arad for thousands of pounds; now I am selling him for hundreds of thousands. I've watched Marc Newson all along and remember the days when we offered him at auction for tens of thousands. In May 2010, we sold the prototype Lockheed Lounge in New York for over $2 million, a world record for Newson. All this has happened in a very short period of time.

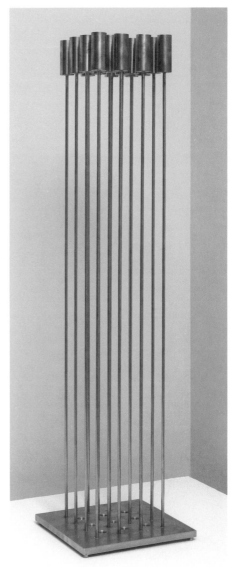

Harry Bertoia
Sonambient sculpture, 1965, Beryllium copper, brass, 39 x 10 x 10 in. (99.1 x 25.4 x 25.4 cm)

We have to seriously look at the essence of these works and their true value. Compared to so much contemporary art – Andy Warhol for example – contemporary design is still inexpensive. As a collector, you need to understand that for a tenth of what you might spend on certain contemporary art, you can acquire highly important contemporary designs.

overleaf: **Carlo Mollino**
Table and four side chairs, ca. 1954, table: oak, 31 ⅜ x 31 ¼ x 31 ¼ in. (79.7 x 79.4 x 79.4 cm), chairs: oak and brass, 36 ¾ in. (93.3 cm) high

At the same time, I am determined to continue illustrating the importance of earlier designers like Paulin, Colombo and Sottsass. We cannot forget these tremendous artists. We cannot forget the Bauhaus, a movement I'm particularly passionate about. It has a consistent, solid market price, and it continues to drive forward, slowly but surely.

A Maria Pergay sofa selling for over $400,000 at auction (one-arm daybed Banquet, ca. 1967, 13 December 2007)

When we first saw Maria Pergay becoming fashionable, we took the foot off the gas. I refused to consider a designer of her stature as a mere object of fashion. I did not want to drive her market in that way. I wanted her *designs* to drive her market. So we held back, and when we had an important work, we presented it cautiously in the market-place and got the results we did because we believed in that particular work. Yes, the daybed we sold for $400,000 in 2007 is one of her best pieces – I would not say it is the ultimate piece, but it is up there, one of her most important works. All it takes is two bidders, and we had about ten on the phone.

Immediately after the sale, the Pergay market began to evolve, but just for her iconic works like the Flying Carpet daybed and the Ring Chair. We'll have to see how the market continues to react to the world record we set. It is important to realise there are times when some designers do not have good days, so we need to make sure that we are selling the best possible examples of their work.

Where this market will be in ten years

We'll all be in a highly exciting place. We will have watched the market evolve, prices increase, new collectors appear. Ten years from now I see the collectors in design growing tenfold – I really do. Our auctions on both sides of the Atlantic will still offer the most exceptional examples of design from the 20th and 21st centuries.

Beyond that, I think design and architecture, very importantly, will be a total force in the art market. I look forward to the very exciting days to come.

Ron Arad
This Mortal Coil bookshelf, 1993,
blackened tempered steel,
87 x 86 ⅝ x 13 in. (221 x 220.5 x 33.1 cm)

overleaf: **Marc Newson**
Lockheed Lounge, 1988, prototype handmade
by Marc Newson, fibreglass-polyster
resin core, riveted sheet aluminium, paint,
34 ½ x 65 ¾ x 24 ½ in. (87.6 x 167 x 62.2 cm)

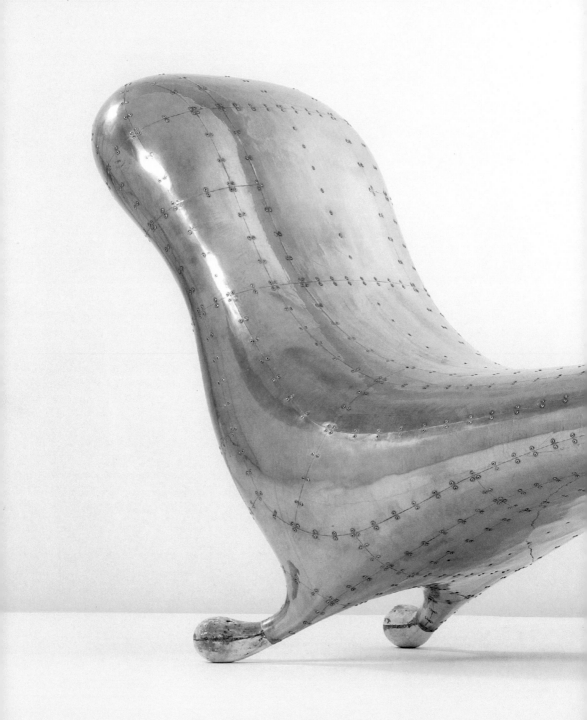

Richard Wright

Auction expert – Wright, Chicago

Richard Wright started one of the first auction houses exclusively specialising in modern and contemporary design. Based in Chicago, Wright auction house pioneered glossy catalogues and higher prices for collectible design objects that only a few years before had been considered "vintage furniture". He has been a leader in developing numerous market trends from Italian design to the work of Harry Bertoia.

Appeal of collecting design

Design offers accessibility to many people for whom Art with a capital A is very intimidating. Design objects offer an immediacy that they respond to – they are not afraid to give an opinion on a chair and they respond very personally to furniture and other objects they live with, whereas with art, I think, it is harder for people to view a painting and feel comfortable that they are qualified or even to have the courage to voice an opinion.

There is so much baggage that comes with art. I am not saying that design is better than art, art is a wonderful pursuit and, in many cases, a higher pursuit. But when I think of what I like about design, I like the accessibility – that is a big part of it.

When did collecting design evolve?

I think you could argue that 1998 or so was the start of the real design market. If you go back to 1995 or 1996, prices were very low. The market was small, it was largely in New York City, and mostly involved a group of artists and underground buyers, sellers and collectors, although some Europeans were active then like Bruno Bischofberger and the Vitra Design Museum.

Vitra is a major museum in Germany, owned by Rolf Fehlbaum and his director, Alexander von Vegesack. When Ray Eames died in 1988, Vitra acquired the estate and the archives, so all of that material left the United States and went to Europe. All the American institutions were late to recognise the importance of mid-century design. Vitra was on the scene early, though, and it has very impressive holdings in design like the classic prototypes of Isamu Noguchi, Charles and Ray Eames and George

George Nelson & Associates
Marshmallow sofa no. 5670, 1956,
vinyl, enameled metal and steel,
31 x 52 x 31 in. (78.7 x 132.1 x 78.7 cm)

Nelson. Vitra is a major business as well, in that Rolf's family produces the Herman Miller and Eames furniture for Europe. I think that at a personal level, Rolf Fehlbaum understood the historical importance of these works, which says a lot about this outstanding company.

Going back to collecting design, in 1998 when a Marshmallow Sofa sold for $40,000 – a George Nelson design – it was a big event at the time because it was very rare for any-

> "Is that piece worth a million? What is any of this stuff worth? What is your Warhol worth?"

thing to break the $10,000 auction mark. By 2005, I'd sold a marble-top Noguchi coffee table for $630,000. To illustrate the historic rise, I sold one of the same form in 1996 for $9,000 – evidence of the change within a decade.

Harry Bertoia: designer or artist?

Harry Bertoia is shown at Christie's and Sotheby's in the art sales, not the design sales, so he is a perfect example of someone who did not play the art game well. Bertoia was a humble man who produced much of his work himself; he was a good craftsman but not a good self-promoter. He sold his work through Knoll and in the 1950s he introduced his wire mesh Diamond chair to the furniture world.

The fact that he went to the Cranbrook Academy of Art, worked with Charles and Ray Eames and designed a hugely successful line of chairs that are in damn near every museum cafeteria in the world actually hurt his standing as an artist when it should not have. Think of it, he designed chairs early on that are masterful, no one would argue that, and he was a sculptor before and a sculptor afterwards. He is both a designer and an artist.

Enzo Mari
Autoprogettazione (Do-it-yourself) dining table, 1975, pine, 28 ½ x 78 ½ x 31 ¾ in. (72.4 x 199.4 x 80.6 cm). Built by Mari in 2007

Value of design

For the big picture, I think assets tend to go up and accrue value over time, given inflation and other "time-value" factors that relate to an investment. When you make a significant purchase with the idea that you are buying an asset, say a work of great art or design that has true historical importance, they will stand the test of time and should appreciate in the long run.

I also think that any market is cyclical and will rise or fall at any time, as will the desirability of a given piece. Added to that is the question of liquidity; depending on when you want to sell, and how to sell a piece, can very much affect what you get for it and what it is worth.

Thinking about the future value of a design object is important and is part of the collecting process; we are not dealing with inexpensive items. The spectacular gains in the art market of late made a lot of money for a lot of people, and there has been much discussion about treating art as an investment vehicle. But when the Wall Street types have tried to run "art investment funds", the actual return

André Dubreuil
Ram chair, ca. 1985, steel, leather,
35 x 28 x 36 in. (88.9 x 71.1 x 91.4 cm)

– if one is seriously trying to invest and resell large amounts of money in the art market – is very hard to realise...it breaks down as an inefficient investment vehicle.

If your goal is investment, I think there are far superior ways to invest your money. But if you have the money and you love the design, it is a great pursuit that will give you great rewards and *can* appreciate over time.

The new design collectors.

The broadening design market is not just in New York, and not just among people who are avant-garde collectors. Through the internet, through magazines and the press, Mid-century modern, for example, is widely dispersed and people understand how design could be collectible and worth a lot of money, so the market has taken off and really grown.

Concurrently, the auction houses have risen in prominence. Ten years ago, the dealers were very strong and led the market. When the LVMH money came into Phillips in late 1999, Phillips upped the game and we saw design take off. I opened in 2000, and by 2003 Sotheby's decided to jump into the game.

The buzz, the cachet, seems to be part of the whole emerging contemporary art and design scene. I think that people are conceiving of a new way of living, recognising that the cultural signifiers and the things you want to surround yourself with extend to design – and what can be more exciting? Many top art buyers, decorators and people in the entertainment world are collecting design, there is a cool factor to it.

Joe Colombo
Tube chair, 1969, Arcipiuma plastic with coated foam upholstery, steel and rubber clips, 24 x 44 x 24 in. (61 x 111.8 x 61 cm)

At the same time, contemporary gallerists and designers are realising that they can market their design work like art, and I think that is where you get into the area of

valuations and what something is worth. Clearly, many of the cues on how to create value and how to market contemporary design are taken directly from the contemporary art market. So designers have started to realise: "I'll make small limited editions, I'll create a special variation..." This offers great possibilities to designers and has brought a new vitality to the market.

If you think of designing only mass-produced pieces for Knoll, Herman Miller, Kartell, and selling a thousand pieces of an object, that is very valid, but it can also be constricting in what it allows the designer to do. So now we have one-of-a-kind objects, edition-produced pieces and mass-produced pieces (both original and reproduction) – all creating a variation of design access and value.

Gio Ponti and Piero Fornasetti
Lounge chair, 1950, lithographic transfer-printed skai, ash and brass, 32 x 27 x 28 ½ in. (81.3 x 68.6 x 72.4 cm)

Appeal of contemporary design today as an investment

Part of what creates the energy and part of what is exciting is that we do not know what is going to stand the test of time. Like contemporary art, you go out and make your choices, being informed by your own sense of design history and by your own taste, and you buy just what you *want* to buy. Some of it will emerge to become important and will stand the test of time, and some of it might not look as good years from now.

I think Larry Gagosian and his show of Marc Newson obviously stands as a turning point. Also, when Christie's put the Marc Newson piece [Pod of Drawers sold for $1,048,000 in May 2007] into their most important sale, in the hottest art market on record – that was a statement. Was it good for my business? Oh, absolutely, it was good for me. Was it good for design? That is harder to know, it will cut both ways. Lower pricing can actually have a good effect on the work. Is it good for Marc? In the short term it is, in the long term, again, I do not know. None of us knows the future. Is that piece worth a million? What is any of this stuff worth? What is your Warhol worth?

A few years ago, I moved to a new house that is being furnished in a mix of historical and contemporary design. I bought some Maarten Baas, a clay coffee table, and I ended up buying the very first one that he produced and signed, "Number One". He will

Philippe Hiquily
Bassinet, 1987, bronze, 56 x 44 x 20 in. (142.2 x 118 x 50.8 cm)

produce others but this was the very first one. I thought it was reasonably priced at $5,000, and it looks incredible in my living room; I had not experienced that form before, it has a great dialogue with the house and with my other historical pieces, and it really makes everything look better. For me, that translates the value of the piece as one which is useful to me, has design impact or dialogue with my other pieces, and that also is part of my collection.

Will it go up in value? Yes, I've got to tell you I think it will. Sure, there is something appealing about that. The same thing is happening in contemporary art, it's very valid to support Maarten's work and watch him evolve as an artist – you do not want it to go down in value, but what does it matter? It's a great thing to buy.

If the table had been $50,000, that becomes a much harder problem, a much bigger commitment. I don't know, I would not have bought it then because I would worry if it would stand the test of time; is it going to be worth $50,000 in five years if I want a change and decide to sell it? And, you know, at those numbers it would matter to me, whereas at $5,000 it does not, it does not have to appreciate in value.

André Dubreuil
Paris chair, 1988, enameled steel,
37 ¾ x 22 ½ x 25 in. (95.8 x 57.2 x 63.5 cm)

overleaf: **Maarten Baas**
Clay Furniture, 2006, industrial clay,
hand-modeled on metal skeletons,
lacquered surfaces, table: approx.
30 x 98 x 50 in. (76.2 x 248.9 x 127 cm),
chairs: approx. 28 in. (71.1 cm) high

James Zemaitis

Auction expert – Sotheby's, New York

James Zemaitis is the director of 20th Century Decorative Arts and Design at Sotheby's. Having begun his career at Phillips de Pury, he subsequently was wooed away to Sotheby's where he has successfully built the 20th Century Design department. *The New York Times* **has referred to him as the "Chair man"; his stylish auctions and gregarious charm have helped to attract a new generation of clients to contemporary and modern design at investment prices.**

Does the designer have a message?

I think someone like Carlo Mollino absolutely had a message. He was the Leonardo of the 20th century. Nobody in the world of furniture design was as multi-talented as Mollino. He was not only a furniture designer, he was also an architect, a fashion designer, shoe designer, photographer, a pornographer, a ski champion, race car driver and race car designer...nobody was more eclectic. He almost epitomises the Renaissance approach to doing everything and doing it well. His furniture was, in most cases, designed either for himself, for one of his own fantastic interiors or for a specific client. Some of it was done – very much as Charlotte Perriand did – for architectural commissions, places like student dormitories, auditoriums and ski resorts.

Mollino's furniture often expressed a message with a zoomorphic and anthropomorphic look that had everything to do with the women that he was photographing with Polaroids, and with the clothing that he was designing for them. He was after a very important, over-encompassing style that covered everything he did, while sending out a message of his own kind of sensuality.

The range of 20th century design at auction

To list the categories we sell, we start with the Art Nouveau – names like Hector Guimard, who did the Paris Metro stations, for instance. Then, the furniture designers like Louis Majorelle. There were the great architects like Victor Horta in Belgium and Antoni Gaudi in Barcelona, who was the subject of an exhibition at the Metropolitan Museum of Art in 2007. The basic aspect of Art Nouveau, of course, is naturalism

André Arbus
Console table, ca. 1948, sycamore and bronze, 29 ½ x 75 x 21 ¾ in. (74.9 x 190.5 x 55.3 cm)

– it was influenced by the early industrial era so they used industrial techniques, factories and foundries to create vegetative, cool styles.

Then there is the Arts and Crafts movement, which was an international anti-modern movement influenced by the writings of William Morris and John Ruskin in England, and defined by people like Gustav Stickley here in America. To some extent, the early work of Frank Lloyd Wright is part of the Arts and Crafts movement. It was a competing force with Art Nouveau, you might say, from the 1880s to about 1910.

At the same time, you have what most design people consider to be the birth of modernism, which for the most part came about in Austria, with Austrian design. There are many terms for this. Some people call it the Jugendstil, others call it the Wiener Werkstätte. The Wiener Werkstätte was actually a group of people working together as an organisation – Josef Hoffmann, Koloman Moser, but also painters like Gustav Klimt were part of all that. Wiener Werkstätte also operated retail shops, including shops here on Madison Avenue run by Joseph Urban, where you could buy textiles, furniture, you name it. So the Austrians played a huge early role.

The Bauhaus movement came after the Wiener Werkstätte in the early 1920s, led by Walter Gropius and Mies van der Rohe, the white knights of great German architecture and design. The Bauhaus was a school, one that preached a lifestyle and a way to create everything needed in one's life. It was part of the great early 20th century tradition of a school that had divisions within it for studying photography, metalwork, glass, furniture etc. Cranbrook in America, which came a little later in Michigan, basically had the same kind of philosophy. So Bauhaus was about producing designers and artists from a single school. It was in search of a new modernism, and about breaking down the barriers of design that came from previous generations.

What we also sell is the parallel descendent, that is: while the Bauhaus was going on, what followed Art Nouveau was Art Deco. Again, Art Deco reflected various modern aspects by embracing technology and industrial materials, but it also exhibited a love of exotic materials like ivories, tortoise shells and incredible woods. One sees many African influences in Art Deco; it represented a love of great technique as well as being a tribute to Africa. The prominent designers were people like Emile-Jacques Ruhlmann, Edgar Brandt, Pierre Legrain, Eileen Gray, who were mostly French but with a few outsiders, both Americans and British, who exhibited in Paris from the early to the mid-1920s at the annual expositions there.

First American modernists

In America, the next area that we cover in auctions is called – I've really kind of coined it – the American modern of the 1920s and 1930s. These are American industrial designers, some of whom were heavily influenced by Art Deco and so they are called American Art Deco, and others who were influenced by the Bauhaus. Many of the great Bauhaus masters like Marcel Breuer immigrated to America, as well as lesser-known architects who came from Europe and made their names here – like KEM Weber, the great furniture designer, or Richard Neutra or Rudolph Schindler – all of them went to California. Paul T. Frankl, famous for his Skyscraper furniture, came to New York from Vienna and later relocated to Los Angeles.

Emile-Jacques Ruhlmann

Nicolle two-door cabinet, 1926, macassar ebony, red tortoiseshell veneer, ivory dentil decoration, 43 x 36 ½ x 18 in. (109.2 x 92.7 x 45.7 cm)

The American modern movement was America's first great modernist tradition. It produced great cocktail shakers and also great scales and meat slicers; it really epitomises the word design, because people like Russel Wright were marketing themselves as designers and selling everything from dinnerware to furniture. Warren McArthur is also a big part of this because he basically used aircraft factories to make tubular aluminium furniture, which was completely influenced by the Bauhaus and Marcel Breuer's tubular steel designs of the 1920s.

From an auction perspective, next comes the rather squishy French 1930s and 1940s period, which is less about design and more about interior decoration. It starts with Jean-Michel Frank in the 1930s right up through Jean Royère in the 1950s – Royère is frequently exhibited with Prouvé and Perriand, but Royère was an interior decorator.

The art dealer Larry Gagosian has a huge private collection of Royère, I think his whole office is Royère. In Paris, if you go to a museum like the Museum of Decorative Arts at the Louvre, there are huge rooms of furnishings from these designers, and they are also very popular in America. Some of them go in and out of fashion like Gilbert Poillerat, who was in fashion for a while, and now he's out. Then you also have the more cult-like people who have now become huge, like Line Vautrin.

Jacques Adnet is another one – he somewhat ran his own retailing firm at Companie des Arts Francais. For years, people thought that the leather for his furniture was made by Hermes, but it was not, their leather was made for Paul Dupré-Lafon who was very much a part of that time. He was known as the "decorator for the millionaires". He was all about injecting a bit of modernism; he had a sense of fun, it was industrial design but then he wrapped it all in leather and used incredible, beautiful stone surfaces and rare materials. Essentially, he was an interior designer. He did interiors, just like Jean-Michel Frank, whether it was for the Rockefellers here in New York or for other clients.

> "The Memphis movement... remains, from a secondary market perspective, the one true blue commercial failure of our era."

Jean-Michel Frank, Dupré-Lafon and Jean Royère are interior designers because none of them mass-produced anything. Take somebody like Ron Arad today – he is mass-producing for one group of clientele, making limited editions for others, and also doing one-offs for a few people who are really close to him. The same applies to Marc Newson. Designers like Frank or Royère are not really any different from Peter Marino, the exception being that the level of craftsmanship of their time is not possible today.

Post-war era

Next comes the Post-war era. Suddenly comes the birth of Mid-century modern and we see several parallel movements at the same time. The great American Mid-century modern movement includes Charles Eames, George Nelson, Isamu Noguchi, and what's interesting about that, of course, is that someone like Noguchi personifies and foreshadows everything we have today.

Noguchi had extremely successful lines of furniture for Herman Miller and for Knoll – the glass high-end 1944 coffee table that is *the* most successful coffee table of the 20th century, and probably the most famous coffee table, and rightfully so. It is biomorphic, it's gorgeous, it is not too expensive to buy, about $2,500 from Design Within Reach, and it epitomises the post-war, atomic age look and feel. What else does it look like? It looks like a Noguchi sculpture. So at the same time that Noguchi was making these pieces to be mass-produced for Herman Miller – every year one could go to the Merchandise Mart showroom in Chicago and buy the latest Noguchi – he was also doing one-off unique pieces of furniture that are very close to being pure sculpture.

Some of the unique pieces are worth well over $1 million, if they were available. Perhaps the most famous one is the Conger-Goodyear table that he did for the glass house out in Westbury, Long Island, which was almost torn down in 2001. It was basically a prototype of his famous coffee table, but much taller, like a dining table, and it is one of the holy grails of 20th century design. The dealer Christina Grajales

Poul Kjærholm
Chaise lounge PK 24, ca. 1965, chromium-plated
steel, cane and leather, 31 ½ in. (80 cm) high

found the table in a private collection in Florida and
I think she probably sold it for over $1 million. If I had
it at auction I would put it at over $1 million.

But again it's Noguchi whom we see as a sculptor, being sold in America in modern art
auctions, working as both a sculptor and as a furniture designer for a specific interior
commission. At the same time, on the side, he was making paper lamps for Akari, you
know, items that you could buy for five dollars. He was the first great artist/designer of
the modern era, the one who really had it down.

What sells today from that period?

As a collectible, we never sell the mass produced pieces. Rather, we look for the mis-
takes, the prototypes and the commercially unsuccessful experiments like the famous
sofas that Noguchi did for Herman Miller, which they wanted to mass produce, but they
made only five or six of them, nobody knows exactly how many. Each one was hand
built underneath the structure because they could not figure out a way for the factory
to produce it successfully. What happened was that it was shown in all the catalogues
and was to be released as a mass production sofa, but each one looked and felt different,
they couldn't get their act together, and so Herman Miller and Noguchi pulled the plug
on it and said: "Ain't working." Those are valuable pieces because they are still beautiful
and still incredible and rare works of design.

On the other hand, Charles Eames and George Nelson are more strictly designers
because Eames was an architect as well as a designer. Nelson was a pure designer, an

industrial designer *par excellence*. He did everything – plates, textiles, metal, even clocks – he made it all. He had a huge office here in New York and he was one of the first designers to have a huge team working for him where others did the pieces and then he took the credit, basically.

As for being collectible, his market went down because when we first started selling Nelson in 1999 and 2000, we didn't really know how common or how rare a lot of the furniture was. We knew only that there were certain things that we saw again and again, and some things that were quite iconic and in every museum catalogue; there were very famous examples of MoMA-style, Post-war design that we didn't see very often – things like the ESU Unit from Charles and Ray Eames, the four-stacker, or George Nelson's Marshmallow Sofa – things that everybody knew were powerhouse icons. But we didn't know how many were produced.

Well, it turned out that in some cases there were thousands, in other cases, only a few hundred. No one really knew what the quantities were. All we knew was that the piece was made, say, for three years, or ten years, by Herman Miller. Then the first time that those pieces went on the market, they got huge prices. An ESU Unit went from fetching $6,000 or

Fernando and Humberto Campana
Teddy Bear chair, 2004,
stuffed teddy bears and tubular metal,
40 in. (101.6 cm) high

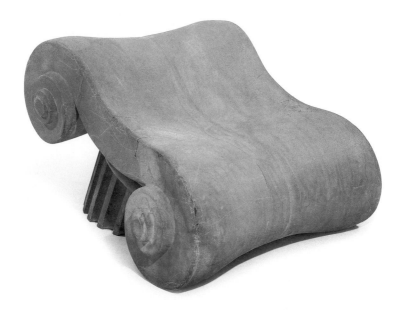

$7,000 dollars in 1997 to $40,000 or $50,000, even $60,000 to $70,000 by 2001. Now they are back down to $10,000 to $15,000. What happened was that too many came out, and they came out via the same exact source, eBay.

The 1960s and on at auction

Those who followed in Eames' and Nelson's footsteps, working both as designers and as decorators, are people like Vladimir Kagan and lesser known figures like Paul McCobb. The next important trend in America would be the Post-war craft movement, developed by furniture designers who were trained either as artists or as craftsmen, not necessarily as industrial designers. Some of them grew up in other ways; George Nakashima started as an architect; Harry Bertoia studied at the Cranbrook Academy of Art with Eames and Saarinen and was a mass-production furniture designer before he mutated into doing sculptures and craft. I call this the American Post-war craft movement for lack of a better term, because we're dealing with certain furniture people who primarily saw themselves as pure craftsmen and furniture makers.

Nakashima is the big presence above all of it. Actually, he was preceded by Wharton Esherick who was kind of the father of the movement. Esherick's work dates from the 1920s all the way up to his death in 1970. But the main figures of the Post-war movement were George Nakashima on the West Coast, Sam Maloof in California and a very young Wendell Castle in upstate New York. People who follow in Nakashima's wake include, in Pennsylvania, the eccentric Paul Evans and to a lesser extent Phillip Lloyd Powell who is just starting to be discovered – he died fairly recently in March 2008, at age 88.

Studio 65
Capitello, ca. 1971, medium polyurethane foam, 30 in. (76.2 cm) high

overleaf: **George Nakashima**
Arlyn table, 1988, redwood burl top with free form edge, fissures and madrone burl butterflies, American black walnut base with butterflies, 26 x 89 x 91 in. (66 x 226.1 x 231.1 cm)

George Nakashima

I think that the market for Nakashima represents the perfect story of 21st century collecting. More than *anybody* – and that includes the French Post-war designers, the Scandinavians, the Italians...forget Mollino, forget Prouvé, forget any of those others – Nakashima is the signature blue-chip Post-war designer, and that is because his appeal is universal.

Why is Nakashima so hot? Because I have never seen one designer appeal to so many collecting categories of people in the auction house world. We have traditional Americana collectors who think he's great, they consider him the modern heir to the early American cabinetry. We have American paintings collectors, and you can't overlook what they are spending these days, who think of Nakashima as somebody American, like part of our native soil tradition. There are also the Japanese and the Koreans, who obviously see the heavy Eastern influence in Nakashima's work. His work is very Post-war and it has a biomorphic aspect that puts him in the same kind of breath as Noguchi.

For the most part, Nakashima was available only to folks who lived in New York, New Jersey and Pennsylvania, and 95 percent of what he did, for 40 years, was found only in the tri-state area. The original owners of Nakashima's furniture were people who went out to New Hope in the 1960s and 1970s to meet him, and he would sketch for them and invite them into his house saying: "Let me show you around, let me make you a table." All those people are first generation owners, either in their 70s or 80s, and they are now downsizing, or moving into retirement homes, or dying. At the same time, we have multiple generations of collectors from all corners of the world who want his work – we sell to Switzerland, England, Paris, Korea, Japan in every sale. In America, we sell to the West Coast like crazy because those collectors see Nakashima as a kindred spirit to that kind of West Coast environmental style.

Post-war European designers

At the same time that all this was happening in America, we have the Post-war French, and in addition to the continuing tradition of the decorators, you have the French architects and industrial designers. There was Charlotte Perriand who lived the entire century, so she just went on and on and on. You have Jean Prouvé, of course, who is one of my personal gods. There is the great lighting designer, Serge Mouille, who really was both an industrial designer and an artist, a sculptor – I love what he does. And then you have a host of lesser lights in France.

One of the most important areas to touch upon involves the Danish designers of the Post-war era. To this day, they have not had the recognition they deserve, perhaps because they did not have the right dealers to hype them or the right galleries in America to promote them. They have never had museum exhibitions in America, and yet one would think they would have, but they haven't. The Danish designers of the Post-war era are still under-priced, ridiculously so in some cases – it's amazing.

In order of importance, first is Poul Kjærholm, who synthesised the Bauhaus tradition with Danish cabinetry and furniture-making excellence. He put the two together by creating pieces

Paul T. Frankl
Skyscraper bookcase, ca. 1928,
mahogany and lacquered wood,
71 x 34 x 14 in. (180.4 x 86.3 x 36.6 cm)

that had the perfect line, the perfect minimalist sensibility, and yet were unbelievably well constructed, mostly involving steel with a little bit of marble but he also did some work in wood as well. I think Poul Kjærholm's work – he was mostly a furniture designer but also an architect – is perfection.

After Kjaerholm would be Hans Wegner, one of the great chair designers of the century. He died at age 92 in Copenhagen, in 2007. Big production line, but there are also wonderful rarities from our perspective, and there are rare Wegner chairs that come up all the time. He is in the $50,000–$60,000 range. His chairs are so famous that he himself refused to name them, he thought that was over the top. He'd say, "well, that's model number" whatever, and so today's collectors have created

"There really are no Ruhlmanns today."

an entire vocabulary of nicknames. In fact, one chair is so famous that we just call it the "Chair-chair". It's the one that Kennedy and Nixon sat in and debated in the first Presidential televised debate in 1960 – it is a beautiful Danish round chair and it is just called "The Chair". How much cooler does it get? Then there is the Ox Chair, the Shell Chair, the Flag Halyard Chair...his work transcends naming, it's so good.

My next choice would be Arne Jacobsen, architect, industrial designer, creator of the famous SAS Hotel in Copenhagen and its interior, which is sometimes referred to as the birthplace of his Egg and Swan chairs which he created as part of his work there. All of these people are very actively sought after by American decorators. Do you know who has the great Jacobsen collection – Bruno Bischofberger, he has some of the very best Jacobsen pieces. All of these Danish designers exhibited every year at an annual furniture makers exhibition in Copenhagen. Again, what we look for are the exceptional pieces. Some of the stuff became famous, some of it not. And then there was work that was famous but never

Wharton Esherick
Dining table and extension table/server,
1957, walnut, 28 ⅜ x 77 ½ x 36 ½ in.
(72.1 x 196.9 x 92.7 cm), extension:
28 ⅛ x 22 ⅝ x 44 ⅜ in. (72.4 x 57.5 x 112.7 cm)

Hans J. Wegner

Flag Halyard lounge chair model GE 225,
ca. 1950s, chromium-plated and
enameled steel, fabric upholstery, wool
and halyard, 31 in. (78.7 cm) high

got produced. It won the awards, but for some
reason, was not put into production. We look for
the rarities, basically.

And finally from that period, the Italians like
Carlo Mollino, Gio Ponti, what I like to call the Turinese organic designers like Ico Parisi.
It started out in the 1950s as furniture, but the thing to remember is that Italy is responsible for the world's greatest Post-war household product designs of the 1950s and
1960s. There was the Vespa but you also had the espresso maker. Everything that represents good design from the 1950s to the 1970s came out of Italy. And Italy played a
major role in later movements like the Pop movement and the Post-modern movement.
From the 1960s on, you have figures like Joe Colombo, the designer of the "total living
units" and installations, and others like Achille Castiglioni.

Then there is Ettore Sottsass, who is allied with the Italian tradition although he was
born in Austria, like Verner Panton who is Danish, but not associated with the Danish
group because he is considered a Pop designer. And when people think "Pop design",
they think of Italy and we hear: "Oh, all Pop is Italian, probably a little bit of French and
American thrown in." Panton lived in Switzerland for the second half of his life and so
his furniture is produced in Switzerland, Italy, France and in Denmark. Panton and
Sottsass are two giants of the Post-war era, but they are associated more with the *movement* they represent rather than their nationality.

The Memphis movement

Most of the designers of the Memphis movement, which Sottsass founded in the early 1980s, were Italian. The Memphis movement emerged basically at the same time as Post-modernism. It remains, from a secondary market perspective, the one true blue commercial failure of our era, in terms of a famous design movement that has been covered regularly by museums, where everybody knows the famous pieces, but it has close to *zero* market value.

Quite simply, it is because the pieces just do not work in people's homes, and it does not matter how colourful the interiors may be, or how radical the colours and forms; just put a work from Memphis in any room and it crushes everything else around it, not because it's great, it simply crushes it and deadens everything, it's so garish and over the top. Memphis' products were meant to be mass-produced and so they were cheaply built. The stuff is like plastic laminate, it's worthless.

The only collector who ever made money from Memphis, who went all out and did it right, and then sold it and did well, was Karl Lagerfeld. Karl sold at Sotheby's Monaco in 1991, in a single-owner sale. He marketed his collection then in the same way that collectors today market Newson and Arad, and so there was this kind of crazy sale of the Memphis collection of Lagerfeld. It was a big sensation and of course after that everyone else tried to do it, but all other attempts flopped. Only Lagerfeld could pull it off, nobody else has been able to.

Pop era and on

The Pop era is very important in terms of the history of 20th century design, important in terms of its links to the culture of the time and because of its commercial appeal, which was vast, but it is hard to collect because much of the greatest Pop installations were just that – installations. Verner Panton's most amazing rooms were mostly destroyed as were those of Pierre Paulin.

French Pop designer Pierre Paulin is one of the great figures, he is the definition of French Pop. The problem is that Paulin will probably never be very valuable because his best work was mass-produced. Like all of the Pop artists, his greatest furniture was upholstered and many of the techniques, the foams and fabrics that were being used, were not built to last forever. So once these pieces lost that original upholstery, the original stretch jersey fabric, or the stuffing hardened on the inside, the piece was finished. Pop designers other than Paulin, like Eero Aarnio and Verner Panton, also had some of their greatest work mass-produced.

Maria Pergay comes later. She is really part of the French interior design tradition, someone who just happened to be, in the 1970s, working in steel. I love some of her pieces, but she is part of the French decorative tradition. She was not a famous designer during her heyday and she is more a kind of hidden cult rediscovery through great marketing of today, which is why I think already you see her market fluctuating, going down and up.

The 1970s were a period that we are discovering again right now, kind of minimalist, with lots of glass, steel, marble, followed by the Post-modern movement in the 1980s which was a reaction to everything in the decade before. It was just a big in-your-face, led by Ettore Sottsass, and it was international in that it included American members

Ron Arad
Rolling Volume, 1989, polished stainless steel, lead weights, 30 ¾ x 35 ½ x 37 ⅜ in. (78.1 x 90.2 x 94.9 cm)

like Michael Graves, the architect who did work for Memphis, and Japanese designers like Shiro Kuramata who first came to international prominence via Memphis. It was a reaction that rates a chapter in every museum survey, but its significance, which I've often said about Memphis, is like owning a record album by Devo, a band that's very post-modern and very equivalent, but one is enough.

The Lockheed Lounge and contemporary design
At the same time that Memphis was rolling along, came one artist who created a series of pieces that really began the contemporary design movement. One person began the whole era with one piece, which has also become the most iconic form of the era, the most Pop culture form of the era and the most expensive piece of the era, and that is Marc Newson's Lockheed Lounge created in Australia in 1986.

Before he arrived in London, after spending a little time in Japan, Newson put together this show at a really obscure art gallery, the Roslyn Oxley9 Gallery in Sydney in 1986.

Here was Newson, working as a jeweller and working as an artist following all these design movements, then creating the Lockheed Lounge and the Pod of Drawers.

Everything about these pieces, the organic qualities that really hark back to the sculptural tradition of the 1950s…it's almost as though he *knew* that collectors would love this form. Think of his use of aluminium, which has always been a kind of radical material that designers have loved to work with and perhaps an unintentional link to aerodynamics and computer technology before computer technology existed. There is a sensual, high-tech look to this chair which, over the course of the next decade, slowly began to be more and more exhibited.

Newson had always intended to make it in an edition, so he started tapping into that thing that everybody does: "Well, maybe I'll create an edition of 10 or 11 of these, I'll have my guys in Australia make them when people order them." And slowly but surely museums began to order the Lockheed Lounge, and slowly but surely it was being included in museum surveys.

Then, a huge moment came when Philippe Starck, who is one of the great 1970s and 1980s designers in his own right, and Ian Schrager, put the Lockheed Lounge in the Paramount Hotel in New York City. One of them had the bright idea that this was one of the great statement pieces you put in a hotel lobby, representing just about everything. For me, it all started there.

The Ruhlmann of the 21st century?

There really are no Ruhlmanns today. In 1925, Emile-Jacques Ruhlmann designed every piece of an interior, he exhibited it to promote himself, and then he worked with a client who bought the work out of that. Actually, if there is a Ruhlmann today – it's an odd choice, but the closest one I can see among the famous boldfaced names of our time, who comes nearest to a Ruhlmann, would be Mattia Bonetti. He does very beautiful watercolour renditions of what he expects to build for you, and works very specifically on an interior or on just a couple of pieces for you, the collector.

Paavo Tynell
Chandelier, ca. 1950, brass, enameled brass,
51 ½ x ø 30 in. (130.8 x ø 76.2 cm)

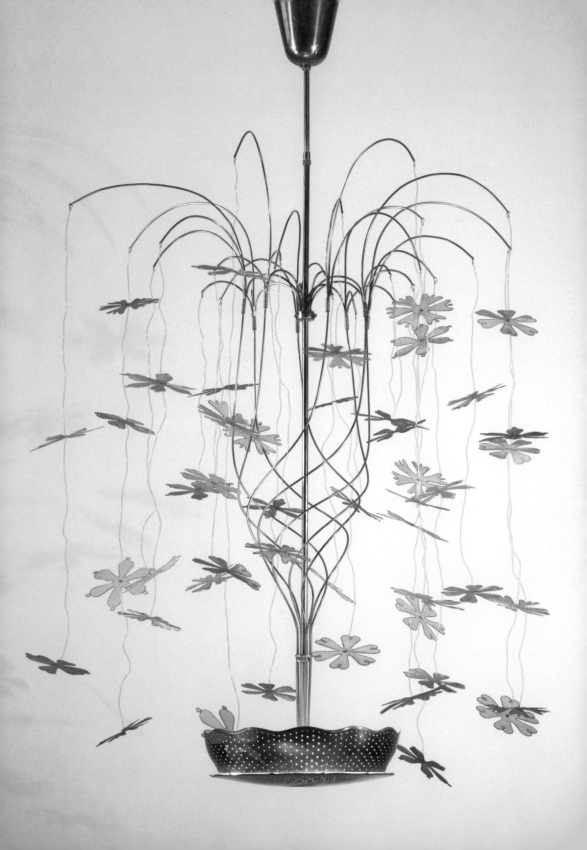

A year in design collecting

Dates of auctions, design fairs and events change every year, so checking online and in newspapers is recommended. A general guide follows:

December **Design Miami, Florida** – Jointly with Art Basel Miami Beach. See June for Design Miami/Basel.

Important 20th Century Design – Sotheby's New York

Important 20th Century Decorative Art and Design – Christie's New York

Important Design – Wright, Chicago

LAMA – Los Angeles Modern Auctions

20th Century Decorative Arts – Artcurial, Paris

January **Design** – Rago Arts and Auction Center, Lambertville, New Jersey

March **Modern Design** – Wright, Chicago

TEFAF – The European Fine Art Fair, Maastricht, The Netherlands. Includes a design section.

Decorative Arts and Design – Artcurial, Paris

Pavillon des Antiquares et des Beaux Arts – Paris

April **Design** – Phillips de Pury & Company, London

20th Century Decorative Art and Design – Christie's London

Design – Rago Arts and Auction Center, Lambertville, New Jersey

20th Century Design – Sotheby's London

May **20th Century Decorative Arts and Design** – Sotheby's Paris

May	**20th Century Design** – Sotheby's London
	20th Century Decorative Arts and Design – Christie's Paris
	ICFF – International Contemporary Furniture Fair, New York. No collectibles here, but a way to see how great designs of the past influence current trends.
	Design – Dorotheum, Vienna. Spring and fall design sales are held during Auction Week.
June	**LAMA** – Los Angeles Modern Auctions
	Design Miami/Basel – Basel, Switzerland. Held concurrently with Art Basel.
	Important 20th Century Design – Sotheby's New York
	Important 20th Century Decorative Art and Design – Christie's New York
	Design – Phillips de Pury & Company, New York
	20th Century Decorative Arts – Artcurial, Paris
September	**Design** – Phillips de Pury, London
	Biennale des Antiquaires – Grand Palais, Paris. Held every second year, the most recent edition was in 2010.
October	**Fine 20th Century Design** – Sotheby's London
	Pavilion of Art and Design – London. Held each year in conjunction with the Frieze Art Fair
	The International Fine Arts and Antiques Dealers Show – New York
	FIAC Paris – Major contemporary art fair, includes design section.
	LAMA – Los Angeles Modern Auctions
	Design – Rago Arts and Auction Center, Lambertville, New Jersey
	20th Century Decorative Arts and Design – Christie's London
	Modern Design – Wright, Chicago
	Decorative Arts and Design – Artcurial, Paris
November	**20th Century Decorative Arts and Design** – Sotheby's Paris
	20th Century Decorative Art and Design – Christie's Paris
	Design – Phillips de Pury & Company, New York
	Design – Dorotheum, Vienna
	Modernism + ART20 – New York. Both fairs show modern and contemporary art and design.

Partial glossary of terms you need to know

American modernism – Began at the turn of the 20th century and continued through the century, with its core between World Wars I and II (see modernism).

Anthropomorphic – Ascribing human characteristics to inanimate objects, animals, deities or abstract concepts.

Applied arts – Idea that the principles of design apply to everything: architecture, photography, fashion, industry and objects of everyday use, whereas fine art refers solely to aesthetic creations.

Arm chair – Chair with side structures to support the arms or elbows.

Armoire – French for a tall cupboard or wardrobe, usually with two large doors.

Art Deco – Term derived from the *Exposition Internationale des Arts Décoratifs et Industriels Modernes* (International Exposition of Modern Industrial and Decorative Arts) held in Paris in 1925, a style of "streamlined" furnishings with sleek lines, repeated geometric motifs, bold colours, mirrored and chrome accents.

Art Nouveau – "New art" developed in France in the late 19th century for works based on natural forms and the female body, often displaying sinuous curves, detailed patterns, ornate and flowing lines taken from nature.

Arts and Crafts – Style that advocated simple utilitarian design and construction, with spare ornamentation and exposed joinery, popular during the early 1900s.

Auction – Public sale in which objects like art, furnishings and other property are sold to the highest bidder, who is charged a commission by the auction house.

Avant-garde – "Advance guard" or vanguard: people or works that are ahead of the majority, particularly in art and culture.

Bauhaus – School of architecture, art and design founded by architect Walter Gropius in Germany, which operated from 1919 to 1933 and promoted unity of the arts through craftsmanship, harmony between design and function as well as the ideal of creating a total work in which all the arts would come together.

Bentwood – Technique in which solid or laminated wood is bent over steam to make curved sections for tables and chair frames, perfected by Michael Thonet (1796–1871) in Austria.

Biomorphic – Resembling or suggesting the forms of living organisms.

Boulle – André-Charles Boulle (1642–1732) was a French cabinetmaker, a master artisan of marquetry. He was later imitated in décor known as boulle work.

Bowfront chest – Chest of drawers with a convex front.

Buffet – French term for a large, heavy sideboard for china, silver, linens, with a top surface used as a serving counter.

Burl – Decorative veneer, produced by thinly slicing a cross-section in a knot or variation in the wood to display a unique pattern.

Cabriole leg – Elongated furniture leg with gently curving S shape, often ending in a stylized claw-and-ball or paw foot.

Chaise longue – French for a chair (formerly upholstered) with an elongated seat for reclining.

Collectible – In *Collecting Design*, something that is recognised by experts to be well designed, superbly crafted and valued because of its rarity. Often unique, it is sought after by collectors and will probably appreciate in value.

Colonial – Early American furniture design, 1700–1780, conservative and less ornate than English and European furniture styles of the same period.

Commode – French term for a low chest with drawers.

Condition report – Document that records the state of a work of art or design piece and is available to potential buyers.

Console – Table with at least one straight side that is designed to be set against a wall; the thin and tall version is often placed behind a sofa.

Contemporary – Furnishings known as "contemporary" are defined by sleek and clean lines, use of glass, metal and chrome rather than wood or leather, with few decorations, wall hangings or other adornments.

Cranbrook Academy of Art – Founded in 1932 in Bloomfield, Michigan, known for its architecture and Arts and Crafts movement style, with influential artists like Eliel and Eero Saarinen, Ray and Charles Eames and others.

Curator – The custodian of a collection as in a museum, library or gallery. Also the creator and supervisor of an exhibition.

Decorative arts – Classification for objects that are designed to function or serve a purpose, vs. fine arts like paintings that are solely for aesthetic appeal.

Design art – Term coined at Phillips de Pury & Company to describe works that were functional pieces as well as artistic and cultural expressions (see chapter with Alexander Payne).

De Stijl – Dutch for "The Style", a magazine and group founded in 1917 by Theo van Doesburg and other architects and artists, which became a movement that focused on linear planes and primary colours. Prominent members were Gerrit Rietveld and Piet Mondrian.

Deutscher Werkbund – German progressive organisation, founded in 1907 in Munich to promote modern design and improve the quality of German design in industry.

Dismountable – A building designed and built to be movable rather than permanently located.

Dovetail – An interlocking fan-shaped wedge used in wood furniture to join two pieces of wood at right angles to increase strength and stability.

Early American – Rudimentary utilitarian furniture, 1640 to 1700, made from local woods.

Fauteuil – French term for arm chair; correctly a specific type of arm chair, upholstered, with open sides, developed in the late 1600s in France.

Functionalism – Doctrine that the function of an object should determine its design and materials; in architecture, that a building's use should determine its form and structure.

Gilding – Decorative finish, or ornamenting with gold leaf or gold dust.

Gueridon – A small, elaborately carved stand or table.

Industrial design – The design of mass-produced objects.

Inlay – Cutting a shape out of a surface and inserting a piece of another material, cut exactly the same size and shape, in its place, to form an overall design.

Joinery – From cabinetmaking: joining together two pieces of wood using different techniques for furniture and other items.

Jugendstil – Literally "youth style", similar to Art Nouveau, popular in German-speaking areas of Europe during the late 19th and early 20th centuries.

Laminated – Bonding or gluing together thin layers to form a composite material, like laminated plywood.

Limited edition – Production of a limited number of pieces that replicate the designer's original piece, as opposed to mass-production.

Marquetry – Decorative surface made by inlaying pieces of wood in different colours and shapes, or mother of pearl, unusual metals etc., to form a pattern.

Memphis – Milan-based collective of furniture and product designers led by Ettore Sottsass, originally dubbed The New Design, and known for furniture made from flashy colourful plastic, industrial materials, printed glass, celluloid, neon tubes, often displaying flamboyant colours and glitter.

Mid-century modern – Design and architecture that began after World War II through the 1960s, often called "mod", and marked by simplicity, clean lines, organic forms and materials such as wood, metal and plastic. The style flourished with designers like Eero Saarinen, Charles and Ray Eames, Florence Knoll, George Nelson and others.

Minimalism – Style in which the simplest and fewest elements are used to create the maximum effect with basic shapes, monochromatic colours, clean lines.

Modernism – Term for a wide range of trends that broke with the past in a search of new forms of expression, seen especially in late-19th to mid-20th century styles which rejected old notions of form, line and ornamentation.

Organic design – Defined by Eliot Noyes of MoMA in 1941 as design in which there was "an harmonious organisation" of the parts "according to structure, material and purpose". The term "organic architecture" was used often by Frank Lloyd Wright to state that a building should grow naturally from its environment.

Patina – Soft, mellow colour and texture of wood surface resulting from age, wear or rubbing.

Peroba – Brazilian wood found in a range of various colours.

Plywood – Layers of wood glued together under pressure, with the grains running in different directions.

Pop design – British and Italian design movement of the 1960s characterised by its use of bright colours, synthetic materials and throw-away objects.

Post-modernism – A movement that started in the 1960s and remained through the 1990s, which reacted against earlier modernist principles by re-introducing traditional or classical elements of style.

Post-war design – Generally the period from the end of World War II in 1945 through 1975 (see mid-century modern).

Prototype – An original type, form or example which may be followed by a series, or produced in additional numbers.

Restoration – Renewing a worn or damaged object to its former state or to a condition as close as possible to the original.

Scandinavian – Furnishings that encompass several Nordic styles, largely produced in wood with light and fresh colours.

Secretaire – French for a free-standing writing cabinet, often with a slim drawer beneath the top and a fall-front writing surface.

Sideboard – Serving piece with a long, flat top and a lower section used for storage, similar to a buffet table but usually longer and narrower.

Traditionalist style – Generally refers to design styles popular in the 18th and 19th centuries.

Veneer – Very thin layer of fine and often exotic or expensive wood that is applied to another wood surface to form beautiful patterns.

Wardrobe – Large cabinet or cupboard for hanging clothes.

Wiener Werkstätte – "Vienna Workshops" which evolved from the Vienna Secession, founded by Josef Hoffmann and Koloman Moser in 1903 to bring together architects, artists and designers who were committed to producing well-designed and well-made furniture, metalwork, graphics, bookbinding, jewellery, textiles, art. The Werkstätte espoused a direct relationship between designer and craftsman. Its aim was to make all human life one unified work of art and its output affected all aspects of society of the day.

Zoomorphic – Something shaped in animal form.

Index

Biography of the author
Acknowledgements

DEDICATION
To Charlotte, it was your idea, I hope you like it.

BIOGRAPHY
Adam Lindemann is a private investor and influential collector of contemporary art and design. He is also the author of *Collecting Contemporary,* which was published by Taschen and dubbed the "most talked-about art book" of 2006. In partnership with designer Marc Newson, he re-launched Ikepod, a Swiss watch design company. He also writes a monthly column on collecting for *The New York Observer.*

ACKNOWLEDGEMENTS
I would like to thank Iris Chekenian for her invaluable support in the research and editing of all the bits and pieces into a coherent tome. Special appreciation goes to Hans Werner Holzwarth who designed the book and was vital in the final selection process. Last but not least, my thanks to all the participants who shared their love of collecting with me, and the many designers who helped to make this book possible.

The Lunar Rock
Edition by *Marc Newson.*

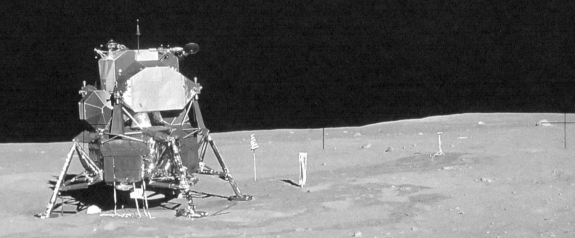

Meteorites from the Moon are exceptionally rare. There are only 58 lunar meteorites known and their total combined weight is less than 30 kilograms, making them millions of times rarer than gem-grade diamonds. However, most lunar meteorites reside in museum collections and research institutions, leaving only 10 kilograms or so available to collectors worldwide. Since acquiring an Apollo Moon rock is impossible, the only realistic way to own a piece of the Moon is to acquire a lunar meteorite.

In order for a piece of Moon rock to get to the Earth, it must be blasted off the lunar surface with enough velocity (approximately 1.5 miles per second or 5,400 miles per hour) to escape the Moon's gravity. The rock or meteoroid must intersect the Earth's orbit, possibly hundreds of thousands or millions of years later, and be captured by its gravitational field into a decaying or unstable orbit. Eventually, friction from the atmosphere will degrade the kinetic energy of the meteoroid so much that it will spiral down to the Earth's surface in a fantastic fiery display which is called a meteor.

If the meteor reaches the surface, it will be called a meteorite. However, less than one in a trillion meteors that enter the atmosphere will reach the Earth's surface – which explains the incredible rarity of extraterrestrial rocks on our planet.

2/3 of all meteorites fall into the ocean and every single lunar meteorite recovery to date has been from a desert where such meteorites are more readily identified.

Of the 58 distinct lunar meteorites known, 16 were found by scientists in Antarctica. Owned by a consortium of countries, not one gram of Antarctic material will ever be available to the private sector.

In conclusion, portions of the Moon are among the rarest substances on Earth, and only a fraction of this material is available to the public.

The Lunar Module,
lunar surface, July 20, 1969.

More Precious than Gold

A piece of the Moon: one of the rarest substances on Earth

Each of the 12 Lunar Rock Editions comes with an authentic and documented specimen of lunar rock, all ranging in weight, size and coloration.

Copy no. 1,969 includes a complete Lunar Meteorite weighing in at 348 grams. One of the largest lunar meteorites ever found on Earth, this is an extremely rare item as nearly all meteorites have been cut into smaller portions for sale or study.

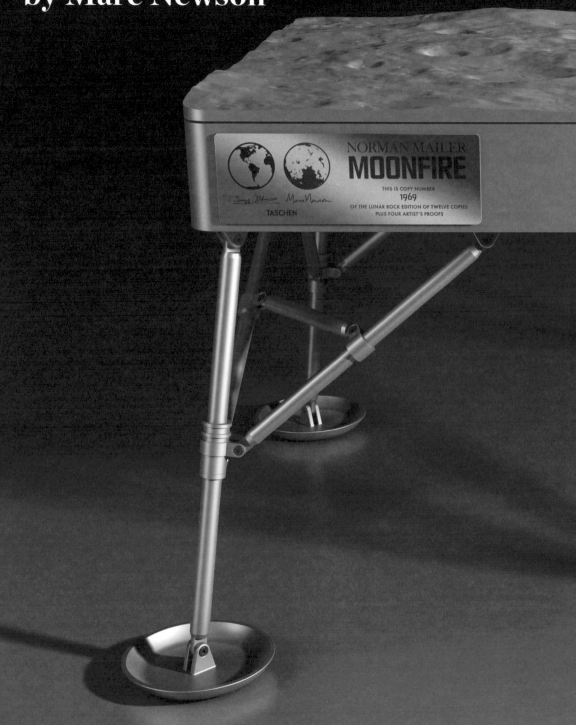

An edition of only 12 copies
by Marc Newson

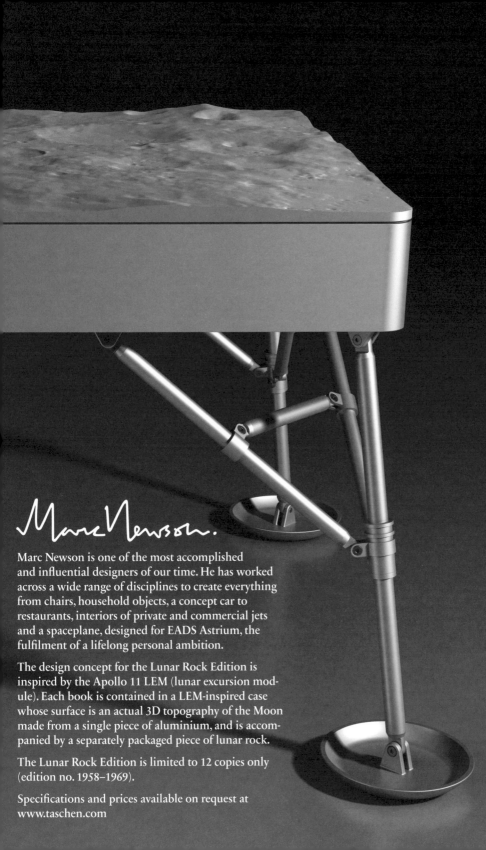

Marc Newson.

Marc Newson is one of the most accomplished
and influential designers of our time. He has worked
across a wide range of disciplines to create everything
from chairs, household objects, a concept car to
restaurants, interiors of private and commercial jets
and a spaceplane, designed for EADS Astrium, the
fulfilment of a lifelong personal ambition.

The design concept for the Lunar Rock Edition is
inspired by the Apollo 11 LEM (lunar excursion module). Each book is contained in a LEM-inspired case
whose surface is an actual 3D topography of the Moon
made from a single piece of aluminium, and is accom-
panied by a separately packaged piece of lunar rock.

The Lunar Rock Edition is limited to 12 copies only
(edition no. 1958–1969).

Specifications and prices available on request at
www.taschen.com

Photo credits

p. 2 → Courtesy Artcurial p. 4 → Courtesy Sotheby's p. 9 → Courtesy Demisch Danant p. 11 → Photo Brad Bridgers. Courtesy Dennis Freedman p. 19 → Collection Bruno Bischofberger, Zurich p. 20 → Collection Bruno Bischofberger, Zurich p. 21 → Collection Bruno Bischofberger, Zurich p. 22 → Collection Bruno Bischofberger, Zurich p. 24/25 → Collection Bruno Bischofberger, Zurich p. 27 → © Christie's Images Limited 2009 p. 28 → Courtesy Phillips de Pury & Company p. 29 → Courtesy Sotheby's p. 30 → Courtesy Sotheby's. © VG Bild-Kunst, Bonn 2010 p. 31 → Courtesy Sotheby's. © VG Bild-Kunst, Bonn 2010 p. 32 → Photo Chandler Strange. Courtesy DeLorenzo p. 33 → Courtesy Barry Friedman Ltd. © VG Bild-Kunst, Bonn 2010 p. 35 → Courtesy Galerie Ulrich Fiedler p. 36 → Courtesy Phillips de Pury & Company p. 37 → Courtesy Sotheby's. © VG Bild-Kunst, Bonn 2010 p. 38 → Courtesy Sotheby's. © VG Bild-Kunst, Bonn 2010 p. 39 → © Christie's Images Limited 2005 p. 40 → Courtesy Sotheby's p. 42 → Courtesy Phillips de Pury & Company p. 43 → Courtesy Sotheby's. © VG Bild-Kunst, Bonn 2010 p. 45 → Photo Brad Bridgers. Courtesy Dennis Freedman p. 46 → Photo Brad Bridgers. Courtesy Dennis Freedman p. 47 Photo Brad Bridgers. Courtesy Dennis Freedman p. 49 → Photo Jon Lam, New York. Courtesy Friedman Benda p. 50/51 → Photo Brad Bridgers. Courtesy Dennis Freedman p. 52 → Photo Brad Bridgers. Courtesy Dennis Freedman p. 53 → Photo Brad Bridgers. Courtesy Dennis Freedman. © VG Bild-Kunst, Bonn 2010 p. 55 → Courtesy Dakis Joannou p. 56 → Courtesy Dakis Joannou p. 57 → Courtesy Dakis Joannou p. 58 → Courtesy Dakis Joannou p. 59 → Courtesy Dakis Joannou p. 61 → Photo Steven Sebring. Courtesy Paul Kasmin Gallery. © VG Bild-Kunst, Bonn 2010 p. 62 → © Christie's Images Limited 2002. © VG Bild-Kunst, Bonn 2010 p. 63 → Courtesy Demisch Danant p. 64 → © Christie's Images Limited 2001 p. 65 → Courtesy Sotheby's. © VG Bild-Kunst, Bonn 2010 p. 67 → Courtesy Sotheby's. © The Isamu Noguchi Foundation and Garden Museum/VG Bild-Kunst, Bonn 2010 p. 68 → © Christie's Images Limited 2002 p. 69 → Courtesy Sotheby's p. 70/71 → Courtesy Sotheby's p. 73 → Courtesy Wright p. 77 → Photo Chandler Strange. Courtesy DeLorenzo. © VG Bild-Kunst, Bonn 2010 p. 78 → Photo Chandler Strange. Courtesy DeLorenzo p. 79 → Courtesy DeLorenzo p. 81 → Photo Ellen Robin Silverman. Courtesy DeLorenzo p. 82 → Courtesy DeLorenzo p. 83 → Courtesy DeLorenzo. © VG Bild-Kunst, Bonn 2010 p. 85 → Courtesy Demisch Danant p. 86 → Courtesy Demisch Danant p. 87 → Courtesy Demisch Danant p. 88 → Courtesy Demisch Danant p. 89 → Courtesy Demisch Danant p. 91 → Courtesy Demisch Danant p. 92/93 → Courtesy Demisch Danant p. 95 → Courtesy Galerie Ulrich Fiedler, Berlin p. 96 → Courtesy Galerie Ulrich Fiedler, Berlin p. 99 → Courtesy Galerie Ulrich Fiedler, Berlin. © VG Bild-Kunst, Bonn 2010 p. 100 → Courtesy Galerie Ulrich Fiedler, Berlin p. 101 → Courtesy Galerie Ulrich Fiedler, Berlin p. 103 → Courtesy Friedman Benda p. 104 → Courtesy Friedman Benda p. 105 → Photo Eric & Petra Hesmerg. Courtesy Friedman Benda p. 106 → Courtesy Friedman Benda p. 107 → Courtesy Friedman Benda p. 108/109 → Courtesy Phillips de Pury & Company p. 111 → © DR. Courtesy Galerie Kreo p. 112 → © DR. Courtesy Galerie Kreo p. 113 → Image © Paul Tahon/R & E Bouroullec. Courtesy Galerie Kreo p. 114 → Image © Fabrice Gousset. Courtesy Galerie Kreo p. 115 → © Morgane Le Gall. Courtesy Galerie Kreo p. 116 → Courtesy Phillips de Pury & Company p. 117 → Image © Fabrice Gousset and Konstantin Grcic Industrial Design (KGID). Courtesy Galerie Kreo p. 118 → Image © Morgane Le Gall. Courtesy Galerie Kreo p. 119 → © Nicolas Register/Nimrod. Image © Fabrice Gousset-Marc Newson Ltd. Courtesy Galerie Kreo p. 120/121 → Image © Morgane Le Gall. Courtesy Galerie Kreo p. 123 → Photo François Dischinger. Courtesy R 20th Century p. 125 → Photo Sherry Griffin for R 20th Century. Courtesy R 20th Century p. 126 → Photo

Sherry Griffin for R 20th Century. Courtesy R 20th Century **p. 127** → Courtesy Sotheby's **p. 128** → Photo Sherry Griffin for R 20th Century. Courtesy R 20th Century **p. 129** → Courtesy Sotheby's **p. 131** → Courtesy Moss **p. 132** → Courtesy Moss **p. 133** → Photo Studio Job. Courtesy Moss **p. 134** → Photo Studio Job. Courtesy Moss **p. 135** → Courtesy Moss **p. 136** → Courtesy Moss **p. 137** → Photo Swarovski Crystal Palace. Courtesy Moss **p. 138** → Courtesy Artcurial **p. 139** → Courtesy Moss **p. 141** → Courtesy Galerie Patrick Seguin **p. 142/143** → Courtesy Galerie Patrick Seguin. © VG Bild-Kunst, Bonn 2010 **p. 144** → Courtesy Galerie Patrick Seguin. © VG Bild-Kunst, Bonn 2010 **p. 145** → Courtesy Galerie Patrick Seguin. © VG Bild-Kunst, Bonn 2010 **p. 146/147** → Courtesy Galerie Patrick Seguin. © VG Bild-Kunst, Bonn 2010 **p. 149** → Courtesy Sotheby's. © VG Bild-Kunst, Bonn 2010 **p. 151** → Courtesy Galerie Patrick Seguin. © VG Bild-Kunst, Bonn 2010 **p. 153** → Photo Kalpesh Lathigra. © Established & Sons Limited **p. 154** → Photo Mark C. O'Flaherty. © Established & Sons Limited **p. 155** → Photo Mike Goldwater. © Established & Sons Limited **p. 156/157** → Photo Andy Barter. © Established & Sons Limited **p. 161** → Photo Jerôme Faggiano and Nils Herrmann. Courtesy Jacques Grange **p. 162** → Photo Arnaud Carpentier/Galerie Vallois, Paris. Courtesy Jacques Grange. © VG Bild-Kunst, Bonn 2010 **p. 163** → Photo Arnaud Carpentier/Galerie Vallois, Paris. Courtesy Jacques Grange. © VG Bild-Kunst, Bonn 2010 **p. 164** → © Galerie du Passage. Courtesy Jacques Grange. © VG Bild-Kunst, Bonn 2010 **p. 165** → © Gio Ponti Archives, Milan. © Galerie du Passage. Courtesy Jacques Grange **p. 166** → Photo Arnaud Carpentier/Galerie Vallois, Paris. Courtesy Jacques Grange **p. 167** → Photo Arnaud Carpentier/Galerie Vallois, Paris. Courtesy Jacques Grange **p. 168** → © Galerie du Passage. Courtesy Jacques Grange **p. 169** → © Galerie du Passage. Courtesy Jacques Grange **p. 170** → Courtesy Demisch Danant **p. 171** → Courtesy Sotheby's. © VG Bild-Kunst, Bonn 2010 **p. 172/173** → Courtesy Sotheby's **p. 174** → Courtesy Galerie Patrick Seguin **p. 175** → Courtesy Demisch Danant **p. 177** → Courtesy Sotheby's **p. 178** → Photo © Paul Tahon and R. & E. Bouroullec. Courtesy Galerie Kreo **p. 179** → Courtesy Sotheby's **p. 180** → Courtesy Sotheby's **p. 181** → © Ductal by Lafarge and Honeycomb. Image © Fabrice Gousset. Courtesy Galerie Kreo **p. 183** → Courtesy Sotheby's **p. 184** → Courtesy Sotheby's **p. 185** → Courtesy Peter Marino **p. 186** → Courtesy Jacques Grange and Galerie du Passage **p. 187** → © Christie's Images Limited 2006. © VG Bild-Kunst, Bonn 2010 **p. 188/189** → © Christie's Images Limited 2007 **p. 190** → © Christie's Images Limited 2000 **p. 191** → Photo Christopher Burke Studio. Courtesy Paul Kasmin Gallery. © VG Bild-Kunst, Bonn 2010 **p. 192** → © Christie's Images Limited 2008. © VG Bild-Kunst, Bonn 2010 **p. 195** → Photo Mark Lyon. Courtesy Robert Rubin **p. 196** → Courtesy Sotheby's **p. 197** → Courtesy Sotheby's **p. 199** → Photo Mark Lyon. Courtesy Robert Rubin. © VG Bild-Kunst, Bonn 2010 **p. 200** → Courtesy Sotheby's. © VG Bild-Kunst, Bonn 2010 **p. 203** → © Christie's Images Limited 2005 **p. 204** → Courtesy Wright **p. 205** → Courtesy Wright **p. 206/207** → Courtesy Adjaye/Associates **p. 208** → Courtesy Wright **p. 211** → © Christie's Images Limited 2006 **p. 212** → Courtesy Sotheby's. © FLC/VG Bild-Kunst, Bonn 2010 **p. 213** → © 2008 Estate of Scott Burton/Artists Rights Society (ARS), New York. Courtesy Max Protetch Gallery, New York **p. 214** → Courtesy Wright **p. 219** → Courtesy Dorotheum **p. 220** → © DR. Courtesy Dorotheum **p. 221** → Courtesy Dorotheum **p. 222** → Courtesy Dorotheum **p. 223** → Courtesy Dorotheum **p. 225** → © Christie's Images Limited 2002 **p. 226** → © Christie's Images Limited 2009 **p. 227** → © Christie's Images Limited 2006. © ADAGP/FAAG, Paris/VG Bild-Kunst, Bonn 2010 **p. 229** → © Christie's Images Limited 2006 **p. 230** → © Christie's Images Limited 2001 **p. 231** → © Christie's Images Limited 2005. © VG Bild-Kunst, Bonn 2010 **p. 232** → © Christie's Images Limited 2006 **p. 233** → © Christie's Images Limited 2006 **p. 234/235** → © Christie's Images Limited 2006 **p. 237** → Courtesy Los Angeles Modern Auctions (LAMA) **p. 238/239** → Courtesy Los Angeles Modern Auctions (LAMA) **p. 240** Courtesy Los Angeles Modern Auctions (LAMA) **p. 241** → Courtesy Los Angeles Modern Auctions (LAMA) **p. 242, 243** → Courtesy Los Angeles Modern Auctions (LAMA) **p. 245** Courtesy Phillips de Pury & Company **p. 246** → Courtesy Phillips de Pury & Company **p. 247** → Courtesy Phillips de Pury & Company. © VG Bild-Kunst, Bonn 2010 **p. 248/249** → Courtesy Phillips de Pury & Company **p. 251** → Courtesy Phillips de Pury & Company **p. 252/253** → Photo Clint Blowers. Courtesy Phillips de Pury & Company **p. 255** → Courtesy Wright **p. 256** → Courtesy Wright **p. 257** Courtesy Wright **p. 258** → Courtesy Wright **p. 259** → Courtesy Wright **p. 260** → Courtesy Wright. © VG Bild-Kunst, Bonn 2010 **p. 261** → Courtesy Wright **p. 262/263** → Courtesy Moss **p. 265** → Courtesy Sotheby's. © VG Bild-Kunst, Bonn 2010 **p. 267** → Photo Chandler Strange. Courtesy DeLorenzo **p. 269** → Courtesy Sotheby's **p. 270** → Courtesy Sotheby's. © VG Bild-Kunst, Bonn 2010 **p. 271** → Courtesy Sotheby's **p. 272/273** → Courtesy Sotheby's **p. 275** → Courtesy Sotheby's **p. 276** → Courtesy Sotheby's **p. 277** → Courtesy Sotheby's **p. 279** → Photo Eric & Petra Hesmerg. Courtesy Friedman Benda **p. 281** → Courtesy Wright

To stay informed about upcoming TASCHEN titles, please request our magazine at
www.taschen.com/magazine or write to TASCHEN America, 6671 Sunset Boulevard, Suite 1508,
USA-Los Angeles, CA 90028, contact-us@taschen.com, Fax: +1-323-463.4442. We will be happy
to send you a free copy of our magazine which is filled with information about all of our books.

Editorial direction: Hans Werner Holzwarth
Editorial team: Lutz Eitel, Elisabeth Hofmann, Julia Schneider, Grace Needleman
The interview with Karl Lagerfeld was first published in Art+Auction; the interviews
with Jacques Grange, the Krzentowskis and Patrick Seguin are originally in French
and translated by the author
Design: Hans Werner Holzwarth, based on the *Collecting Contemporary* design
by Sense/Net, Andy Disl and Birgit Reber
Production: Ute Wachendorf, Cologne
Printed in China
ISBN: 978-8365-1993-9